BLACK
DOMERS

BLACK
DOMERS

*African-American Students at Notre Dame
in Their Own Words*

Edited by

DON WYCLIFF AND DAVID KRASHNA

Foreword by

REV. THEODORE M. HESBURGH, CSC

UNIVERSITY OF NOTRE DAME PRESS   NOTRE DAME, INDIANA

CONTENTS

* Deceased

PREFACE TO THE SECOND EDITION

With this updated edition, *Black Domers* comes to what the editors always believed was its natural home: the University of Notre Dame Press. The story of how African-Americans came to be part of the Fighting Irish is a tribute to Notre Dame's Catholic Christian ideals and deserved to be published by its own press. We are grateful to Stephen Wrinn, director of the Notre Dame Press, for his support of and commitment to this project.

Likewise, we thank Jim Langford, Class of 1959, whose Corby Books published our first edition in 2014. Jim was able to do then what an academic press could not: take a volume produced on a tight deadline, getting it into print and ready for sale only three months after receiving the manuscript.

There have been some noteworthy changes at Notre Dame and among our contributors since the first edition.

Most notably, Father Ted Hesburgh died, marking the end of an era of unparalleled progress at Notre Dame and in American social and political history. *Black Domers* co-editor David Krashna retired as a superior court judge. And Ron Irvine, one of our essayists, died unexpectedly. Not only was Ron a contributor to this book; he also was one of its most active promoters.

When the first edition was published, David Krashna was the only African-American ever to have been elected Notre Dame's student body president. In 2016, he became the first of two, when Corey Robinson, Class of 2017, was elected to the position. We are pleased that Corey, along with half a dozen others, have added theirs to this compilation of Notre Dame stories told from the perspective of her African-American students.

Aside from those few exceptions, the accounts that follow were written in late 2013 for publication in the first edition of *Black Domers*. As a result, there are references to events and experiences that may now seem dated. We have chosen not to attempt to update or revise these references, but simply to ask readers to recognize that some situations, events, and even writers' opinions may have changed between then and now.

Readers should also note that four essays in the first chapter were not written by the Domers themselves because they had died by the time the first edition was being assembled. The profiles of Frazier Thompson, Joseph Bertrand, Goldie Ivory, and Aubrey Lewis were written by volume editor Don Wycliff.

This volume is a labor of love and celebration. Love for the hallowed spot of ground in northern Indiana that is the Notre Dame campus. Love for the community of scholars who inhabit that campus and pursue knowledge and wisdom and holiness there. Love for the spirit that infuses that community and that campus, the spirit of Notre Dame.

And the celebration? This year, 2014, is the seventieth since the first African-American student arrived on that campus and became a member of that community. His name was Frazier L. Thompson. A Philadelphian, he came to Notre Dame as part of the United States Navy's V-12 program to produce officers for service in World War II. The war ended in 1945, and Thompson stayed on at Notre Dame, earning varsity letters in track as he worked his way toward a degree in preprofessional studies. He graduated in June 1947.

In the seven decades since Thompson's arrival, the number of African-Americans among the Fighting Irish has grown from one to hundreds. They have been student body president, valedictorian, Heisman Trophy winner. They quarterbacked the football team to its last national championship and to the threshold of two other championships. They have broadened and deepened the educational experiences of all at Notre Dame by bringing their experiences and perspectives as African-Americans to her classrooms, dormitories, teams, clubs, and religious life.

In the pages that follow, the stories of seventy of these black daughters and sons of Notre Dame are related: how they came to the university; how they survived and thrived — or didn't; how their Notre Dame experiences have affected their lives since graduation.

Not all of these stories are happy. For many black Domers, Notre Dame was a hard place to be; they felt racially and culturally isolated, and sometimes experienced garden variety racism. And yet all of these stuck it out, earned their degrees, and went on to lives of success and, in many cases, great distinction.

This book is the brainchild of one of those seventy, co-editor David M. Krashna, Class of 1971. During his senior year, Krashna was Notre Dame's first, and still its only, black student body president. He went on to the law school at the University of California at Berkeley. He now is a superior court judge in Alameda County, California.

The other co-editor, Don Wycliff, graduated from Notre Dame in 1969 and went to graduate school in political science at the University of Chicago. While there he discovered his true vocation, journalism. He spent thirty-five years in the newspaper business, including five as a member of the editorial board of the *New York Times* and nearly ten as editorial page editor of the *Chicago Tribune*. The last six years of his working life he taught journalism at Loyola University Chicago. Five of his family members have followed him to Notre Dame. He and his youngest brother, Brian Wycliff, Class of 1985, have endowed a scholarship at the university in their parents' names.

Those whose stories are told here were selected from among almost 250 candidates nominated by members of the Black Alumni of Notre Dame and Notre Dame staff members with deep institutional knowledge. Especially noteworthy among the latter are Melvin Tardy of the Office of the First Year of Studies, and Daniel Saracino, the longtime head of the Office of Admissions.

It goes without saying that the integration of African-Americans at Notre Dame could not have happened without support from the top, beginning with the president at the time of Frazier Thompson's matriculation, Rev. J. Hugh O'Donnell, CSC, and continuing with each of his successors: Rev. John J. Cavanaugh, Rev. Theodore M. Hesburgh, Rev. Edward A. Malloy, and Rev. John I. Jenkins.

It was during the administration of Father Hesburgh, however, that adding black daughters and sons to the legions at du Lac became not just a matter of acceptance, but of pursuit. Civil rights, diversity, and inclusion were to be pursued not just in Washington and on the national stage, but also at home, on the campus at Notre Dame. And these things were priorities not just for the sake of justice—although that would have been reason enough—but also for the sake of the university's fundamental mission: to foster the intellectual, spiritual, and moral growth of all her daughters and sons. For Notre Dame must be catholic as well as Catholic; it must embrace all.

That Notre Dame today is more catholic than seventy years ago is a tribute to all who helped bring about the change. But it is especially a tribute to those African-American students who, like the ones whose stories are told in this volume, came and studied, came and persevered, came and succeeded.

Besides the addition of women, the most dramatic change in the character of Notre Dame's student body in my lifetime has been its growing racial and ethnic diversity. Black students, in particular, have grown in numbers from one in 1944, when Frazier L. Thompson enrolled as a member of the US Navy's V-12 program, to hundreds now, seventy years later.

This change, achieved through great and deliberate effort, has benefitted not just the black students but all of our students. The Notre Dame educational experience has been enhanced by the presence in classrooms, dormitories, dining halls, chapels, and all aspects of university life of students from many backgrounds, whose life experiences often differ substantially from those of students in the American economic and racial mainstream.

I am privileged not just to have witnessed this change, but also to have helped create it. In 1970, challenged to find financial aid for a then-record 119 admitted black freshmen, I proposed and the university's board of trustees approved ending our forty-five-year ban against participation in postseason football bowl games. We lost to the University of Texas in the 1970 Cotton Bowl, but the money we received for that appearance allowed us to fund financial aid for the largest class of black freshmen in the university's history to that point.

In 1985, when it seemed to me that we needed to redouble our efforts to enroll and make our black students feel at home on campus, I convened a group of black alumni for a three-day conclave about how to do those things. Besides producing ideas for improving the lives of black students, that meeting gave rise to the Black Alumni of Notre Dame, an official part of the Notre Dame Alumni Association. Membership in the Notre Dame family does not end at graduation, but continues throughout the graduate's life. The BA of ND helps foster those post-commencement ties to Our Lady's university and its ideals.

All of these efforts—and many others since I departed the presidency in 1987—have been undertaken for the sake of justice, the same ideal that motivated me to spend fifteen years on the United States Commission on Civil Rights and to work in a host of other human and civil rights activities.

But even more they stemmed from Notre Dame's commitment to be, as the Catholic Church strives to be, inclusive of all of our nation's and the earth's peoples—every race, nationality, and ethnicity. At Notre Dame, we seek to embody the Christian principle that we are all sisters and brothers to one another, with God as our loving father.

This volume, conceived and edited by two of our black alumni, rightly celebrates the growth of the black presence at Notre Dame over the last seventy years. It was David Krashna, Class of 1971, whom I sent nationwide in the late 1960s to recruit black students and who came to my office one night to report that bumper crop of 119 applicants. Don Wycliff, Class of 1969, had a distinguished career of nearly four decades as a newspaper journalist and has taught journalism for the last six years at Loyola University Chicago.

The seventy individuals whose stories are contained in these pages describe their personal struggles and triumphs, joys and sorrows as Notre Dame students of various eras. In the process, they allow all who cherish Notre Dame's tradition as an avenue to advancement for the despised and marginalized to see how that tradition has been renewed and extended by a new group in a new era.

We are justly proud of these newest of Our Lady's daughters and sons, for as surely as any of those who came before them, *they are Notre Dame.*

Rev. Theodore M. Hesburgh, CSC
President Emeritus
University of Notre Dame

A REFLECTION ON SEVENTY YEARS
OF BLACK DOMERS

I grew up in a predominantly black city, Washington, D.C., in the early stages of the civil rights movement. I played on a highly successful high school basketball team (Archbishop John Carroll) that was known as the first freely integrated one and that was adopted by the local media as a model for the future.

When I came to Notre Dame as an undergraduate student, I found a much different reality. Black students were few in number, and their cumulative impact on the campus was generally limited to certain athletic teams and selective friendship groupings.

When I was elected president of Notre Dame in 1987, I set, as one of my most important priorities, the racial and ethnic diversification of every aspect of the institution's life. This included: a substantial increase in African-American students and faculty; the creation of effective support structures; the revisioning of appropriate areas of the curriculum; the recasting of the administrative, alumni, advisory, and governance structures; and the creation of a more welcoming environment overall. Thankfully, we made progress in all of those areas, some more rapidly than others.

I am delighted that in this book we have such a talented and successful cross section of black students to draw upon to share their experiences of Our Lady's university. While some of their stories contain elements of pain and frustration, I am proud that they have earned their degrees and, in the process, have enriched our campus with their talent, energy, commitment, and love of Notre Dame.

Rev. Edward A. Malloy, CSC
President, 1987–2005

REFLECTION

Black Domers: Seventy Years
at Notre Dame

If I could change one thing about this book, it would require reliving our history to make the number of years in its title—seventy—far greater. We started too late, but I am grateful for those seventy years and for the story this book tells.

Much has changed for the better at Notre Dame since 1944; this collection offers a narrative of that progress. I know it has not been easy. That progress required struggle and sacrifice on the part of many, and mostly from African-American students, faculty, and staff. The most important thing I want to say is: "Thank you. Thanks to all those who helped make Notre Dame a richer place through their presence."

I'm proud of many accomplishments. I was proud in 2010, for instance, to preside over our 165th Commencement and to listen to the address of our first African-American valedictorian, Katie Washington. Two years later, I was proud to greet the incoming freshman class of 2016 by announcing that it was the first at Notre Dame in which one in four members was a student of color.

We must go farther and we will. But as we do, we must remember the contributions of so many people over the past seventy years to make Notre Dame a more richly diverse and inclusive place. For this is not a matter of mere numbers; it is, in the words of the Notre Dame diversity statement, a "moral and intellectual necessity," an affair of the mind and the heart. As such it is a very human story. Insofar as we live it, we become more what we say Notre Dame is. We respond to a call. I thank all those who have gone before who have helped us hear this call and respond to it.

Rev. John I. Jenkins, CSC
President, University of Notre Dame
December 10, 2013

ACKNOWLEDGMENTS

Besides the essayists themselves, numerous people assisted us in producing this book. They include, from the Notre Dame staff: Paul Mueller, Don Bishop, Joseph Smith, Charles Lamb, Angela Kindig, Michael Bertsch, John Heisler, Carol Copley, Tomi M. Gerhold, Deborah Gabaree, Joseph Mulligan, Melanie Chapleau, Joan Bradley, Sarah A. Gotsch, Bridget Keating, Ann Firth, and Elizabeth Hogan.

Matthew Dowd, our editor at the University of Notre Dame Press, was unfailingly helpful and encouraging as we prepared the updated edition.

Of special assistance, especially in the early stages of the work, were Daniel Saracino, retired assistant provost for enrollment, and Melvin Tardy, academic advisor in the First Year of Studies. Both were invaluable in providing institutional memory about the growth of black enrollment at Notre Dame over the last several decades.

Among the alumni essayists, several went beyond simply writing their stories to put us into contact with people we had been unable to reach and to provide editing help in the last stages of the project. These include Richard Ryans, Phyllis Washington Stone, Ben Finley Jr., Tommy Hawkins, Iris Outlaw, Percy Pierre, and Clyde Jupiter.

Relatives of several deceased alumni provided us with photographs and information, including Joseph Bertrand Jr., Ann Lewis, Angie Winston, and Mary Drye Bell.

Finally, we leaned heavily—at times unreasonably so—on family members, including our wives, Pamela Wycliff and Gina Coronel Krashna. Pam kept track of the myriad administrative details that inevitably are involved in a project of this sort. And Gina handled all of the photography, including bringing back to life some old photographs that our essayists submitted. Andre Walker Krashna, one of David's sons, first recommended that we use the BA of ND's Black Shamrock in the book.

CHAPTER 1

The 1940s and 1950s

Before World War II the Notre Dame campus was off-limits to young black men aspiring to college; as a result of the war, the university's doors were finally opened. Notre Dame's first black student came to study for war as a Navy V-12 program enrollee; he remained to prepare as a pre-med student for a life of healing.

The early years of black enrollment at Notre Dame were full of ironies like those, as was the era in which they occurred.

Those years were called the "postwar era"—there was no need in those days to say which war—but in retrospect they appear to have been an early stage of an age of permanent war.

The USSR, so recently America's ally in World War II, rapidly morphed into our rival, and then our mortal enemy. With their nuclear arsenal and their Warsaw Pact, the Soviets erected a figurative "Iron Curtain" across Europe, which they had helped liberate from Hitler's Nazis. With our nuclear arsenal and our NATO, America opposed them and the totalitarian ideology they espoused and enforced within their orbit.

We on our side and they on theirs learned to duck, cover, and hold our breaths as we all lived under the shadow of "the bomb." We developed and became familiar with a whole litany associated with this geopolitical standoff: "communism," of course, but also "Cold War" and "Sputnik" and "megaton" and "mutually assured destruction."

We also learned a darker litany as a result of fears and suspicions spawned in American society by this Cold War: "traitor" and "black-list" and "card-carrying member" (of the Communist Party) and "fellow traveler." In the end, this resulted in another coinage, "McCarthyism," for the US senator from the heartland who fearmongered his way to national political prominence and, then, finally and mercifully for the nation, to ignominy and disgrace.

At home in America, the end of World War II gave rise to a sustained period of economic growth and new prosperity, fueled by demand pent-up from the war years and the Great Depression before it. The GI Bill of Rights, one of the greatest strokes of political genius in American history, gave returning service members access to higher education and housing, both critical elements in the creation of a durable middle class.

Among those returning service members were thousands of Negroes, who had fought to save the world from fascist tyranny and yet found themselves denied at home the rights to decent education, to housing outside of ghettos, to service at lunch counters, to lodging in hotels and motels.

It soon became clear that something was stirring among Negroes in the postwar era, a determination to throw off second-class status and win the place in American society that they had been denied for centuries and to which they knew they were entitled.

That determination manifested itself first in the courts, where Thurgood Marshall and his cohorts at the NAACP Legal Defense and Educational Fund systematically challenged the legal underpinnings of segregation and won victory after victory. The greatest of those victories came on May 17, 1954, when the US Supreme Court declared in *Brown v. Board of Education* that racial segregation had no place in public education.

Then, on December 1, 1955, the battle for equality spilled into the streets—literally. Following the arrest of Rosa L. Parks, a Negro seamstress, for refusing to yield her seat on a Montgomery, Alabama, bus to a white passenger, the city's black citizens mounted a boycott. It lasted 381 days and finally forced the Montgomery bus system and the city's white power structure to their knees. It also thrust into national prominence the man who over the next thirteen years became the most recognizable face of the civil rights movement, Dr. Martin Luther King Jr.

In 1957, in a show of support for the Supreme Court's *Brown* decision and after South Carolina Senator Strom Thurmond's longest-in-history filibuster (twenty-four hours and eighteen minutes), Congress passed the nation's first civil rights act since the post–Civil War Reconstruction period.

It was a modest bill, but it had one important result from the perspective of Notre Dame: it created the United States Commission on Civil Rights. After signing the bill into law, President Dwight Eisenhower tapped Father Theodore M. Hesburgh, the young president of Notre Dame, to serve as a charter member.

Hesburgh had been inaugurated as Notre Dame's president five years earlier, in 1952. He took over an institution with an endowment of $9 million, a student body of about five thousand, and a reputation mainly as a football school. He would leave the presidency thirty-five years later, having transformed Notre Dame into a modern university among the first rank in American higher education.

Part of that transformation included welcoming Negroes, providing them access to the American mainstream. But it was a slow and painful process. When Hesburgh took over in 1952, there were fewer than a dozen Negro students at Notre Dame. By the end of the 1950s, there were only a few more than that. But progress was being made. A black man, Aubrey Lewis, had been a starter and a star on the football team, and, in 1957–58, the captain of the track team, the first black captain of a Notre Dame athletic team. Another black man, Tommy Hawkins, had been Notre Dame's first basketball All-American and first black basketball team captain. And another black man, the celebrated diplomat Dr. Ralph Bunche, had become the first black recipient of an honorary doctorate from Notre Dame.

A black presence had taken root in the old sod at Notre Dame, and the tender shoots of a new multiculturalism had begun to appear.

FRAZIER L. THOMPSON

(Class of 1947)

THE STORY WAS ONLY THREE PARAGRAPHS LONG AND IT APPEARED at the bottom of page 31 of the March 23, 1946, edition of the *Baltimore Afro-American*. But it attested to the importance of the University of Notre Dame in the national consciousness at that time and, consequently, the importance of a twenty-year-old Philadelphian who had enrolled there almost two years earlier.

Under the headline "Sprint Star Blazes Trail at Notre Dame," the newspaper reported that Frazier Leon Thompson of Philadelphia, "first colored athlete to compete in Notre Dame athletics," had run the sixty-yard dash in 6.2 seconds in a recent triangular meet among Notre Dame, Marquette, and Michigan State. That feat, the paper said, was evidence of Thompson's status as "one of the outstanding sprinters in the school's track history."

Whether he realized it or not, Frazier Thompson was carrying the hopes of a whole people on his shoulders when he arrived on the Notre Dame campus in July 1944 as a member of the US Navy's V-12 officer training program. His was the age of black breakthroughs, of barrier-breakers and "firsts."

It was the time of Joe Louis, the Brown Bomber, who loomed large as a hero in the hearts and minds of black Americans. It was *before* the time of Jackie Robinson, who didn't shatter the most potent cultural barrier of all—baseball's color line—until 1947, three years after Thompson's enrollment.

It was before Kenny Washington, a former UCLA football star, would be signed to a contract with the NFL champion Los Angeles Rams, making him the first black player signed to play in modern professional football. (Ironically, Washington's signing was reported on the front page of the same March 23, 1946, edition of the *Afro-American* that reported Thompson's success in that sixty-yard dash.)

Notre Dame, a perennial national sports powerhouse since the days of Knute Rockne, was college football's New York Yankees, its heavyweight champion, and as big a deal as any professional football team at the time. To have a black man involved in athletics at Notre Dame was of huge symbolic importance to black Americans. A black man on the football team would have been the ideal, but any black man performing in any sport was significant.

Of course, Thompson's athletic success was in the nature of a lagniappe, a little extra. His greatest significance lay in the fact that he had cracked the enrollment barrier at Notre Dame. Although it seems never to have been written university policy, it had long been understood among black Americans that Notre Dame did not admit Negroes, apparently for fear of alienating white students from the South.

But that barrier fell before the demands of the Navy, which engaged Notre Dame and dozens of other colleges and universities around the nation to prepare young men for service as officers in the World War II naval forces. The V-12 enrollees were to be provided an intensive, accelerated college education, so they could be rushed into the fight against the Axis powers.

That Thompson's matriculation at Notre Dame was assisted by the Navy was more than a little ironic, since the Navy, more than any of the other services, resisted enlisting blacks even as the war raged. Only after President Franklin Roosevelt pushed the Navy into it—and Joe Louis helped embarrass it into it—did the Navy relent.

Even so, it's not clear that Thompson's enrollment at Notre Dame was intentional on the Navy's part. President Emeritus Rev. Theodore M. Hesburgh, in a 2008 interview with the *Wall Street Journal*, said the Navy "thought he was white when they invited him to the program, and when they swore him in, they found out he was black."

As it turned out, Thompson was discharged from the Navy in October 1945, three months after the war ended. Invited by university officials to stay on, he did. He majored in pre-med and ran track, becoming in 1945 the first black athlete to win a Notre Dame monogram. He lived in Morrissey Hall and chaired an organization called the South Bend Youth Congress, besides running track.

At least two other black students also enrolled at Notre Dame in 1944, but later in the year than Frazier Thompson. Carl Coggins, of

Warren, Ohio, was one of them. Coggins ended up earning a bachelor's degree in naval science; he graduated in June 1947, along with Thompson. He was commissioned a Navy officer and served for several years before returning to Notre Dame to earn another bachelor's degree, in civil engineering, in 1952.

Rev. Edward Williams, pastor of a South Bend AME congregation, enrolled in Notre Dame's journalism program in late 1944 and received his degree in August 1947, a few months after Thompson and Coggins had gotten theirs.

Speaking late in his life about his status as Notre Dame's first black student, Thompson was quoted in a black alumni newsletter as saying, "I wasn't trying to prove anything. I just wanted to be me. I just wanted an education. I wasn't trying to prove a point."

After graduation, he returned to the Philadelphia area. His Notre Dame degree did not immediately work the magic that it has for subsequent generations of black alumni: he ended up going to work for the US Postal Service, not to medical school at Temple or the University of Pennsylvania, as he had told the *Afro-American* he hoped to.

In 1955 he changed jobs, going to work for ILC Corporation of Dover, Delaware, where he spent the rest of his career. Among other things, he helped test space suits used by American astronauts.

Ben Finley, Class of 1960, a founder of the Black Alumni of Notre Dame, tracked Thompson down at his home in Dover in the late 1980s and spent several hours talking with him about his experience as Notre Dame's first black student. Thompson was ill at the time, suffering from cancer.

"He was very proud of being the first African-American graduate," Finley said. "He talked about living in Vetville," the area on campus where veterans were housed.

Because of his illness, there was no possibility that Thompson would be able to attend the first Black Alumni Reunion, which was being planned at the time. So Finley asked the aged pioneer whether there was anything he would like from Notre Dame.

"He asked me to send him a Notre Dame stadium blanket," Finley said.

Frazier Thompson died in Dover on September 25, 1991. He was 65.

In 1997, the Black Alumni of Notre Dame created the Frazier Thompson Scholarship Fund. In 2008, Notre Dame honored Thompson at a football game. One of his two sons, Paul Thompson, presented the colors before the game.

An interesting footnote: In May 1947 the *Baltimore Afro-American Magazine* sent a reporter to Notre Dame to write about the impending graduations of Frazier Thompson and Carl Coggins. The resulting story contained this prescient observation, attributed to "close observers" of the racial change at Notre Dame.

Those observers, it said, "point out that an opening wedge has been made and that it is reasonable to assume that in time other qualified men will be admitted, and some will eventually make the celebrated football team."

They didn't know the half of it.

CLYDE JUPITER

(Class of 1951 MS)

Clyde Jupiter came to Notre Dame in autumn 1949 from New Orleans. He was a graduate student in physics with an undergraduate degree from Xavier University of Louisiana. After receiving his Notre Dame degree, he married, served in the Army, and later focused on radiation detectors, accelerators, and nuclear safety research. He organized and managed JUPITER Corporation, a technical service company, for twenty-five years. He and his wife, Pat, now live in Salt Lake City, Utah.

HURTLING THROUGH THE BLACK NIGHT IN LATE AUGUST 1949, amid the rumbling of the swaying coach and the high-pitched screeching of steel wheels on iron rails, I lazily scanned occasional distant lights of farmhouses and towns, wondering how my new adventure would unfold. I was a welcome captive on the Panama Limited—the fastest rail transport on the Illinois Central Railroad, speeding overnight from New Orleans to Chicago.

I was traveling in the company of a friend, Charlie Bell, and my brother, Clarence. The three of us had secured bachelor's degrees from Xavier University of Louisiana and were en route to fulfill a dream we had audaciously harbored since our youth—without family precedent for accomplishment of such fantasies. Clarence was to begin graduate studies at the Art Institute of Chicago, and Charlie was accompanying me to the University of Notre Dame, where he would be in his third year of graduate study in mathematics and I would begin work toward a master's degree in physics.

As I mulled over my future away from home, I tried to visualize the Notre Dame campus environment and how I might adapt to my new off-campus home in South Bend. I recalled the events leading to this moment: preparing to graduate from Xavier the previous June with a BS in physics and without monetary resources for graduate school tuition, I would have to either postpone school for a year while working to save money, or secure support from the school.

Accordingly, I applied to a dozen universities outside the Jim Crow South that had reputable science curricula, seeking scholarship or fellowship assistance. I planned to accept the best financial offer. I considered no other criteria such as religion or racial composition of the student body; in 1949, all of the larger universities were predominantly white anyway. In response to my application, Notre Dame offered me a physics teaching fellowship with an annual stipend of $2,000, which I happily accepted.

The preceding weeks had been a blur of preparations—purchase of a wardrobe trunk and suitcase, packing for a long stay away from home, goodbyes to family and friends, and taking every opportunity to savor my mother's home cooking.

The train conductor's shout of "Kankakee!" roused me from my musing and informed me that we were nearing our destination. Upon arriving in Chicago, Charlie and I accompanied Clarence to his dormitory at the Art Institute, where we stayed overnight before taking the train to South Bend. Charlie had used his contacts from the previous year to arrange affordable lodging for us at the economical rate of $7.00 a week in a blue-collar rooming house on East Sorin Street, near the corner of Eddy—and within walking distance (about a mile) of the Notre Dame campus.

It was an aged two-story cottage with two bedrooms and one bath that had been converted to accommodate five tenants and the landlady, Mrs. Zoe Smith, who ran a tight ship with sternly enforced house rules. Charlie and I occupied the choice front upstairs bedroom. Our colorful cohabitants in this dwelling included Thurston, a big-time spender from East St. Louis who worked at the Studebaker plant; Joe, a gay house painter; and an older man employed at the Bendix factory. These guys regaled us with stories that were both entertaining and revealing about people and situations that were foreign to us.

We all had use of the kitchen on a restricted schedule and could prepare our own food. Charlie and I set a figure of $13.00 a week as our (impossible) food budget, with me doing the cooking based on untested knowledge garnered by watching my mother in her kitchen. We survived this arrangement only because of the kindness of some local black families, who proudly observed the presence of a few black students enrolled at Notre Dame. Charlie and I received dinner invitations from several families. We became expert at accepting such invitations, scoring about two engagements per week. However, the key benefit for us was the friendliness and emotional support from members of South Bend's black community, who welcomed the belated integration of their hometown university; they wanted to help us be successful. It was common to encounter an elderly black stranger at the bus stop in town and hear expressions of appreciation for "our boys at Notre Dame."

Arriving on campus, I found myself to be the lone black student in the physics department, and only one of six black students on a campus of about five thousand. The group included Charles B. Bell (mathematics), Alton Adams (engineering), George Rhodes (education), Tony Horne (history), Aaron Dyson (physical education), and me.

My professors and many white classmates were friendly enough, but we were not friends—a consequence of racial inhibitions on my part as well as theirs. I was not part of a study group, and we did not socialize off campus. My closest relationship within the physics department was with a Chinese student, Leslie Ho, who experienced similar social isolation. The physics department head, Father Henry J. Bolger, CSC, was cordial, but distant.

My daily routine was to attend class, study alone in the library, and return to my room on East Sorin Street to do homework. Weekends afforded some pleasant social interactions with black townspeople and a relief from the isolation of the campus community. The six of us black students got together very infrequently—usually in smaller groups.

The physics department sponsored a monthly social with pizza, piano music, and group singing. My thermodynamics professor noticed that I was humming instead of singing—I didn't know any of those songs—so he invited me to suggest songs for the group. I happily provided titles of several songs ("Gypsy," "I'm True") that were popular among my college classmates, but found that white Notre Dame students didn't know any of them. So they went back to singing theirs.

The academic work was challenging because my undergraduate physics preparation was a bit substandard. Accordingly, I made a strong effort to catch up and was assigned two remedial undergraduate physics courses as a supplement to my graduate courses—which helped immensely. I found my mathematics skills to be competitive with other students since Xavier had a strong mathematics program. As a teaching fellow, I assisted in undergraduate physics laboratory instruction and grading laboratory experiments and test papers. This was a particularly useful experience. Physics department seminar discussions of current departmental research were very enlightening. This peer review process provided a pattern for my later use in evaluating research projects.

In September 1950 a few additional black students appeared on campus, including Entee Shine and Joe Bertrand, both of whom played on the basketball team; Bill Johnson, a chemistry student; and others.

The only negative experience I had with the university was a threatening warning received from a university official to withdraw an affidavit that I and other black citizens had signed with the local district attorney, citing the manager of a dance hall in South Bend for unlawfully refusing us admission to a "white" dance. We took this action rather spontaneously, to oppose illegal discriminatory practices in South Bend. Evidently the DA had contacted the university to get me off the case, so the town could continue with its status-quo practices. I was disappointed and outraged that the university official would take such a position against me for supporting law enforcement.

Consequently, I focused on graduating and leaving the university, which I did in August 1951 with a master's degree in physics. For the next fifty-eight years, I never visited the campus or engaged in Notre Dame alumni activities. However, in 2009 I met Dr. Ani Aprahamian, professor and director of the nuclear physics laboratory at Notre Dame. We were attending a working meeting of a US Department of Energy nuclear science advisory committee, for which she served as co-chair.

As a result of her friendship and encouragement, I visited the Notre Dame campus during the 2009 alumni gathering and received an escorted tour of the campus—including the nuclear accelerator lab.

The highlight of my visit was participation in a black alumni dinner meeting. It was exhilarating to find myself in a room on the Notre Dame campus crowded with black alumni—so different from past experiences wherein I might encounter one or two black students per month, other than my roommate Charlie. My initial thought was: "Where were you all in 1949?"

Following graduation from Notre Dame in August 1951, I accepted my first professional job as an aerodynamicist with Douglas Aircraft Company in California. My career was indeed helped by my credentials as a Notre Dame graduate—either because people recognized Notre Dame's academic standing or because they were impressed by its football team (or both). This initial professional acceptance opened up work opportunities that led to valuable on-the-job training in nuclear physics research and development at the Lawrence Radiation Laboratory in Livermore, California, with subsequent opportunities in corporate project management and marketing, as well as university-level teaching.

Publication of research papers in journals and proceedings of several professional societies provided me recognition in the technical community, and I was elected to the grade of Fellow in the American Nuclear Society. My career was capped by my organizing and leading a successful technical service company for twenty-five years and registering two patents.

My Notre Dame student experience was somewhat stressful because of racial inhibitions on my part as well as that of the university staff and the predominantly white student body. However, I gained a good education and carried recognized academic credentials that afforded me excellent job opportunities that benefitted my career. I am grateful for having received a physics teaching fellowship from Notre Dame that enabled my entry to graduate school. I will always be grateful to the black families—particularly the Riddle, Moxley, Smith, Toodle, and Allen families—in South Bend whose friendship and hospitality played a significant role in maintaining a degree of normalcy in my life. I hope that my life, and those of the other black pioneers at Notre Dame, have rewarded the pride and trust that they placed in us.

ALTON A. ADAMS JR.

(Class of 1952)

Alton Adams came to Notre Dame in autumn 1948 from St. Thomas, Virgin Islands. He was a transfer student from Syracuse University. He majored in civil engineering. After graduation, he served as an Air Force pilot and operated his own engineering firm for many years. He lives in Atlanta.

MY FIRST VISIT TO THE NOTRE DAME CAMPUS WAS IN 1948, when I transferred from Syracuse University in my sophomore year. Upon disembarking from the taxi, the sight of the Golden Dome and the Basilica was the most inspirational moment of my young life. It has remained with me at Notre Dame as a student and throughout my adult life.

After considering enrolling in several Catholic universities (Georgetown, Catholic University, Fordham, St. John's in Minnesota) Notre Dame was recommended by a high school teacher because of its size, national recognition, and scholastic excellence.

I was one of six children born to Alton and Ella Adams and raised in St. Thomas, Virgin Islands. My father, a prolific musical composer, music critic, author, entrepreneur, and hotelier, was the first black US Navy bandmaster. My mother was a homemaker devoting all of her time, love, and efforts to raising the family.

I was assigned to Badin Hall, at that time a senior dormitory. While one of the older buildings, it was considered the most desirable living quarters on campus. Father Bernard Furstoss, the rector, and

Father Theodore Hesburgh, one of the dorm prefects, were popular and well liked.

The student population consisted to a great extent of former military men enrolled under the GI Bill of Rights. They brought a sense of maturity to us eighteen-year-old students. The most common attire was former military uniforms, purchased from military surplus stores.

In 1948 Aaron Dyson (Class of 1953), who was a World War II veteran, and I were the only African-American undergraduates at Notre Dame. There were nine Negro graduate students. Dyson was very popular, not only with the athletes but with students in general. He supplemented his GI funds by delivering the *South Bend Tribune* on campus.

While there was general acceptance of their Negro fellow students by the majority of the white students, there was at times outspoken resentment by some, together with a few members of the South Bend business community. A white former US Navy officer—a law school student—with whom I became friends, invited me once to join him at a popular off-campus beer joint frequented on Friday nights by students, only to be refused service. Together with several others, we left under some unpleasant conditions.

This incident, supported by some in keeping with their Southern culture, was expressed in the *Scholastic*. Two Notre Dame administrators, Father Hesburgh and Father Edmund Joyce, together with athletic director and basketball coach Edward "Moose" Krause and some members of the football and basketball teams, championed the cause for equal social justice. One way was to recruit outstanding high school basketball athletes.

Entee Shine, an Indiana all-state basketball and football star from South Bend Central High School, was recruited by Frank Leahy for the football team. Shine left the football team because, he said, he became "uncomfortable," and joined the Notre Dame basketball team instead. Joe Bertrand, a St. Elizabeth Chicago High School All-American, was recruited and joined the basketball squad that included Dick Rosenthal, who later became the Notre Dame athletic director. In 1950 Bertrand and Shine became the first Negroes to play one of the major sports at Notre Dame.

They often complained about being accommodated apart from the rest of the squad at Knights of Columbus facilities when the team traveled, even when they were playing Catholic colleges and universities. Father Hesburgh, upon becoming president of the university, immediately corrected this practice.

Aaron Dyson, Bengal Bouter and a member of the football B Varsity Team, at the encouragement and insistence of members of the football team, played in the final 1951 home game and is considered to be the first African-American football player in Notre Dame history. I personally witnessed that moment. The student body responded with great applause and cheers.

I have many fond memories of student life at Notre Dame, among which was the mandatory thrice-weekly attendance at mass in the dormitory chapel that required our signatures. This act of devotion has remained as a constant obligation to sustain me and my faith, instilled through the teaching of Christian principles emphasized at Notre Dame. My class in marriage and ethics has also been of great importance and meaning throughout fifty-six years of marriage.

As civil engineering students, we were required to earn 140 credit hours for graduation, including many laboratory courses, at times demanding Saturday morning classes that on home football Saturdays were difficult to accept. Additionally, we were required to participate in summer land-surveying classes, most of which were conducted outdoors in a remote peach orchard, competing with dragonflies enjoying the fruit that fell to the ground.

Father Hesburgh was installed as president in June 1952. As a member of the August 1952 summer graduating class, I was informed by Karl Schoenherr, then dean of the School of Engineering, that the first diploma signed by Father Hesburgh was that of Alton Adams.

On the occasion of my sixtieth class reunion in 2012, I had a private visit with Father Hesburgh. He was kind and gracious enough to again sign a copy of my 1952 diploma, after reminiscing over sixty years of progress and, in particular, some yet-to-be-achieved goals in increasing the numbers of Hispanic Notre Dame students.

I am today so proud and honored, recognizing what Father Hesburgh means to Notre Dame and his contributions to education, social and civil rights, national service, expansion of the physical plant of the campus, and spiritual programs.

Father Hesburgh's influence sustained my desire to continue activities and services within and to the diocese of the Virgin Islands and my parish. For those I was given special blessing by Pope John XXIII. There was also the opportunity to consult and work with two bishops with strong connections to the Virgin Islands, who later were elevated to cardinals (Bernard Law and Sean O'Malley, both of Boston).

I was among the first group of graduates presented with the "Black Notre Dame Exemplars" recognition that hangs prominently and proudly on the wall at my home and, before that, hung in my office.

Negro student enrollment at Notre Dame was unusual in 1949 and of such interest that *Ebony* magazine, in its February 1950 publication, used the subject as its cover story. The article, in some detail, covered the history and campus life of the nine Negro students and the first two graduates—Frazier Thompson and Rev. Edward B. Williams.

Negro students were often invited by radio and print media to talk about their experience. At that time, attendance at Notre Dame by Negroes was considered a novelty. Radio station WWCA, in Gary, Indiana, was frequently visited.

Social life and activities on campus were rather limited or non-existent. Off-campus South Bend families—the Moxleys, Smiths, Riddles, Whites, and Bells—provided much of the social life for Negro students.

After my graduation from Notre Dame, I spent a year with Lockheed Aircraft as a junior structural engineer. I then entered the US Air Force and earned my wings as a pilot, flying for six years. Upon honorable discharge I worked with the Civil Aeronautics Administration, was executive director of the Virgin Islands Port Authority, and finally was founder and president of Alton Adams Jr. Inc., an engineering firm, for thirty-eight years.

JOSEPH BERTRAND

(Class of 1954)

FOR MANY A CATHOLIC KID GROWING UP ON THE SOUTH SIDE of Chicago, going to college at Notre Dame has been the fulfillment of a lifelong dream and the gateway to professional success.

And if the kid was black? Well, he could do all right, too.

Joseph Bertrand is a case in point. In fact, Joe Bertrand was the *first* case in point.

He arrived at Notre Dame in the fall of 1950, recruited as a basketball player from St. Elizabeth, a small, black Catholic high school on Chicago's South Side. Despite its relatively tiny size, St. Elizabeth was a basketball powerhouse, largely thanks to Bertrand. During his senior year he reportedly scored more points than any other player in the Chicago area except one: Johnny Lattner, who also went to Notre Dame and won the Heisman Trophy in 1953 as quarterback of the football team.

Like so many black families in Chicago, Bertrand's family were migrants. They came from Biloxi, Mississippi, where he had been born, in pursuit of jobs and freedom.

Timothy O'Hara, a 1954 classmate of Bertrand's who became a friend when they both worked together in Chicago city government, said that, during his youth, Bertrand became a protégé of Roger J. Kiley, a longtime, highly influential member of the legal community in Chicago who ended his career as a judge of the United States Court of Appeals, appointed by President John F. Kennedy. Kiley was a Notre Dame graduate and had played football under Knute Rockne. It was Kiley who apparently steered Bertrand to Notre Dame.

Bertrand was one of two black basketball recruits in the freshman class of 1950. The other was Entee Shine, a two-sport (football and basketball) star at South Bend Central High School. Together they made history when, in the autumn of 1951, in their sophomore years, they took the floor as starters for the Fighting Irish.

Shine, along with two other members of the team, became academically ineligible after that first semester of his sophomore year. He eventually left Notre Dame. But Joe Bertrand continued. Not only did he become the first black man to win a monogram in basketball, he also was named an honorable mention All-American after his senior season. And he *endured*.

In *Echoes on the Hardwood: 100 Seasons of Notre Dame Men's Basketball*, author Mike Coffey quotes Jim Gibbons, a teammate of Bertrand's, about an incident that occurred during a road trip to Louisville, Kentucky:

> After the game, Joe Bertrand and I went out to eat. We got into a restaurant and sat down at the counter. We sat there and sat there and sat there, until finally the guy that was the maître d', so to speak, came up and said, "Excuse me, but you'll have to leave. We don't serve blacks here." Joe didn't say a word. He handled it like a champion. We got up and walked out and didn't cause any problem. That was my first experience with racism. It had never happened to me before, and I wouldn't have imagined it in a hundred years.

After graduation, Bertrand remained at Notre Dame for two years as a coach, and then spent two years in the Army. After the Army, he returned to Chicago and went into the banking business. He also began working his way up in Chicago and Cook County government and politics. His Catholicism and his Notre Dame pedigree stood him in good stead as he became a ward committeeman and an alderman and, after being chosen for the Democratic ticket in 1971 by Mayor Richard J. Daley, he was elected Chicago city treasurer. That made him the first black person elected to a citywide office in Chicago. He served as treasurer from 1971 to 1979.

Asked about his father's time at Notre Dame, Bertrand's son, Joseph Bertrand Jr., said his father "developed some meaningful relationships that carried him through life."

But Catholicism and Notre Dame and those relationships could not shield him against all negativity. According to the *Chicago Tri-*

bune, Bertrand applied in 1963 to become a member of the Knights of Columbus and was rejected. Only after the grand knight of the Chicago Council, Eugene Liner, resigned in protest was Bertrand accepted for membership. One more barrier broken down by the black kid from the South Side.

Joseph Bertrand died much too young on Nov. 8, 1990. He was fifty-nine.

Wayne Edmonds

(Class of 1956)

Wayne Edmonds came to Notre Dame in autumn 1952 from the western Pennsylvania coal town of Canonsburg. He became the first black player to earn a monogram for football. He majored in sociology and, after graduation, went on to earn a master's degree in social work at the University of Pittsburgh. He had a long and highly successful career in social work, education, and physical fitness. He lives now with his wife, Dorothy, in Harrisburg, Pennsylvania.

BY THE TIME I REACHED SENIOR YEAR OF HIGH SCHOOL IN autumn 1951, I had attracted the attention of several college football programs. I visited Penn State, Penn, and Colgate, but I really expected to go to the University of Pittsburgh, where I had the promise of a full scholarship and a commitment for graduate school if I wanted to go. (I had even been contacted by the University of Georgia, which obviously didn't realize I was black. What a visit that could have turned into!)

Then, thanks to scouting reports and information from Notre Dame supporters in western Pennsylvania, I got a call from Coach Bob McBride, an assistant to head coach Frank Leahy, at Notre Dame. He invited me to visit. And so, on a lark, I went with my Canonsburg High School teammate Jim Malone to South Bend.

I knew Notre Dame had never before had a black football player, but I was impressed by the campus and the academic program. And I knew Coach Frank Leahy had had black players on his team at Boston

College and so would probably be open to minority players now that he was coaching at Notre Dame.

In the end, the biggest hurdle to my going to Notre Dame was my mother, Grace Edmonds, who was afraid Notre Dame would turn her Baptist son into a Catholic. Coach McBride promised that he would see that I got to Baptist services every Sunday, and that was good enough for Mom. In fall 1952, I set out to Notre Dame—again with my teammate Jim Malone.

My Notre Dame years were full of difficult challenges and unforgettable experiences. Joining me on the football team in autumn 1952 was another young black man from western Pennsylvania, Dick Washington. Freshmen weren't allowed to play in those days—we were to concentrate on our studies. Dick washed out during sophomore year, so I became the first black player to remain at Notre Dame long enough to earn a monogram in football. With the support of the Notre Dame athletic department and the administration, I made desegregation of the football team a reality and set the pace for other young black men who wanted to come to South Bend to play.

I went to Notre Dame as an end but was moved to tackle in my sophomore year. I achieved monogram status three years, including with the 1953 national championship team.

In 1953, Notre Dame's season-opener was at Oklahoma. No hotel could be found in Norman that would accommodate the entire team— black players and white—so we stayed at a hotel an hour or so outside the university town. On game day, as the team buses drove to the stadium, Coach Leahy used that fact to whip up the players' enthusiasm to beat Oklahoma, which we did by a score of 28–21.

The 1953 Notre Dame–North Carolina game also was memorable; not because it was a close game, but because Dick Washington and I were the first blacks to appear in Kenan Stadium in Chapel Hill. The black fans, seated in a segregated section of the stands, roared as the two young black men ran onto the field with the Notre Dame team.

Still later in the 1953 season, Notre Dame was to play Georgia Tech, which had a thirty-one-game winning streak and the number-one ranking at the time. It was to be a home game for Georgia Tech, but Tech said Notre Dame couldn't bring me or Dick Washington onto the field in Atlanta.

Our Lady stood strong. If Georgia Tech wanted to play Notre Dame, Frank Leahy said, it would have to come to South Bend and play the *entire* Notre Dame team. They came. Notre Dame won, 27–14.

After the 1955 game with the Miami Hurricanes, in a special exception to the sanctity of the Notre Dame locker room, Jake Gaither, the legendary coach of Florida A&M University, came in, got me, and took me with him for a celebration of the Notre Dame victory in the Miami black community. The experience was like something out of *Cabin in the Sky*—I enjoyed the music and the adoring fans, signing autographs and getting back to the hotel in Miami in the wee hours of the morning.

I never knew who engineered that experience, but figured it had been arranged by Coach Leahy or Father Ted Hesburgh, both of whom looked out for me while I was at Notre Dame. Nobody, even Jake Gaither, gets into the locker room without someone higher up approving.

Off the football field there were ups and downs. I recall walking back to campus one day with another black student when one of the Notre Dame priests, known as Father Mac, stopped his car and told us we were in a "restricted" part of town where Notre Dame students weren't supposed to be. (In other words, we were in the black section of town.)

I replied, "We went to get a haircut—you know the campus barbershop only cuts white hair." That got us off the hook with Father Mac, but the Notre Dame barbershop did not change its discriminatory policy for many years after that.

In the 1954–55 academic year, I had the privilege of living in Sorin Hall in the room that had been occupied in the 1920s by Harry Stuhldreher of "Four Horsemen" fame. One afternoon, while visiting his son who was then at Notre Dame, Stuhldreher showed up to look at his old room. I had the chance to meet and talk with him a bit, an amazing experience for any Notre Dame football player. What a thrill!

In that same hall that year, there was a fire one Saturday caused by a sunlamp that had been left on. I was in the dorm at the time and helped those in the hall to get out. Among those I helped was a "don," a residential advisor, who lived in the hall. This don was a professor who had flunked me in an English literature course the prior year.

When I complained to the athletic department, they said that, if they had known, they would have warned me not to take that professor's course because he was known not to like football players.

After I "rescued" the don from the dorm fire, he asked me to take his course again. I did so and got an acceptable, accurate grade. And maybe the don's prejudice against football players ended. One could only hope!

When I came back to campus in autumn 1955, I was disturbed, as was most of America, about the murder in Mississippi of Emmett Till, a fourteen-year-old black boy from Chicago. But I heard no discussion of the atrocity in class or anywhere on campus.

As it happened, I was taking a speech course that semester and I decided to do a speech on the Emmett Till murder. I enlisted a couple of classmates to raise their hands and hold up dollar bills when I came to the part of the speech where I would ask for donations to help achieve some justice in this awful situation. I ended up getting the then-enormous sum of fifty dollars. I was prepared to refund it to the donors, but the professor said, "No, you need to see that the NAACP gets the money."

I had no idea how to do that, but I had a friend and mentor in South Bend, Art Hurd, a labor organizer and business owner, and I knew he would know what to do. That was how I first got involved with the NAACP. I remained involved throughout my adult life, eventually serving as chair of the Canonsburg chapter.

(As an aside, at a class reunion many years after the Till murder, several of my classmates told me their parents had selected Notre Dame for them partly because it would be a safe place for them during the coming civil rights upheaval. So they were shocked when I walked into the classroom on the first day.)

My father and my brother had been to the campus for a few games, but my mother had never visited Notre Dame until my graduation in 1956. I graduated from the College of Arts and Letters. My major was sociology, supplemented with courses in my other interests—history, English, and philosophy.

Since my earliest years in the Number Nine coal patch and the little town of McDonald, Pennsylvania, my ambition had been to become a social worker. I had seen how social service agency staff treated the people they visited. I vowed I would do things differently.

During Christmas my senior year, I wrote the dean of the School of Social Work at the University of Pittsburgh, inquiring about entering the MSW program in the fall of 1956. Those plans took a brief detour as inquiries came in from professional football teams, including the Green Bay Packers, the Philadelphia Eagles, the Chicago Bears, and my hometown team, the Pittsburgh Steelers. I was the second of eight players from the 1956 Notre Dame team to be drafted, taken by the Steelers in the ninth round. I was the first lineman to receive a signing bonus from the Steelers, the handsome sum of $500. But while at the Steelers' training camp, my dad brought me a letter from Pitt, admitting me to the School of Social Work. So I left training camp and set about to begin my career in social work.

And what a career it was! Fittingly for a child from the coal fields, I spent a substantial part of it working with and for the United Mine Workers, administering health and benefit programs. I worked in academia, as a professor and a dean at Pitt's School of Social Work and at California State University in California, Pennsylvania. And eventually I found my way into physical fitness, administering at the state level programs for youth, senior citizens, and disabled Pennsylvanians.

In December 1991 I retired or, as I like to say, "graduated" to tend my garden, enjoy the company of my wife and my four daughters, ten grandchildren, and nine great grandchildren—so far.

In 2009, when the Notre Dame athletic department celebrated "60 Years of Success by Black Athletes" at the university, I had the honor of presenting the flag in pre-game ceremonies before the ND–San Diego State season opener. I did so alongside one of the sons of Frazier Thompson, who earned the first monogram by a black athlete in 1947 in track.

My experiences at Notre Dame reinforced values I grew up with— that with hard work and good relationships, you can go a long way. Notre Dame gave me an opportunity to see where I had something to give to others.

GOLDIE IVORY

(Class of 1956 MA)

IT IS ONLY HALF-TRUE THAT NOTRE DAME DID NOT ADMIT women as students until 1972. The university had a long tradition before then of educating women, mostly members of religious orders, in graduate programs. But it was not until 1956, nine years after Frazier Thompson became Notre Dame's first black graduate, that the University of Notre Dame awarded a graduate degree to a black laywoman.

She was Goldie Lee Ivory, a South Bend resident who, on July 31, 1956, received a master's degree in sociology. Mrs. Ivory was thirty at the time, married to an autoworker, Sam Ivory, and the mother of twin five-year-old sons, Kevin and Kenneth.

She was a native of Chicago and a graduate of South Bend Central High School. She had earned a bachelor's degree in social services from Indiana University Bloomington. She already had broken a barrier by becoming one of the first two black people to be employed in the St. Joseph County probation department. When she received her Notre Dame degree she was working as intake supervisor at the county's juvenile department.

"N.D. Degree Goes to First Negro Woman" read the headline on a *South Bend Tribune* story about her achievement. A picture accompanying the story showed Mrs. Ivory wearing what appears to be a black robe and with a mortarboard on her head, seated on a sofa next to her admiring husband and with their two little boys standing by.

In the article she credited her husband for standing by her and encouraging her, first to get her IU degree and then to endure the three summer sessions and a winter of evening classes to earn the Notre Dame degree. Not only did she have to care for their two sons and work a full-time job while studying for the master's, but her husband had to find new employment after being laid off from his job at the then-mighty Studebaker-Packard Corp. in South Bend.

"I almost cracked under the strain," Mrs. Ivory was quoted as saying. And even though she was not a Catholic, she credited two religious medals—of St. Christopher and St. Francis of Assisi—and a lot of coffee with keeping her going.

Sociology, of course, fit well with her professional focus on youth and the justice system. But after earning her Notre Dame degree she went on to a variety of other professional pursuits as well. She taught at Goshen and Saint Mary's Colleges, and worked for many years in the Elkhart Community Schools system, where she started out as an attendance worker and retired in June 1987 as director of human relations.

A grandniece, Angie Winston, described Mrs. Ivory as "a very driven person" to whom "education was very important."

She was a well-known figure in the South Bend and Elkhart communities. A photo on the website of the South Bend alumnae chapter of Delta Sigma Theta sorority shows her among ten charter members of the chapter. And she was an active member of Greater Holy Temple Church of God in Christ in South Bend.

Goldie Ivory died on December 17, 2010, in South Bend. She was eighty-four.

LEMUEL JOYNER

(Classes of 1957, 1969 MFA)

Lemuel Joyner came to Notre Dame in 1951. He majored in fine arts and graduated in 1957 with a bachelor of fine arts degree. He later earned a master of fine arts at Notre Dame. He taught for several years at St. Mary's College and worked in liturgical art and as an art therapist in private practice. He and his wife, Barbara, live in South Bend.

IN THE SPRING OF 1951 — IT WOULD HAVE BEEN MAY OR June — my father, Dennis Joyner, dropped me off at the front of the Notre Dame campus. He and my older brother, Dennis Jr., then turned around and headed home to Nashville, Tennessee. I headed into the campus. I had $35 in my pockets and the name of a contact, a priest.

As I wandered the campus, I encountered a priest and asked his help to find my contact. He went off for a short time to see what he could do. When he came back he said he had had no luck and he explained, "There are many priests on this campus; there's no way for me to find this one."

He then asked whether I had had anything to eat. I told him I was planning to find a restaurant and get a bite to eat. He took me to Corby Hall and we ate. While eating dinner we discussed where I would stay. I was given a key and spent that first night in Sorin Hall.

The next day this priest, whose name I cannot now remember, sent me to the university's business manager, who had contacts at Bendix and other big South Bend employers and routinely connected

Notre Dame students and others with them. Bendix at the time was on layoff, but the business manager sent me to a foundry on the West Side of South Bend, where I was hired for the summer months. I lived that summer with a black family in the city, the Herrings.

So began my life in South Bend and my relationship with Notre Dame, where I enrolled as a student in September 1951.

Notre Dame was my second college. I had enrolled at Tennessee State immediately after high school and completed about two-and-a-half years of study before dropping out to support my first wife, Mattie, and our three sons, Lemuel Jr., John Michael, and Christopher Anthony.

It was one of my employers who urged me to go back to school. You'll never be able to support your family the way you want to unless you get an education, he told me. So I decided to resume my education. I wrote to three colleges: UCLA, Michigan State, and Notre Dame. Only Notre Dame responded.

I entered Notre Dame at age twenty-three, intending to major in architecture. I was going to be a black Frank Lloyd Wright. My wife and children were not with me that first semester, when I lived in Farley Hall. My daily routine was going to classes during the day (I was taking twenty-one credit hours), then working from 3:30 p.m. until midnight at Bendix, and studying after that.

One day, as I was studying for exams, I became involved in conversation with one of the hall rectors, Father Victor Dean. When he saw my schedule, he was shocked. "There's no way you can keep this up," he said.

At the end of my first semester, we had a conference. I was there with my father and my brother, along with Father Dean; Father Charles Sheedy, who had been named dean of the College of Arts and Letters, and Father Ted Hesburgh, who would become the president of the university. They said that, given my need to work to support my family, I would need to change majors to something less demanding than architecture. I would be given a semester to prove myself. So I switched to fine arts.

My family came up from Nashville the second semester, and we lived in Vetville, the family housing created after the war to serve veterans and their families. At that time there were only four black students at the university that I knew of.

I worked in the storeroom at Bendix, and I usually ate lunch in the storeroom. But one day some Notre Dame fellows invited me to go with them to a restaurant close by. We got there and the owners told me I couldn't eat there because I was black. So I returned to eating in the storeroom.

I recall two encounters with African students while I was in school. I went one day to the swimming pool at the Rockne Memorial and saw this tall dark person standing and I knew I had a brother to bond with. I went up and introduced myself, and he replied, "I'm from Africa. I'm not American Negro." I said, "Excuse me!"

On the other side of the coin, there was a fellow from Africa who came over without his family. He lived in Vetville also, and one night he locked himself out of his apartment—left his key inside—and I pushed him up through a window. He said to me, "Brother of my mother." I didn't know at first what he meant by that. But I later learned it was a saying that meant he was really close to you. He was a fantastic guy. He went back to Africa after graduation. After about two years, I heard he had died.

There were only three art professors in the fine arts program at that time. Ivan Mestrovic didn't come until later, so I didn't work with him. No one but graduate students worked with Mestrovic at that time. He was a great man, but when he worked he did not want to be disturbed.

Father Hesburgh was a very compassionate man. He made all the difference in the world to me. If you saw him on campus and talked with him, he would always try to do whatever he could for you. At graduation Fr. Hesburgh handed me my diploma and said, "You made it!"

Soon after graduation, Mattie and I purchased a home on Corby Boulevard. By this point our family had grown to five boys. The two younger sons were Dennis Louis and Victor Paul.

I was still working for Bendix when I graduated. After graduation it proved hard to find a job in my field. Finally, however, I found work at St. Christopher's Workshop in Bremen, Indiana, creating liturgical artwork for many churches in the United States and for the Vatican as well.

While I was working there Sister Rose Ellen Morrise, director of the Art Department at St. Mary's College, asked me to teach there during the summer of 1965. By the fall I was employed full-time! I taught for four years at St. Mary's in the late 1960s and early 1970s, thanks to Sister Rose Ellen. God only knows what she must have gone through to bring a black man to an all-girls college.

The priest who had given me the name of that contact when I first came to Notre Dame was Father Kevin Roe, a Franciscan. He was at St. Vincent de Paul Church in Nashville. He later was moved to Louisiana, to the church at Grambling University. I created a mural and the stained glass windows for his church there.

My thesis for my MFA at Notre Dame was done while I was teaching at St. Mary's; it was the design and development of a slab glass panel. I had to show how I designed, developed, and produced the slab glass. I also did a lot of community work while I was at St. Mary's, including Upward Bound and classes we called "Creative Soul."

In the late 1960s my first wife and I divorced; she is now deceased, as is my son John Michael. In 1974 Barbara and I married. She already had a son, Lonnie C. James. So between us we had six sons.

When I was an undergraduate, Notre Dame offered students the opportunity to dedicate their lives and their work to the Blessed Mother in a special way. Along with about fifty of my classmates, I took that opportunity. We attended a mass at Sacred Heart Church, where I formally dedicated my life and my work to the Blessed Mother.

Notre Dame will *always* be in my heart.

JEROME GARY COOPER

(Class of 1958)

Jerome Gary Cooper came to Notre Dame in autumn 1954 from Mobile, Alabama. He majored in finance and was a member of the Naval ROTC program. After graduation he became a Marine Corps officer, retiring with the rank of major general. He served as US ambassador to Jamaica during the Clinton administration. He and his wife, Beverly, live in Mobile, Alabama.

GROWING UP IN A DEVOUT CATHOLIC FAMILY IN SEGREGATED Mobile, Alabama, I had never heard of the University of Notre Dame until I was eleven or twelve years old. It was 1948 when Archbishop Fulton Sheen of New York, with a police escort, pulled up in front of my home on a dirt street in a black neighborhood in Mobile. He was accompanied by Clare Boothe Luce, the wife of the publisher of *Time*, *Life*, and *Fortune* magazines. My daddy was raising funds to build a hospital for black folk, and the archbishop heard of the effort and wanted to help. Under Jim Crow laws at the time, black women were not admitted in hospitals in Mobile and had to have their babies at home. My daddy, a graduate of Hampton Institute, had plans to change that.

A popular radio personality, Archbishop Sheen was a nationally known figure and helped raise funds. While visiting, he asked me if I had heard of the University of Notre Dame. I told him I had not. Then he told me that it was a great college and one day, if I wanted to attend, he would be happy to write a letter of recommendation and help me get a scholarship.

In 1950, Mobile's first African-American hospital opened not far from my home. It was named Blessed Martin De Porres Hospital. By then, Notre Dame had become my college of choice. A few years later, I wrote Archbishop Sheen, and he wrote back: "Thank you for your kind and warmhearted letter, which brought to mind the happy occasions when I visited with your wonderful family in Mobile. . . . You have my hearty approval to use my name on your application to Notre Dame University. I shall be delighted to recommend you." I still have the letter today.

So with the help of an academic scholarship, I headed to Notre Dame in the late summer of 1954, climbing aboard the all-black "Jim Crow car" on a train from Mobile to Chicago. It was called the Hummingbird. On the train, after eating the fried chicken lunch Mom fixed, I decided to see what the dining car was like. There was one table designated for blacks. When I sat down, they pulled a purple curtain around the table to segregate me from the white diners. The Hummingbird took me to Chicago, and then I took the South Shore for a ride to South Bend.

When I walked onto the campus, it was a revelation. I still remember clearly seeing the Golden Dome for the first time. This trip to Notre Dame was my first time outside the segregated South. I thought I had died and gone to heaven. Until I reached Notre Dame, I don't think I'd ever been in a room with three white folks. On campus there were no "colored" or "white" signs on the drinking fountains or bathroom doors. People were friendly, and Father Theodore Hesburgh, the thirty-seven-year-old president, was determined to make sure my experience was positive.

Notre Dame was a great experience! Those four years laid the groundwork for all the achievements that followed. I would become a Marine general and the first African-American to lead a Marine infantry company in combat. That helped open other doors for me in government, business, and diplomacy, including a presidential appointment as the first African-American ambassador to Jamaica.

I majored in finance, and I am convinced that my Notre Dame education and exposure to diversity gave me the credibility that was essential to the success that followed in the Marines and my other appointments to corporate boards, such as those of U.S. Steel and PNC Bank.

I had attended all-black Catholic schools in Mobile and, thanks to the Dominican sisters who taught us and my parents' emphasis on education, I was prepared academically when I went to college. If I had missed out on anything, it was the ability to understand and know different people, but I was lucky enough to go to Notre Dame to pick that up, because at Notre Dame I got a chance to live with people from all over the country, all over the world. It was a school developing diversity. Consequently, when I got to the Marine Corps—where I was one of just six blacks among twenty thousand Marine officers—working closely with people of all colors really was not a serious problem for me.

In my freshman class at Notre Dame, I was one of three African-Americans out of 1,500 students. Another of the three was my roommate, Mervin "Corky" Parker, who studied organic chemistry, became a chemist, and worked almost his whole career with Gillette. He and I remained friends and, over the years, rarely would a week or two go by when we did not get in touch. The other was Aubrey Lewis, a star halfback on the football team and a star hurdler who became the first black captain of an athletic team at Notre Dame—the track squad. He recently was named athlete of the century in New Jersey. He was also the first African-American FBI agent.

I was six-feet, six-inches tall and in good shape, but I was no collegiate-level athlete. That was clear—and a humorous memory from my Notre Dame years—when I made a brief tryout for the basketball team. At the end of the practice, the coach said I needed to learn three things: how to shoot, how to pass, and how to dribble. "That means you need to learn how to play basketball," said Corky.

End of tryout.

I recall Father Hesburgh or another priest would drop by and check on us in the dorm in the evenings. At first after he left, Corky and I would look at each other and say, "Why is he checking on us?" But it soon became clear that he just wanted to make sure we were OK. Integration on campus was still relatively new and it was important that it go smoothly.

While the campus atmosphere was friendly, I found social life for African-American students was minimal at best. There were only two or three black female students at Saint Mary's, and in the 1950s, even at Notre Dame, it still did not seem like a good idea for me to ask white female students for a date.

Every Sunday afternoon at LaFortune Student Center there was a mixer. The students from Saint Mary's would come and we would go to meet them. After attending a few of these events, I stopped going because there were never any black girls at the mixer. Coming from Alabama, I still have not gotten used to asking a white girl to dance.

One Sunday afternoon, my friend Bob Moretti from Detroit knocked on my dorm door and shouted, "Cooper, get dressed! There's a black girl at the mixer." I immediately got dressed and ran from Dillon Hall to the mixer. I walked in and laid eyes on the most beautiful sister in the world. Her name was Pat LaCour. Pat was tall, smart, and beautiful. Not only did that make my day, it made my year. Pat and I remain friends today. She is a great person, and we laugh about meeting that Sunday evening.

But as it happened, the girl who became my wife and the mother of my three children—son Patrick and daughters Joli and Shawn—was a student at Marquette whom I met while working a summer job in Chicago, thanks to Father Hesburgh.

He wanted to make sure we had work during the summer months, and I didn't have anything lined up—in Mobile or anywhere else. So in 1956 he arranged for me to work that summer at U.S. Steel's Chicago mill. I was a "stamper," a physically tough job that involved putting an identifying number on the white-hot steel as it went by. Years later, when I served on U.S. Steel's board of directors, I was able to joke with the other board members by saying I was the only one who had actually worked in a mill.

It was at Notre Dame that my career as a Marine officer began. When I arrived on campus, I didn't even know the ROTC existed. But then I saw these guys wearing blue uniforms, some with Marine emblems. I learned about the Naval ROTC program, which allows you to choose the Marine Corps for your junior and senior years. So in the spring of 1958, when I graduated, I also was commissioned as an officer in the Marine Corps, the first African-American to do so at Notre Dame.

After graduation I left Notre Dame for the Basic School at Quantico, Virginia, but my heart never left the campus at South Bend. My fondness for Notre Dame has only grown over the years, and I am thrilled that my daughter Joli also chose Notre Dame, where she graduated in 1981, as did her son Ashley Cooke III, who graduated in 2011—making us the first African-American family with three generations graduating from Notre Dame.

Over the years I have returned often to attend black alumni programs and other university events. At a reunion in 2011, Joli made sure I heard the stories of recent black graduates who would not have been able to attend Notre Dame without financial help. Joli's friend, the wonderful Ramona Payne, was in the development office, so I am sure they all had this planned. But these incredible young people moved me with their stories and accomplishments. They inspired me to donate $100,000 and, with my wife, Beverly, endow the J. Gary Cooper Family Scholarship Fund.

I also visited Father Hesburgh and took a photograph of him with my daughter Joli and grandson Ashley. While in his office, I noticed that he had a crystal bowl on his bookshelf with his memorabilia. For me, this was not just any crystal bowl—it was a gift he had received from a great friend of Notre Dame, Archbishop Fulton Sheen. I smiled, as I felt like my Notre Dame journey had come full circle.

AUBREY LEWIS

(Class of 1958)

NOTRE DAME'S FIGHTING IRISH DIDN'T NEED ANY EXTRA motivation when they arrived in Norman, Oklahoma, on Nov. 15, 1957. They were smarting from a defeat the previous week at the hands of the Michigan State Spartans. And they were going up against an Oklahoma Sooners team that, under the legendary Bud Wilkinson, had won forty-seven straight games.

They didn't need extra motivation, but they got it when they arrived at the hotel where they were to spend the night before the game on Saturday, Nov. 16. The hotel management informed them that everyone on the team was welcome to stay except for one person: starting left halfback Aubrey Lewis, the sole black player on the Notre Dame roster.

With that, President Father Ted Hesburgh, who was traveling with the team, announced that no one from Notre Dame would stay at the hotel. He found accommodations for the team at a Catholic Church–related facility. Those accommodations were not, one team member later recalled, exactly four-star.

The next day, the Irish went out and took out their disgruntlement on the Oklahoma Sooners, winning 7–0 and staging one of the greatest upsets in Notre Dame and college football history.

Interesting as it is, that incident was no more than a footnote in Aubrey Lewis's distinguished career as a Notre Dame student-athlete. Not only was he a running back in the same backfield as Heisman Trophy winner Paul Hornung, but he was a world-class hurdler and the first black captain of an athletic team at Notre Dame, the 1957–58 track squad.

Lewis came out of Montclair High School in New Jersey, where he was an all-American halfback and a major track star. He reportedly attracted more than two hundred college scholarship offers, from among which he chose Notre Dame. He enrolled in the fall of 1954, when freshmen were still barred by NCAA rules from varsity competition.

He became a starter on the football team in his sophomore year and remained so through most of his collegiate career, despite nagging injuries. He reportedly had planned to forego football his junior year if he made the US Olympic team as a hurdler. However, he came up short in that ambition. News reports indicate he was leading in the 400-meter hurdles trial when he stumbled at the last hurdle and finished out of the top three.

Lewis reportedly was bright, gregarious, and immensely popular. A story in the September 27, 1957, issue of the *Scholastic*—"A Goodwill Tour: Aubrey Lewis in Europe"—described his activities the previous summer as a member of a National Amateur Athletic Union track team. He spoke of conversing with Adolpho Consolini, a 1948 Olympic gold medalist in the discus from Italy. Neither spoke the other's language, so, Lewis said, they spoke in French.

He described contending with traffic as an American pedestrian in London, where cars came from a direction different than he was accustomed to. And he described the difference between American and European attitudes about athletic competition by women. "Over there," he said, "the female athlete is honored and given respect just as men are here. And as a result they turn out some very good women track stars."

After graduating from Notre Dame, Lewis returned to New Jersey and spent several years teaching and coaching at schools in Montclair, Newark, and Paterson. In 1962, he was recruited as one of the first two African-Americans to be trained as FBI agents. Five years later, the F. W. Woolworth Co. hired him as an executive recruiter. He remained with Woolworth until he retired as a senior vice president in 1995.

He held a wide range of civic and governmental appointments, including as a commissioner of the New Jersey Sports and Exposition Authority and the Port Authority of New York and New Jersey. In 2000, the *Star-Ledger* of Newark named him New Jersey's offensive football player of the twentieth century.

He served for several years as a member of the Notre Dame board of trustees.

He was once quoted as saying of himself, "I wanted to do a lot of things, to challenge life. I came along at a time when there were many doors to be opened by the black man, and that was a challenge to me."

Aubrey C. Lewis died December 10, 2001. He was sixty-six. In 2002, he received posthumously a distinguished alumnus award from the Notre Dame Alumni Association.

BOOKER RICE

(Class of 1958)

Booker Rice came to Notre Dame from Chicago in autumn 1954. He majored in economics and finance and was a member of the track team. After graduation, he enjoyed a highly successful career in the insurance industry. Later he formed his own executive search firm and enjoyed success in that field as well. He and his wife, Carolyn, live in Lakewood Ranch, Florida.

THE YEAR WAS 1954. GAS WAS 22 CENTS PER GALLON; THE average cost of a car was $1,700; the average cost of a house was $10,000; Eisenhower was president; Nixon was vice president; and the US Supreme Court was about to rule in *Brown v. Board of Education* that segregation in public schools is unconstitutional.

I was an eighteen-year-old non-Catholic from a working class family, attending Wendell Phillips High School on the South Side of Chicago. I was a track and field athlete, a hurdler, and I had been offered scholarships by dozens of colleges across the country. I was excited about an opportunity to go to any first-class university. But the fact that Notre Dame showed an interest in me was particularly exciting.

I knew Notre Dame only as a Catholic institution, a highly acclaimed academic and football powerhouse. The only person of color I was aware of who had ever attended Notre Dame was Joe Bertrand (Class of 1954), an All-American basketball player who also hailed from Chicago.

During a pre-enrollment visit to the campus I found that there were fewer than a handful of black students, among them Wayne Edmonds (Class of 1956) and Lem Joyner (Class of 1957). However, during my visit I was impressed with the genuinely warm and friendly reception I received from the coaches, the students, and everyone I met.

Thanks to Father Theodore Hesburgh's leadership in equal opportunity and diversity, that handful of blacks grew with my incoming class. My first year there were approximately six new black students on campus. Over the next few years, the black student population doubled to more than a dozen students.

During my years at Notre Dame I can honestly say I never felt uncomfortable in the midst of the overwhelmingly white student population. I did not have a problem fitting into the track team. I was involved in campus clubs. Father Thomas Brennan's philosophy class was very helpful in my rapid adjustment to campus life because he took a strong personal interest in me and in most of the athletes.

Dorm life was a positive in many ways. In my freshman year I was in Cavanaugh Hall. The rector was Father James Doll, who was very supportive and made me feel welcome and did many things to assure that I felt I was a "Notre Dame man." I received similar support and encouragement from Father Shulte, whose first name I cannot now recall, and Father Laurence Broestl.

I actually enjoyed living in the dorm because there were so many opportunities to build personal relationships with my dormmates, which led to a strong sense of community. As a scholarship student, one of my jobs was to work with the rector in room checks. Another was to deliver mail to the dorm mailboxes. This job made the one who did it very important and popular, because you often were bringing love letters from girlfriends and money from parents. These duties allowed people to get to know you as a person. I had a number of dorm- and classmates who became lifelong friends.

In retrospect, the dorm rules served as a great lesson in maturity. In freshman year you had to be in your dorm by 10:30 p.m. and lights were turned off at midnight. As you matured into an upperclassman, you could stay out to after hours, but you still had to sign in with the night watchman.

The only negative as an all-male student body was the lack of dating and normal social life. Saint Mary's College was all white, and biracial dating was not in vogue in the 1950s. As a result, we black students were forced to find dates in South Bend or invite friends from our hometowns to a football weekend or to such events as the annual Commerce Ball or the Arts Ball.

Among my memorable experiences were meeting high-profile people who visited our campus. For example, I met Louis Armstrong, Senator John Kennedy, and presidential candidates Adlai Stevenson and Richard Nixon. No matter what your political leanings, this was great exposure for a nineteen- or twenty-year-old college student.

The student body support is exemplified by a situation in which a South Bend restaurant refused to seat me and several other black students for dinner on a football weekend, ostensibly because we did not have a reservation. But historically, reservations had never been required. It was a clear case of racial discrimination, which got back to the student body. Paul Hornung, the quarterback of the football team and the reigning Heisman Trophy winner, took the lead in obtaining a public apology from the restaurant owner.

My professors at Notre Dame were supportive in every way. This was especially true with priests. I can honestly say I was proud to be a Notre Dame student for so many reasons, including the many friendships I acquired and the fact that it was always fun to go home for the holidays wearing the blue and gold jackets with bold letters spelling "Notre Dame" on the back. You would always get admiring looks from the people around you.

I was able to use my Notre Dame education to build a rewarding career as an insurance executive with one of the largest firms in the world, Prudential Insurance. In the early part of my career the Notre Dame Club of Chicago was very instrumental in my success. I became a star salesperson, which catapulted me into multiple prime management assignments. Much of the club support came as a result of the relationships I had developed in my campus dorm life. Being known as a Notre Dame man helped me become the first African-American vice president of Prudential, the world's largest insurer, and a first in the insurance industry.

After thirty-three successful years as a senior executive, I took an early retirement and took some time off. Then I established a successful executive search firm, catering to Fortune 500 companies. When you tell people in business or social situations that you are a Notre

Dame man they usually are immediately impressed. I am often amazed with the power of the ND brand.

The strong foundation I acquired as a Notre Dame student has been critically important to my growth and development as a businessman and family man. The first-class education, the broad cultural exposure to students and professors from around the world, the personal relationships, and the fun experiences—all combined to make Notre Dame right for me. It was not perfect, and there were ups and downs, but it worked for me in the changing decade of the 1950s.

TOMMY HAWKINS

(Class of 1959)

Tommy Hawkins came to Notre Dame in autumn 1955 from Chicago. He majored in sociology and was the Irish's first black basketball All-American. After graduation he spent ten productive years in the NBA — six with the Lakers and four with the old Cincinnati Royals. He later was a television and radio broadcaster. He spent the last eighteen years of his career as vice president of communications for the Los Angeles Dodgers.

ON THIS, THE SEVENTIETH ANNIVERSARY OF THE ENROLLMENT of Notre Dame's first black student, I have celebrated my fifty-fifth-year class reunion: All hail the men of 1959!

Back in 1955 I was one of two black students in our freshman class of 1,200. At that time, there were only ten blacks attending the all-male university. Please keep in mind, this was before President Barack Obama was born and before Rosa Parks' and Rev. Dr. Martin Luther King Jr.'s Montgomery bus boycott. My matriculation at "the Dome" preceded by nine years the passage of the landmark Civil Rights Act of 1964. It followed by just one year the US Supreme Court's unanimous ruling in *Brown v. Board of Education* outlawing segregation in public schools. Despite that ruling, integration was by no means the law of the land; for the most part, segregation ruled.

Having grown up in Chicago, just ninety miles west of South Bend, the spectacle of the Fighting Irish of Notre Dame always loomed brilliantly before me. However, I never thought that one day I would become a part of the great Irish tradition.

In deciding to accept a four-year scholarship to Notre Dame, considerations of race and religion were not factors. I had already experienced four years of first-time integration (1951–55) at Parker High School in Chicago, where I served my school as a racial ambassador, mediating student racial conflicts. At the same time, I led all basketball players in the city in scoring my senior year and was named Chicago's most valuable player. At good ol' Parker High, I was coached by the gregarious Irish Catholic Eddy O'Farrell, who had grown up in the Windy City with my collegiate Irish Catholic coach, Johnny Jordan. So maybe my die was cast.

I grew up in a single-parent, Protestant home, the proud grandson of a Methodist minister. Both O'Farrell and Jordan were surrogate fathers to me. My choice of Notre Dame from among all of the scholarships offered did not sit well with many of my family members. My mother, however, was delighted. I was honored.

The moment I set foot on the Notre Dame campus, I had a sense of belonging. There I was, a hopeful young black teenager beneath the Golden Dome at one of the most prestigious universities in the world, which happened to be led by a steadfast and resilient civil rights–minded president, Father Theodore M. Hesburgh. Father Ted always preached the dignity of man regardless of race, creed, or color. He marched with the champion of human rights, Dr. King. Father Hesburgh was far ahead of society. He made it perfectly clear to the nation that anywhere Notre Dame's minority students weren't welcome, neither was Notre Dame.

With that as a foundation and imbued with a pioneering spirit engendered by Major League Baseball's barrier-breaker Jackie Robinson, I embarked on my mission. My goals were to get a great education, become a basketball All-American, and prepare myself to become a productive black man in a man's world.

The four years were full of challenges and life-shaping experiences. I feared not making the grade and letting a lot of people down. I told my mom that if I flunked out, not to expect me to return to Chicago to face all of those people—it would be the French Foreign Legion for me! She frowned and said to get back to work.

Through it all, I always felt that I was a respected Notre Dame man in the making, getting a sound, personalized education. Of course

I felt the pressure of being the face of my race. I came to realize that the first and only real black contact that most whites on campus had ever experienced was me. So integration at Notre Dame was a work in progress and I wore a hard hat. I was the only black on the basketball team for four years, the team's first black captain, and a two-time All-American. In fact, I was the only black in every class I attended.

Looking back over my bountiful Notre Dame career, my cup runneth over with indelible memories. My dormitory rectors were watchful and caring. I especially recall my freshman rector at Cavanaugh Hall, Father Robert Pelton. He said to me, "Please let me know immediately if you're having any problems. We're counting on you to be successful on and off the court." My freshman student advisor, Bill Burke, stressed keeping tabs on my academic problems and getting to him early on. Logic professor Henri DuLac invited me to take his class and promised it would help to organize my thinking and my life. English composition professor Joseph X. Brennan insisted that I dig in and develop the raw talent he saw in me. Father Tom Brennan, the hard-nosed philosophy professor, taught me in the classroom and helped me with my free-throw shooting. English literature professor Chester A. Soleta told us that poetry was his specialty and he would make it live in our souls. Boy, did he ever. Social psychology professor Raymond Murray hammered home that as human beings we all have some psychological frailties. "If," he said, "there is anyone present who insists this doesn't apply to him, please leave the room; there is nothing I can do to help you."

A criminology professor I had was a former warden at Indiana State Penitentiary. He pointed out that prejudice and racism are pervasive, from the psychopathic killer on death row to many of us sitting in his classroom. Kudos to anthropologist and senior thesis advisor Dr. James Crowley, who insisted that I delve into my African heritage and examine the Dahomey and Asante tribes of West Africa. My protector and teammate John Smyth, now Rev. John Smyth and president of Notre Dame College Prep in Niles, Illinois, was a six-foot, five-inch enforcer who made it known that if you messed with me, you had to go through him.

I have never had a more meaningful knock on my door than the one delivered by Notre Dame's All-American football great and Heisman Trophy winner Paul Hornung. I answered the knock, and there stood "the Golden Boy."

"Hawk," he said, "because of you I'm missing out on the best pasta and pizza in town."

Father Hesburgh had put a particular restaurant off-limits to Notre Dame students after I was refused service because of my race. The ban was to be in effect until I got a public apology. Hornung went and secured that apology and the restaurant's doors were opened to all. Talk about All-American performances!

Then there was fellow Chicagoan and teammate Ed Gleason, who bristled during a 1958 NCAA "Elite 8" trip to a still heavily segregated Lexington, Kentucky. The team left the hotel together to go to a nearby theater and, when we arrived, the ticket seller told us we were all welcome: whites on the main floor and blacks in the balcony.

"Bullshit!" shouted Eddy. "Where can we go where we can all enjoy a movie—together?"

"In the black section of town," answered the ticket seller.

Eddy hailed two cabs and we were off to share an integrated evening in the segregated mid-South.

I give credit to 1960 black engineering graduate Ben Finley for starting Notre Dame's first black student union, which was first jokingly called the NND—the Negroes of Notre Dame. Ben, a born organizer, insisted that all the men of color meet in my room (309 Badin Hall) one day after dinner. Those who were interested crammed into my room and the meeting was on. The session, however, was interrupted by a knock on my door. Enter two Caucasian classmates and close friends of mine: Joe Mulligan, the pride of Cincinnati, Ohio, and longtime Chicago basketball buddy Dick Chrisgalvis. They criticized us for our separatist efforts and refused to be excluded from all proceedings. So the founding of the NND was an integrated affair. This story always gets a hearty laugh from my audiences.

I close by paying tribute to my all-time best friend, basketball teammate, and roommate: Eugene Raymond Patrick Duffy. Duff died of cancer at age thirty-three. God, I miss him! I have never been more connected with another human being in all of my life. I stand six-feet, five-inches and Duff stood five-feet, six-inches. We were compared to the cartoon characters Mutt and Jeff. We were poster boys for athletic achievement and integrated friendship. Duff was a baseball All-American and co-captain of the basketball team. We loved being Notre Dame men and prized each other's friendship. Duff's life story puts the movie *Rudy* to shame.

How do I feel about my Notre Dame experience? The greatest four years of my life! I still get choked up when they play "Notre Dame, Our Mother" and the Notre Dame Fight Song. Black, white, or polka-dot: "WE ARE ND!"

CHAPTER 2

The 1960s

"Let the word go forth from this time and place, to friend and foe alike, that the torch has been passed to a new generation of Americans. . . ."

President John F. Kennedy obviously had his own generation—the so-called greatest generation—in mind when he spoke those words in his 1961 inaugural address. It was, as he put it, a generation "born in this century, tempered by war, disciplined by a hard and bitter peace, proud of our ancient heritage—and unwilling to witness or permit the slow undoing of those human rights to which this nation has always been committed, and to which we are committed today at home and around the world."

But there was another generation also listening that day—one born in the years after World War II, nurtured amid an affluence their parents never could have imagined as children, terrified by constant threats of nuclear annihilation and communist takeover, and, thanks in no small measure to the penetration of television, rendered at least mildly skeptical of the notion that their nation had "always been committed" to human rights, either at home or around the world.

The 1960s would become to a large degree a contest between those two generations' notions of America—what it ought to be at home and what it ought to do in the world. The contest was never as simple as a "generation gap," the term that came into vogue to describe what often was depicted as a conflict within households between conservative parents and their rebellious offspring. Life is never so simple as that.

In a very real sense, Kennedy was himself the embodiment of a challenge to the old order. True, he was white and male. But he was forty-three when he was elected president—the youngest person ever elected to the office. And most important, he was Catholic—a radical departure from the Protestant norm that had prevailed since the founding of the republic.

Kennedy, a Democrat, defeated Richard Nixon, the Republican vice president, in the first presidential election of the decade, in a campaign that featured the first televised debates between the contenders. A marginal factor in American life a decade earlier, television suddenly was one of the most potent factors in our politics, our commerce, our social order.

Its power to compel attention and force change was demonstrated again and again in the sixties, through coverage of events such as the 1963 March on Washington and Martin Luther King Jr.'s stirring "I Have a Dream" speech; John Kennedy's assassination a few months later; the 1964 appearance of the Beatles on the "Ed Sullivan Show" in the first wave of rock and roll's British invasion; the "schoolhouse door" confrontations between Southern governors and federal authorities enforcing the rights of black students to study at the Universities of Mississippi and Alabama; coverage of the beatings of civil rights marchers on the Edmund Pettus Bridge during the 1965 Selma-to-Montgomery marches for voting rights; the bloody combat of the Vietnam War; the marches and mobilizations by mostly youthful protestors against the military draft and the war in Vietnam; the urban riots in Newark and Watts and other American cities; and, in the last year of the decade, the landing of American astronauts on the moon.

Kennedy's brief presidency featured the closest brush the world had ever experienced with nuclear annihilation: the Cuban missile crisis of 1962. It also produced one of the most noble and enduring foreign policy initiatives of the postwar period: the Peace Corps. And it left his successor, Texan Lyndon Johnson, with a problem from hell: a war in a distant land, Vietnam, that ultimately undid his presidency and indelibly marred what otherwise would have been a sterling record of domestic achievement.

For even as Martin Luther King Jr. and his cohorts in the civil rights movement pressed from without for an end to America's shameful regime of segregation, Johnson, to the surprise of many, pressed from within. It was Johnson who, in the aftermath of Kennedy's assassination, called for and won passage of the Civil Rights Act of 1964. It was Johnson who signed the Voting Rights Act of 1965. And it was Johnson who, proclaiming "We shall overcome," pressed for the creation of a Great Society of economic opportunity and equality.

Sadly, it also was Johnson who escalated the war in Vietnam to the point that it broke his presidency.

College campuses were foci for much of the turbulence and conflict that roiled the nation during the sixties. For young men especially, the student draft deferment that went along with college enrollment made the Vietnam War a subject of much more than academic interest.

By comparison with many other college campuses, Notre Dame's was quiescent during the 1960s. That no doubt reflected in large part the relative conservatism of its all-male student body, a large number of whom depended on support from the ROTC to pay their college bills.

But Notre Dame was not simply on the sidelines. Father Hesburgh was a player on the national stage. He was influential in the creation of both the Peace Corps and the Office of Economic Opportunity, the principal governmental engine of the "war on poverty." And his service on the Civil Rights Commission helped pave the way to the great civil rights laws signed by President Johnson. That iconic photo of Hesburgh and Martin Luther King singing, hands clasped, at a rally in Chicago was no accident. It was taken on June 21, 1964, two days after the Senate had passed the great Civil Rights Act. King, of course, would be dead four years later, the victim of the second gruesome political assassination of the decade. And John Kennedy's younger brother, Robert, would die shortly after, victim of the decade's third political assassination.

On campus, black student enrollment grew, but slowly. The freshman class of 1965, with eleven, or perhaps twelve, black students, doubled the total black enrollment. By decade's end, it had doubled yet again, but remained a tiny percentage in an undergraduate student body of more than six thousand. The number of black faculty members could be counted on one hand, with fingers left over. But significantly, the university got its first black trustee (and, wittingly or not, a gay trustee) in 1969, when Bayard Rustin, architect of the great March on Washington, was appointed to the new lay board.

Like young black people on campuses throughout the country, Notre Dame's black students began to press for change—on campus and in the world. They created a black student group, the Afro-American Society. They demonstrated: *against* segregationist Senator Strom Thurmond of South Carolina in a speech at Washington Hall, and *for* greater black representation on the football team on the hallowed turf of Notre Dame Stadium.

Notre Dame in the late 1960s was deriving momentum for change from another source besides Hesburgh and youthful protestors and the changing currents in American society. The Catholic Church, for centuries as dependably static as any institution on earth, had been shaken from its torpor by the action of an Italian farmer's son named Angelo Roncalli: Pope John XXIII.

Shortly after his election in October 1958, Pope John called for a rare ecumenical council of the church. The Second Vatican Council convened in October 1962 and closed in 1965. It loosed the winds of change in the church, calling for a deeper, more robust involvement with the world, especially on the part of lay Catholics.

At Notre Dame this fired minds and imaginations among faculty and students. It gave rise to new and passionate interest in Catholic social teaching. And on a very practical level, it was part of the impetus behind perhaps the most important change in the structure of the university since its creation: the handover of control in 1967 from the Congregation of the Holy Cross to a lay board of trustees. That action set the stage for much of the university's progress in the decades since.

BENJAMIN F. FINLEY

(Class of 1960)

Ben Finley came to Notre Dame in autumn 1956 from Harlem in New York City. He majored in electrical engineering and chaired the campus civil rights committee. After graduation he enjoyed a career of thirty-nine years in the aerospace industry. He was instrumental in founding the Black Alumni of Notre Dame and served as its first chairperson. His son, Ben, graduated from Notre Dame in 1992. He and his wife, Andi, live in Marina del Rey, California.

WHEN I ARRIVED ON CAMPUS IN 1956, EISENHOWER OCCUPIED the White House and Father Ted was the president of Notre Dame, then an all-male bastion. At that time there was a total of twenty Negroes on campus, including the grad students. Segregation was the rule in the South, the civil rights movement was in its infancy, and a slide rule was as close to technology as you could get. As a seventeen-year-old from the North, I was way too naïve to recognize that we were all part of the university's experiment in integration.

I was raised in Harlem, and my high school career had been spent at All Hallows, an all-boys Catholic school located in the South Bronx and run by the Irish Christian Brothers. Even there I was one of two Negro students in my class. So I suppose one could say I was accustomed to white folks. I applied to Notre Dame only because our guidance counselor insisted that we apply to at least one Catholic college. Surprisingly, I was accepted to multiple major universities. I chose Notre Dame because my girlfriend told me that she would rather tell her friends that I attended Notre Dame than the University of Colorado, where I was originally headed because it was the most beautiful place I had ever seen. My acceptance of her preference was a major turning point in my life.

The only thing I knew about Notre Dame at that time was what I had learned from the movie *Knute Rockne All American*. The only rational facet of my decision was that I wanted to be an engineer, which everyone said would require dedication to my studies. Since I had partied my way through high school, going to an all-male institution seemed to be a way to insulate myself from party-like distractions. Little did I know how wrong I would be.

My arrival on campus was filled with the normal freshman anxiety concerning with whom I would be roomed in Zahm Hall, then an all-freshman dorm. My anxiety was relieved when Warren Roche, a six-foot, five-inch brother from New Orleans, walked into the room. So now there were at least two of us. In those days the freshmen arrived on campus a week before the upperclassmen for purposes of "indoctrination." We were exposed to the campus, the traditions, Father Ted Hesburgh, the very strict student life rules, the engineering faculty, and "mixers" with the ladies from Saint Mary's. As could be expected, there were not many black women over there, either. We also met the other two Negro students in our class: Jerry Johnson (Class of 1960) and Wejay Bundara (Class of 1960), with whom we immediately bonded. So now there were four of us. The mixers and the unwritten rule that "thou shall not date a white woman" were a concern that led the four of us off campus on Sunday morning. Dressed in Notre Dame attire, we conveniently strolled past the Baptist church located at Five Points, drew the attention of a few young ladies, and successfully launched our new social lives.

The Negro community, including Professor Adam Arnold and his family, greeted us with open arms, lent us their homes for our parties, and lent us their cars when we dated their daughters. So there went my social insulation objective. For the next four years, I organized most of our off-campus parties and dated St. Mary's students who lived at home in South Bend.

In our era, student life at Notre Dame was driven by an archaic set of rules left over from the postwar Navy program. We had bed checks, curfews (10 p.m. on weekdays, 12:30 a.m. on weekends), dorm lights out at midnight, and wore a coat and tie to dinner. Since there were only twenty Negroes enrolled, we were a few grains of pepper scattered in the salt. With one exception, I never encountered overt racism. That one exception, where the "n-word" was used, resulted in a fight in the lake. With no females to soften the environment, our school spirit was testosterone-driven. Pep rallies were frenetic and everyone went to the football games regardless of the weather, even though we had seasons averaging only three wins and seven losses. Aubrey Lewis (Class of 1958) was the only Negro on the football team.

Personally, I felt so comfortable in the Notre Dame culture that one Saturday, after a loss to Purdue, I found myself, by myself, standing behind Zahm Hall confronting the Purdue band, who were celebrating their victory. Yelling up to my dormmates for help to respond to this disrespect resulted in the whole dorm turning out and my leading Irish cheers until the real cheerleaders arrived to take over the situation.

From the standpoint of us Negroes, we lived, ate, and studied with our roommates and classmates. However, every night after dinner, we gathered in Dillon Hall for an hour or so. These evening sessions allowed us to relax, maintain our blackness, listen to stories and jokes, and plan our next party. During one of these sessions I organized the Nu Nu Delta (Negros of Notre Dame) as the first secret fraternity on campus. I was principally mentored by Gary Cooper (Class of 1958) and Tommy Hawkins (Class of 1959), both of whom taught me useful, functional, and sensible arrogance.

The civil rights movement became energetic during my four years and it impacted Notre Dame. Father Ted, who to this day is one of my personal heroes, was a member of the US Civil Rights Commission. We hosted campus visits by the students who had been beaten while conducting the Southern sit-in demonstrations. Empathizing with the movement, I ended up organizing and chairing our civil rights committee, made up of both black and white students. It ended up being a teaching experience, as many times there would be a knock on my door and there would stand a student from the South who seriously didn't understand "how come y'all want to come South and upset our good nigras." And the lesson would begin.

One night, I had the pleasure of walking across campus having a discussion with Father Ted about a civil rights march by Notre Dame students aimed at getting media attention to indicate support for the sit-ins taking place in the South. Father Ted was not necessarily supportive of our march, which was to go from campus to the South Bend courthouse, because he was concerned that we might encounter violence along the way or that our Southern students might violently object. But with two hundred students in protest, march we did! It was an amazing success.

Academically, to me, Notre Dame was an unnecessarily rigorous environment, which included Saturday morning classes. In the College of Engineering it seemed that the university had developed a program to weed out the unworthy. At many universities they take you by the hand and walk you through the maze. At Notre Dame, they would drop you into the center of the maze and tell you to find your way out. At the first meeting of my Introduction to Engineering class, Professor Emil Schoenheinz told us to "look to your left and look to your right; the students you see will not be in engineering two years from now." And damn if he wasn't right. With few exceptions, I was always the only Negro in my classes. And over the course of my four years, the number of electrical engineering students dropped steadily, in a process that could sometimes be embarrassing. For example, the professors would post grades, by name, outside of their offices, thereby exposing everyone's performance to everyone else. By my senior year, all of the remaining electrical engineers clustered together on the fourth floor of Walsh Hall. We all worked the system as a team to survive. If it weren't for help received from my white classmates, I wouldn't have survived the academics. They are the reason for my professional success. It was because of my Notre Dame experience that I earned a master's in electrical engineering from New York University in 1965.

Being a Notre Dame grad has grounded me during my life, professionally, intellectually, socially, and spiritually. I graduated in 1960, a time when many Negroes with college degrees were still being shuttled off to the US Post Office. However, after John F. Kennedy was inaugurated, affirmative action began. Throughout my thirty-nine-year career in the aerospace industry, I was generally the only black in the room, a situation that Notre Dame had well prepared me for. In fact, every morning in the shower I would say to myself: "How can I mess with the white folks' minds today?"

While I didn't return to campus until our twenty-five year reunion, I always proudly wore the brand. The diploma always hung in my office, my license plate read "Irish 60," and I rarely missed listening to or watching Notre Dame football games. To this day, I informally encourage black high school students to consider Notre Dame. Professionally, being Irish was a huge benefit, as my white managers seemed to have deep respect for the university and were willing to mentor me so I could gain continual promotions. On two occasions, my Notre Dame class ring was the catalyst that allowed me to capture multimillion-dollar business opportunities.

My Notre Dame experience has also driven me to endeavor to expand the life experiences of the American black populace. I have been a co-founder of many predominantly black organizations, such as 4 Seasons West Ski Club, Inc.; the National Brotherhood of Skiers, Inc.; Hughes Aircraft Black Professional Forum; and the Black Alumni of Notre Dame. In 2000 the alumni association recognized my efforts in recruiting and mentoring more than 150 African-American students by presenting me with the Reynolds Award.

There are two black Notre Dame experiences that need to be mentioned. The first was sitting in the living room of Frazier Thompson (Class of 1947), our first black graduate. Listening to his story of his life was like sitting at the feet of my grandfather. The second was at the very first reunion meeting of the black alumni. I left that meeting with the clear recognition that I had just gathered with the most educated and intelligent assembly of black folks that I had ever met.

My ashes will be interred in Cedar Grove Cemetery on campus by my sons, Ben Finley (Class of 1992) and Micah Finley, a prospective applicant for the Class of 2021. My blood is in the bricks!

PERCY A. PIERRE

(Classes of 1961, 1963 MA)

Percy Pierre came to Notre Dame in autumn 1957 from New Orleans. He majored in electrical engineering and played intramural basketball. After graduating he obtained a doctorate in electrical engineering and pursued a career in academic administration, research and development administration, and consulting. He and his wife, Olga, have two children, one of whom, Kristin, was a member of the Notre Dame Class of 1991.

WELCOME, LOUISIANA, IS A SMALL COMMUNITY ON THE WEST bank of the Mississippi River, about halfway between Baton Rouge and New Orleans. That is where my parents, grandparents, most of my great-grandparents, and I were born. As with the rest of the Welcome community, there was a strong Catholic tradition in my family. My father was a laborer whose schooling ended at third grade. My mother was a housewife with an eighth-grade education. Each was determined to give their children opportunities for education and insisted that they do their best.

In 1943 we moved to New Orleans so that my sisters and I could start school. We enrolled at Blessed Sacrament School and later at St. Joan of Arc. I, and each of my two sisters, graduated from St. Joan of Arc as valedictorian of our classes.

When I was in the eighth grade in 1953, I heard about a new high school that had been started by the Josephite priests—St. Augustine

High School. To get into the school, one had to take an exam. The top ten students were promised full scholarships for four years. My parents urged me to take the exam, since the tuition of $7 per month would be a burden on them. I won one of the scholarships and found out later that I had the second-highest score. My mother wanted to know why I was not number one. She fully expected that by the end of my high school career I would be the valedictorian. She was right.

My time at St. Augustine's was the most impactful period of my life. It was there that the priests instilled in me two overriding missions in life. The first was to excel intellectually in engineering, a field that had been closed to African-Americans. There were opportunities for blacks in service professions where their clienteles were also black—such as medicine, law, and education. However, engineers worked for companies, and companies did not hire black engineers at that time, even in the North. Thus I chose engineering. The second overriding mission was to use my career to make a difference in the lives of other African-Americans.

St. Augustine has had a special relationship with Notre Dame. When I was at Notre Dame, there were more African-American students from St. Augustine's than from any other high school. That tradition has continued. I believe that, to this date, no high school has sent more African-American students to Notre Dame than St. Augustine's.

I first heard of Notre Dame when I would listen to their football games on the radio in the 1950s, when they were winning lots of games. I next heard of Notre Dame when Warren Roche, the valedictorian of the St. Augustine class of 1956, chose Notre Dame. Throughout my high school career, I had been prepared to be able to attend the best universities in the country. I was drilled in preparation for the SAT. My teachers wanted me to be the first black student from Louisiana to win a Merit Scholarship. I fell short of that goal, but I was named a "commended" student. That brought me to the attention of the best universities in the country. As a result, I received offers of full scholarships from institutions I had never heard of, such as Princeton University and Amherst College.

Since I *had* heard of Notre Dame, I decided I wanted to go to there. The only problem was that I needed a scholarship. Notre Dame offered me $500 per year, about one-third of what it cost. The state of Louisiana offered me $750 per year for leaving the state and not applying to LSU. Catholic Scholarships for Negroes, a small foundation funded by William Lowell Putnam, provided the rest. Thus, I attended Notre Dame on full scholarship for four years.

In my first year at Notre Dame, I found that I was better prepared than many of my white fellow students. In my freshman religion class of about ninety students, the teacher asked if anyone knew what the "Rig-Veda" was. When no one raised a hand, I gave the answer that Fr. Keenan of St. Augustine's had insisted I know: it was the bible of Zoroaster. From that time on, many of my white friends came to me for help. I did well in my freshman year and earned a place on the dean's list. While I was proud of that accomplishment, it turned out bad for me. In those days, students were allowed three class cuts. More than that could cause you to flunk. However, if you were on the dean's list, as I was during my sophomore year, you could have unlimited cuts. Unfortunately, I slept in more than I should have and did not do well in my sophomore year.

My relationship with Notre Dame is as much about my relationship with one individual, Father Ted Hesburgh, as it is with the institution. Throughout my career I have looked to him for help on various projects focused on using my career status to help black folks in the field of engineering.

In 1959, when I was a sophomore at Notre Dame, I took a civil service exam and won an engineering internship with the Corps of Engineers in New Orleans. Father Ted helped me integrate the on-base dining facility by forcing the Army to convert two separate facilities into one. In my senior year, I suggested to Father Ted that the university discontinue its practice of always housing black freshmen together. The following year the policy was changed.

In my senior year, I took the Graduate Record Exam and did quite well. However, I decided that I was tired of school and wanted to get a job. One day Professor Lawrence Stauder of the electrical engineering department saw me in the hall and asked if I had a job. A week later, I got an offer from a company in New Jersey called Keerfott. That was the same company that had hired my fellow black Notre Dame electrical engineer, Ben Finley, the previous year. Thus I learned that there was at least one company that would hire a black engineer in 1961.

I decided not to take that offer but to continue in graduate school at Notre Dame for my master's degree. One course I really liked was taught by Professor Ruey-Wen Liu. He gave me some special research problems to work on. When I finished the master's in January of 1963, he told me that I should go for the PhD. His advice gave me the confidence to do just that. I entered the Johns Hopkins University in 1963 and received my PhD in electrical engineering in 1967. I have been recognized as the first African-American to receive a PhD in electrical engineering. After gaining my doctorate, I was an engineering researcher at the Rand Corporation, a White House fellow, and dean of engineering at Howard University from 1971 to 1977. From 1977 to 1981, I held a presidential appointment as assistant secretary of the Army for research, development, and acquisition. In this role, I managed the development of most of the current Army weapons systems.

In 1973 I chaired a symposium at the National Academy of Engineering on the problem of bringing more underrepresented minorities into the field of engineering. The principal result of this symposium was the establishment of the National Action Council for Minorities in Engineering (NACME). Fr. Ted was a member of NACME. Over the last thirty years, this organization has raised more than $100 million for the support of minorities in engineering. About that same time, Fr. Ted helped me establish the National GEM Consortium. GEM has supported more than six thousand minority engineering graduate students in the last thirty years. I am recognized as co-founder of both of these organizations.

In 1973 I ran into Fr. Ted on K Street in Washington, D.C. He knew that I had been previously selected as a White House fellow, serving as a deputy to Patrick Moynihan. I was the second Notre Dame graduate so chosen. A year later he invited me to serve on the board of trustees of Notre Dame. In my tenure on the board, I have focused on the welfare of African-American students. I served on the Notre Dame board of trustees for thirty years and continue to serve in emeritus status. During that time I also served as president of Prairie View A&M University in Texas and as vice president for research and graduate studies at Michigan State University.

The creation of the black alumni association of Notre Dame, BA of ND, resulted from an initiative of Fr. Hesburgh that he discussed with me in 1985, when I was on the board of trustees of the university. This has been a very successful program and served as a model for the creation of other ethnic affinity groups, such as the Hispanic Alumni of Notre Dame and the Asian-Pacific Alumni of Notre Dame.

Notre Dame has honored me in various ways. In 1977 I was awarded an honorary doctoral degree. In 2008, I received the Cavanaugh Award for Public Service from the Notre Dame Alumni Association. In 2011, I was recognized at my fiftieth anniversary reunion as a distinguished graduate. By far the highest honor that I have received was not awarded by Notre Dame, but was enabled by Notre Dame: in 2009, I was elected to the National Academy of Engineering, the most prestigious engineering society in the country. That honor validates the two missions that I accepted at St. Augustine. It recognized the engineering work I did in managing the development of U.S. Army weapons systems and the work I did in creating organizations to bring more minorities into engineering.

Although not perfect, Notre Dame has been central to my life.

HOSEA ALEXANDER

(Class of 1962)

Hosea Alexander first came to Notre Dame in autumn 1952 from St. Louis. He majored in engineering. In 1956, one semester shy of graduation, he was forced by illness to withdraw from the university. He returned in 1962 and completed his degree. Before and after graduating, he worked in the aerospace industry and related fields in Southern California. He and his wife, Genevieve, had four children, two of whom graduated from Notre Dame. They live in Los Angeles.

I WAS ONE OF A THOUSAND ST. LOUIS NEGROES WHO CONVERTED to Catholicism after Cardinal Joseph Ritter integrated all churches and schools in the city in 1947. On Thanksgiving Day 1950, I was at home in St. Louis on a three-day pass from my Army post at Fort Riley, Kansas, and attended mass at my home parish, St. Anne's.

Father James Bresnahan, the pastor, preached a good homily, talking about the reasons we should be grateful for the gifts Jesus earned for us on the cross and how we should see Christ in our fellow men and love one another. After mass Father Bresnahan introduced me to a visitor, Father Glenn R. Boarman, CSC, who was working on his master's in liturgical studies at St. Louis University.

"I understand you'll be discharged from the Army next year," Father Boarman said. "What are your educational plans?"

I told him that I intended to be an engineer, that I was already taking some courses at Kansas State College, and that my uncle had invited me to come to Los Angeles and enroll at UCLA.

"Did you ever think of going to Notre Dame?" Father Boarman said.

To which I replied, "If I did it was a fleeting thought, because Notre Dame doesn't admit Negroes."

"That's no longer true," Father Boarman said. And he went on to mention that the Notre Dame Club of St. Louis sponsored a young man each year with a scholarship. "Would you be interested?"

"I certainly would!" I replied.

On his own initiative, Father Boarman applied on my behalf for the Notre Dame Club of St. Louis scholarship. Early in 1951, he wrote to me at Fort Riley. He said that the club had decided not to sponsor a scholarship until the Korean War ended, so as to avoid a situation in which, if the winning student were drafted, the money would be committed for the duration of the war.

Nevertheless, he asked that I have my transcript sent to him from St. Louis' Sumner High School, where I had graduated in 1948 just before entering the Army. I complied.

Shortly after, in February 1951, I received a letter from Mrs. Roger L. Putnam, president of Catholic Scholarships for Negroes in Springfield, Massachusetts. Again, on his own initiative, Father Boarman had applied for a scholarship there on my behalf. Mrs. Putnam was offering me a scholarship to Notre Dame, to be used after I got out of the service the next year.

I informed her that I would be eligible for GI benefits after my service ended, but she told me the scholarship would be available to cover whatever expenses were not covered by the GI Bill.

In May 1952 I was discharged from the Army. That fall I entered Notre Dame as a twenty-one-year-old freshman, intent on studying engineering. My life as a student, both on campus and off, was exciting. Almost daily the African-American students met in the dorm room of one of us, Walter Hall, for "rap" before departing for study.

Two black South Bend families provided us support. The Riddle family, with two beautiful daughters, opened their doors for all students. One of the daughters, Charlotte, married one of the students, Bill Rodgers, who later became a physician. I was Bill's best man.

Mr. and Mrs. J. Chester Allen, both of whom were lawyers, also welcomed Notre Dame African-American students. Mr. Allen was a Democrat; Mrs. Allen was a Republican. Between them, they had all the political bases covered. I tutored their daughter, Sarah, before she went off to Wellesley.

Father Glenn, who by then was back on the Notre Dame campus, was a great friend and advisor. I talked to him of becoming a philosopher. He replied, "If you're a philosopher, it'll happen. But you have a gift in physics. You'll be better able to support a family on an engineer's salary than on that of a philosopher."

During the summer of 1955, while on a visit to Los Angeles, I met Genevieve L. James, the cousin of an Army buddy of mine. On December 26 of that year, the feast of St. Stephen the Martyr, Genevieve and I were married in the Log Chapel at Notre Dame. A little more than a month later, in February 1956, with only a semester left before graduation, I was forced to withdraw from Notre Dame because of a painful flareup of a back injury I had suffered while in the Army.

Despite my lack of a degree, I was hired at North American Aviation in Inglewood, California. And because of my work in thermodynamics at Notre Dame under Professor George E. Rohrbach, I was assigned to work on the X-15, the first manned aircraft to travel outside the earth's atmosphere. I later transferred to Rocketdyne, a designer and producer of rockets, in Canoga Park, California. While there, I designed a patented gimbal.

In 1961, Irving Hirschfeld, one of my supervisors, offered me the chance to take a leave to get my degree at Notre Dame, while keeping full family insurance coverage. If I returned to his development group for two years after getting my degree, he said, he would sponsor my promotion to Rocketdyne's advanced analysis group, the company's think tank.

Chuck Flores, a supportive colleague, bet naysayers in the group that I would find a way to return to Notre Dame. I did, using my own resources, help from my pastor and a brother-in-law, and two scholarships obtained through the intervention of my old thermodynamics professor, George Rohrbach. At my going-away luncheon, Flores gave me a new London Fog raincoat, a new leather briefcase, and $300 cash, the winnings from his bets with the naysayers. "They don't know Notre Dame men, Hosea!" he said in admiration, even though he was not himself a Notre Dame man.

In advocating my readmission to the Notre Dame College of Engineering, Professor Rohrbach told the committee that I was one of only three students who had made As on his Thermodynamics final in 1955. Jerry and Jim Massey, who had been at the top of our graduating class, were the other two. Professor Rohrbach also remembered how Gen and I had sent him a mass card when his mother died after Christmas in 1955.

When I returned to Notre Dame in the fall of 1961, I did so with three children and a wife pregnant with our fourth. During that one academic year, I found another professor who lit my fire just as Professor Rohrbach had.

"If I can do automatic control systems, you can do automatic control systems," Professor Francis H. Raven told our class in automatic control engineering. His words proved prophetic for me. After I had graduated and returned to Rocketdyne in 1962, I was able to convince management and test engineers that we could cut costs and prevent explosions if we used simulated systems, an idea that came from Professor Raven.

Irv Hirschfeld kept his promise. After I had been back on his team for two years, he sponsored my move to the advanced analysis group, which was a joy. Using fundamentals taught me by Professors Rohrbach and Raven at Notre Dame, we attempted—and achieved—a host of improvements and innovations in rocket technology.

In 1967, after solid propellant propulsion had evolved, I resigned from Rocketdyne and went briefly to McDonnell Douglas. Within my first week there, I reviewed a specification relating to the Nike-Zeus anti-ballistic missile system to decide whether a contractor could perform. He could not. I rewrote the specification and redesigned the automated production system to save the company's Nike-Zeus defense contract.

Dwain Spencer, a Notre Dame man, had long pursued me to join the team at NASA's Jet Propulsion Laboratory at Caltech. Despite efforts by McDonnell Douglas to keep me, I decided later in 1967 to go with Spencer and JPL.

In the first of my eleven years there, I won a best presentation award at NASA's Aerospace Mechanism Symposium in Santa Clara, California. Later I was part of efforts that applied scientific and mathematical modeling to a patient admission system for UCLA–Harbor General Hospital in Torrance, California, and I received a NASA certificate of recognition for a health services estimation model.

Later, during eleven years with Hughes Electronics Systems Engineering, I led in performing ready-for-market validation tests to traction control systems for seven models of General Motors vehicles.

In all of these activities, I applied and then extrapolated from principles and fundamentals learned at Notre Dame, and especially from Professors Rohrbach and Raven.

Not unrelated to my Notre Dame experience is my other career — as a permanent deacon of the Catholic Church. In June 1975, I and twenty-four other men became the first class of permanent deacons ordained for the archdiocese of Los Angeles. I continue to work actively as a deacon and, along with my son Edward Andrew Alexander, MD, produce the *St. Martin de Porres Hour*, a local television program.

Not incidentally, Edward and another of my sons, Hosea Alexander Jr., both were members of the Notre Dame Class of 1979, part of the second generation of our family to live and learn in the shadow of the Golden Dome.

Algernon Johnson "Jay" Cooper

(Class of 1966)

Jay Cooper came to Notre Dame in autumn 1962 from Mobile, Alabama. He majored in Latin American history and had a minor in theology. He graduated from the New York University School of Law in 1969. He has three children. He and his wife, bj Hampton, live in Fairhope, Alabama, on the Gulf Coast.

I RECENTLY ATTENDED THE FORTY-SIXTH CONVENTION OF the National Black Law Students Association that I founded while in law school at New York University in 1968. Having finished a lunch featuring a talk by Judge Ann C. Williams of the Seventh US Circuit Court of Appeals, I was reminiscing about my days as a Notre Dame student for this essay.

Notre Dame was stenciled in my mind when my brother Gary (Class of 1958), came home in his Navy ROTC dress white uniform. I was mesmerized by the uniform and the figure he cut. I wanted to be like my big brother. Persuading my parents to allow me to attend a military academy was my first hurdle, finding a Catholic military academy the next. My father finally located a Benedictine abbey, twenty-four-hour boarding school in Aurora, Illinois. I entered Marmion Military Academy in 1958. Marmion turned out to be a good choice. It taught me discipline and provided a great education, and a large number of its graduates went on to Notre Dame. Marmion also taught me that I wanted no part of the military and gave me my first taste of politics when I was elected editor of the academy newspaper, *The Cadet Call*. Importantly, Marmion introduced me to an environment where I was the only black student.

I followed my brothers Gary and William "Billy" (Class of 1962) down South Bend Avenue to the Golden Dome. The trip led me to "the best of times" and the "worst of times," to "the spring of hope" and "the winter of despair." Notre Dame was truly *A Tale of Two Cities*, as only Dickens could tell it.

My schizophrenic time at Notre Dame, from 1962 to 1966, was during the tempestuous and turbulent days of the civil rights movement, women's liberation, and Notre Dame's 1966 national championship football team led by All-American Alan Page. These years included Martin Luther King's standing room-only speech at the Stepan Center in October of 1963, the assassination of John F. Kennedy in November of 1963, a Johnny Mathis concert in May of 1963, and George Wallace speaking at the packed old Fieldhouse at the invitation of several student groups. Then there was Harry Belafonte's tour de force appearance in October of 1964. There was the Civil Rights Act in 1964, followed by the Voting Rights Act in 1965. There was Martin Luther King's "I Have A Dream" speech at the 1963 March on Washington for Jobs and Freedom and the assassination in Mississippi of Medgar Evers.

When my brother Gary arrived on campus in 1954, there were a half dozen or so black students. By 1958, with the arrival of my brother Billy, the number was about a dozen. When I arrived in 1962, there were sixteen blacks, including three football players, two basketball players, and a track star. My first dorm was Farley Hall, room 327, I recall. My roommate, Jay Rini, was from Shaker Heights, Ohio, and we hit it off immediately. We decided to campaign for hall council. Our slogan was "Make Your Vote Pay Off: Vote for Jay Cooper and Jay Rini." With the help of the dormitory room cleaners, who placed flyers under the pillows of every room the night before the election asking for votes, our campaign was successful.

As my second semester began, I noticed that South Bend remained segregated in many respects, from barbershops to bars, with no interference from the university. I began looking at Notre Dame with a more critical eye. I noticed that I was the first and only black member of the Notre Dame Ave Maria Chapter 1477 of the Knights of Columbus.

There was only one black professor, Dr. Adam Arnold, who was in the School of Business. The room cleaners and janitorial staff were all Polish and the number of black students was still miserably low, especially if you did not count the heavily recruited black athletes.

There were several black families in South Bend who wrapped their arms around us and were, indeed, "bridges over troubled waters." One family was that of Dr. Roland Chamblee, a physician. He and his wife welcomed many of us to their dinner table. His daughter Michelle attended St. Mary's Academy, a South Bend boarding and day school that both of my sisters also attended. Michelle became an oncologist and married my roommate, Alphonso Christian, from the Virgin Islands. Al, the smartest person I had met, graduated from Harvard Law. A sports fanatic, he was also, as historians would put it, a "race man."

Notre Dame's president, Father Theodore Hesburgh, was a conundrum to me. His office was right beneath the Golden Dome and, if his light was on, one could walk in and talk with him. He and I spent a number of evenings talking about national politics and civil rights, as well why there were more African students at Notre Dame than Catholic black Americans. We talked about the lack of minorities on the faculty and staff.

We talked about what Notre Dame was doing to help blacks in South Bend. Father Hesburgh's position on the US Civil Rights Commission and the liberal policies that he espoused there put Notre Dame's lack of racial progress in sharp contrast and was very disconcerting to me.

The Civil Rights Commission of the Student Government Association, which I founded, created the Committee on Negro Enrollment (CONE). Father Ted encouraged me and other black students to visit high schools and recruit students, but the University did not put any money into the effort. CONE sponsored a concert to raise money. All of the black students and a number of white students supported the effort, especially the president of the student government, which provided the seed money for the event. CONE's show consisted of Dick Gregory, "Little Stevie Wonder," and Nina Simone. Our hopes were high, but our efforts fell short.

In my junior year, the history department nominated me to become a "Foreign Affairs Scholar" and I was accepted. This was a joint venture by the Ford Foundation, Howard University, Dr. Kenneth Clark's Metropolitan Applied Research Center, and the State Department. The program, located in Washington, D.C., and lasting ten weeks, was designed to recruit blacks to be Foreign Service officers. This experience afforded me the opportunity to meet black college juniors and seniors from all over the country and made for me many lifelong friends.

Returning for my senior year, I encountered a great professor, Father John Cavanaugh, former president of Notre Dame. He taught me in a course on the Great Classics. He was, along with Professors Sam Shapiro and Fred Pike, my Latin American history professors, the most influential, interesting, fascinating personality of my college years.

I had decided to enter law school and naturally researched the law school at Notre Dame. The school had never had a black law student. When I discovered, however, that a former dean, Clarence Manion, was one of the founding members of the John Birch Society, I knew I would not be staying at Notre Dame. Manion founded *The Manion Forum*, a weekly conservative radio broadcast carried over hundreds of stations throughout the country. His favorite guests included Jesse Helms, Strom Thurmond, Harry Byrd Sr., and Stan Evans, chairman of the American Conservative Union, all key players in the rise of the conservative movement. Manion's influence on the law school makes it one of the great bastions of conservative legal scholarship to this day.

One of my great experiences was returning to campus a few years after my graduation, at the invitation of law school dean, William Lawless, to give a speech, which I titled, "To Be Young, Black and Irish: Schizoid Miscegenation." Parenthetically, Dean Lawless, with law degrees from Notre Dame and Harvard, was a New York State Supreme Court justice when I met him while working for a small, black, Buffalo law firm one summer. In his most noteworthy decision, he ruled that the New York state prison system must recognize members of the Nation of Islam as members of a valid religion.

Would I do it all again? Yes. I got a great education, academically and otherwise. The Notre Dame reputation certainly has cachet, but I cannot think of an instance when either the university or a Caucasian alumnus helped me to get a job or a client. Perhaps all of the above are the reasons I strongly feel that BA of ND, Black Alumni of Notre

Dame, should be more assertive in challenging the university to provide greater student, staff, and faculty diversity. This would include sharing the university's wealth by assuring that black architects, contractors, engineers, attorneys, and others are directly engaged by the university and that those with whom the university contracts have both measurable minority set-asides and diversity programs in their executive employment.

RONALD A. HOMER

(Class of 1968)

Ron Homer came to Notre Dame in autumn 1964 from Brooklyn, New York. He majored in psychology, ran freshman cross country and track, and co-founded the Afro-American Society. After graduation, he developed a career in banking and investments. He and his wife, Cheryl, live in Boston and West Palm Beach. They have two sons and five grandchildren.

EVEN THOUGH THE CHOICE WAS SERENDIPITOUS AND SECOND-guessed throughout my first year, attending Notre Dame has played a major role in building the foundation for the most satisfying aspects of my life: my marriage and my career.

Born and raised in the Bedford Stuyvesant/Crown Heights section of Brooklyn, I was the oldest child and the only son of immigrant parents. My mother and father came to New York City as adolescents; they were raised by single mothers from Jamaica and Trinidad, respectively. My father worked his way up from a shipping clerk to a buyer in the garment industry, and my mother was a traditional homemaker.

While my parents stressed the importance of a good education, I would be the first in my family to attend college. I was a good student, attending Catholic schools from kindergarten through high school. However, my preference for college was an Ivy League or Big Ten university with a medical school. The most realistic career choice for a college-educated Negro ("African-American" was not part of the vernacular then) was doctor, lawyer, teacher, or preacher. By default I aspired to be a doctor.

The Jesuits convinced my parents that I would lose my way at an Ivy League or a Big Ten school. So in retaliation I eliminated all the Jesuit colleges, leaving Villanova and Notre Dame as my choices. Never having traveled west of the Pocono Mountains in Pennsylvania and with little or no idea of where Indiana was, I chose Notre Dame and, fortunately, Notre Dame chose me.

My first time on the Notre Dame campus was freshman orientation in September 1964, at the end of a two-day car ride with my parents. It seemed forever. I arrived precisely twenty years after Frazier Thompson had enrolled. The Civil Rights Act of 1964 had just been enacted in July, outlawing major forms of discrimination but also leading to heightened racial tensions and sensitivities. I spent almost a week at Notre Dame before I saw or met another person of color. I finally discovered three other African-American freshmen carefully dispersed among the five disparate freshman dorms. There were a dozen or more African-American upperclassmen with an informal network, but they were located on the South Quad and didn't have much time or motivation to reach out to the newbies. As far as I could tell, the faculty, dining hall workers, maids in the dorms, landscaping crews, librarians, and administrators all were white.

Notre Dame was my first exposure to *de facto* segregation. By the end of my sophomore year, two of my original three freshman black classmates had transferred and the third escaped to Italy to study abroad. Among my white classmates a few were openly hostile, most were indifferent but not too eager to interact, and others were curious but full of perceptions based upon stereotypes. In most instances, I was the first person of color with whom they had had a peer-to-peer relationship, and certainly the first with whom they had shared living space.

Whether from cramming for an Emil Hofman chemistry quiz, playing basketball behind the bookstore, swimming at "the Rock," or sneaking out to Cartier Field to drink beer, I managed to form many friendships based upon shared interests and experiences. The one clear line of separation was dating across racial lines. Even my best drinking buddies disappeared when the coeds came on campus from surrounding schools. Curfews and off-limit restrictions also made it difficult to meet "townies." There were few women of color at St. Mary's and even fewer among the busloads of coeds who came to campus on football weekends.

Against this backdrop, I began dating my future wife, Cheryl, whom I met in Brooklyn during the Christmas break of my freshman year. When we met, Cheryl was a high school senior. After graduation she worked and attended college at night in Brooklyn. During the next two years, we corresponded daily, spent all of our summers and school breaks together, arranged frequent campus visits and fell deeply in love. We married two years later during the mid-semester break of my junior year, and she moved for my senior year to South Bend, where we lived in a small apartment near the campus. We have since raised two fine sons and have five wonderful grandchildren. Together they represent the loves of my life flowing from my Notre Dame experience. On April 22, 2005, we were honored with the University Alumni Family Life Exemplar Award.

I moved to Alumni Hall in my sophomore year to room with Algernon Johnson Cooper ("Jay" or "AJ"), an African-American senior from Mobile, Alabama. Jay's background was quite different from mine, but we shared the same aspirations. He was from a well-to-do family, had two older brothers who had graduated from Notre Dame, and two sisters attending boarding school in the South Bend area. He was well connected to the South Bend and Chicago African-American communities, which made the social life at Notre Dame much more tolerable. Jay always had political ambitions and went to New York University Law School on the way to becoming the first black mayor in Alabama. After graduation he married my wife's cousin, whom he met when we were roommates, but the marriage did not last long. Ironically Jay also played a role in helping me shape my career choices.

Early morning, April 4, 1968, I found myself heading to the South Bend Regional Airport at the request of my former roommate, Jay Cooper. He was working in the Bobby Kennedy presidential campaign, and had called a day earlier. The campaign wanted a black student to ride in the motorcade from the airport to an event at Notre Dame's Stepan Center. While expressing my intent to cast my first presidential vote for Dick Gregory (his brother was a Notre Dame alum), I reluctantly agreed to meet the advance man—it turned out to be Earl Graves, the eventual founder and publisher of *Black Enterprise* magazine—at an ungodly early hour to be driven to the airport and escorted onto the tarmac to greet the Kennedy plane.

To my surprise, I learned that I was not only in the motorcade but would be riding from the airport to campus in a top-down convertible with Bobby and Ethel Kennedy and the mayor of South Bend. For the next few hours I witnessed, upfront and close, the Kennedy charm, acumen, intensity, and mystique. Over the course of the ride Bobby energized and connected with crowds of disheartened but hopeful blacks, frustrated but proud working-class whites, idealistic but skeptical students, and all-knowing academics, all the while soliciting my opinion, pledging his support, and asking for a commitment to work with him toward making America a better place through the expansion of opportunity. By noon Bobby Kennedy had my vote and my heart.

Much later that evening, Cheryl and I eagerly watched the news expecting footage of the motorcade. Instead we saw the footage of a fatally wounded Martin Luther King Jr. and heard Bobby Kennedy making an impassioned plea for peace 140 miles away in the heart of the Indianapolis African-American community. Barely two months later, we again gathered excitedly in front of our nine-inch black-and-white TV to catch the results of the California primary, which would pave the way for Bobby Kennedy's nomination as the Democratic Party candidate for president. Instead we witnessed the assassination of another drum major for change.

During my senior year I came to realize there was not much about medicine that appealed to me aside from the money and the respect. However, I had developed a strong interest in psychology. After a rocky start with the co-heads of the newly formed psychology department, I eventually earned their respect, resulting in an offer of a paid fellowship and full tuition for graduate study at Notre Dame.

However, strongly influenced by the King and Kennedy assassinations, I made a decision to work within one of the poorest and toughest sections of the South Bend community by accepting a position to run the LaSalle Neighborhood Community Center, a part of the federally funded local anti-poverty program advocated by King and Kennedy. After a year of social work and community organizing, I came to the conclusion that poor communities needed economic development as well as social work. So I left to get an MBA so I could learn how businesses work. With my MBA in hand, I turned to banking as a logical vehicle for supporting economic development. The end result, which deserves an essay in itself, has been a sometimes frustrating but always satisfying forty-plus-year career in banking and financial services, with an emphasis on urban economic development.

Nearly fifty years from the day I first stepped onto the campus, my marriage and my career remain strongly rooted in the events that I experienced while at Notre Dame.

Paul Ramsey

(Class of 1968)

Paul Ramsey came to Notre Dame in autumn 1964 from Louis-
ville, Kentucky. He majored in English literature. After gradu-
ation he taught at the high school and collegiate levels before
joining the Educational Testing Service, where he retired in
2009 as senior vice president of the international division. He
now runs a small consulting organization, International Edu-
cators Inc. He lives in New York City with Dr. Richard Co-
burn, his partner of more than thirty years.

THE DATE WAS SEPTEMBER 18, 1964. I DON'T REMEMBER THE
day of the week (maybe a Friday) or the weather (it may have been
raining—after all we're talking about South Bend) or much else about
my mother and stepfather bringing me to Notre Dame. Just that date
and my mother making an incredibly motherly and therefore uncool
suggestion: the campus seemed too dark at night to her. Perhaps we
should buy a flashlight to help me get around.

A flashlight! When were these people going to leave so I could . . .
Could what? Be an oxymoron: a grown-up seventeen-year-old?

Though I don't remember our parting, knowing my mother it was
definitely theatrical. After getting "them" out of my new life that I
hoped would be a dream come true, I must have returned to The Black
Room, 436 Cavanaugh. But more about that later.

How had I ended up at this place? That, too, was my mother's
doing, I'm sure. I think it was in the eighth grade: Father Bowling, the
always-only assistant pastor at our parish, St. Augustine (one of the

two black parishes in segregated Louisville, Kentucky), took two of us—undoubtedly seen as definite credits to our race—to the Catholic Student Mission Crusade (CSMC) Conference held at the most beautiful place I'd ever seen, the University of Notre Dame, in South Bend, Indiana. All I really remember about that experience, other than resolving that I would go to Notre Dame for college, was that when I opened my suitcase there was a sappy note from my mother that would have one think that I had gone to Mars for a lifetime rather than to Indiana for four days.

When I returned home, it was all about Notre Dame and how I had to go there. Knowing my mother, she must have thought this was a good idea, so she decided to seal the deal. She said, "Poor colored boys like you don't go to places like that for college." Her words worked the magic I have, in retrospect, thought she must have intended. When it was time, she had to force me to apply to Villanova and Marquette—it was going to be a Catholic school—because there had been no college other than Notre Dame that I would even consider since my CSMC visit and my mother's challenge.

So my wise, if uncool, mother drove away and I returned to The Black Room. Why do I call it The Black Room? Because it was. Ray Fleming, one of the twelve undergraduates at Notre Dame during my freshman year, had had the room the year before. I need not calculate the odds that two blacks two years in a row out of six thousand undergraduates would end up with the same single by chance.

I've always understood that rooming situation to have been the result of Notre Dame's ever-vigilant eye on its image. It would have done that image no good to have a racial incident: parents or fellow students complaining because the latter had ended up with a black roommate. It would be all right if a black and a white *chose* to room together, but the university wasn't going to put itself out there forcing integration, even though Father Hesburgh, admittedly an outstanding president, was constantly being praised for being on the US Civil Rights Commission—with twelve undergraduate blacks at his university. But this was 1964 at a Midwestern white school that even today remains incredibly provincial. Notre Dame has always been a Catholic institution, but never a truly catholic university.

All I remember about what I thought about that room was that I was disappointed that I didn't have a roommate. I had looked forward all summer to meeting him. In the spirit of full disclosure, I want to report that in the second semester I moved into a room with a white student who explained he wanted to live with me because he was trying to overcome his prejudiced feelings about blacks. You have to give the guy, whose name I don't even remember, a lot of credit. Most of us aren't as honest about our motives and don't push ourselves beyond our prejudices, whatever they may be, as that name-forgotten roommate did.

The first thing I remember about being in that single room after my parents left was hearing the guys in the hallway introducing themselves. I didn't know what to do. I don't know if it's because I was raised as an only child or because, being raised in the segregated South, I was taught for survival reasons to draw as little attention to myself as possible, or for some other reason, but I am not to this day good at introducing myself. I'd rather just be on my own. In this particular dorm situation my shyness had everything to do with being black and alone and frightened to enter a white world that might not accept me.

As I stood in that room wondering what to do, I heard the boys in the double directly across the hall, Bob Bradley and Dennis Morrissey (both of whom became good friends), introduce themselves and name their hometown and state: Little Rock, Arkansas.

For a black person of my age, one of the defining racial incidents in my life had been the hate-filled confrontations around integrating Central High School in Little Rock; the other was the horrific lynching of fourteen-year-old Emmett Till, which was used by every black parent I knew as a parable of the dangers of living in a white man's and woman's world. The lesson: keep your distance and keep your mouth and door shut. And the lesson of Little Rock: those white folks were good at spitting and hitting. I can still see the televised hatred in those Little Rock whites. There was no way I was going to test those waters that night, so I stayed in my room.

The next morning I went to mass in the hall and one of the greatest acts of charity I have ever experienced took place. I entered the chapel and, of course, sat at the edge of a pew alone (as I would do now in a similar situation) when this guy came up to the pew and stood there. I remember looking up at him wondering what he wanted and what I was to do. He said, "Move over." I did and he sat next to me. Finally, human contact. Again, I don't remember his name, but when I think of Christian charity, I think of this white boy demanding to sit next to this lone and lonely black boy.

The next days and years were happy ones for me, until the assassination of Martin Luther King Jr. near the end of my senior year. Though I was part of the group that successfully argued with the university to turn the lights out on the Dome as a tribute to Dr. King and that helped organize a march in his memory—fewer than one hundred from Notre Dame and Saint Mary's attended—I came to realize that I was not affected enough by his death because the community I had come to love and thought I was a part of was not greatly affected. For me a defining moment was when I went alone into the television room in my dorm to watch Dr. King's funeral. As I entered the room I saw the cortege being drawn by those mules for a second, but only a second, because there were two white classmates in the room switching the channel, looking for their afternoon soaps. I backed out of that room and began my leave-taking from that white, Catholic cubicle that is, or at least was, Notre Dame.

I have no idea who I was to be so happy at such an insular place, but I must acknowledge I was. About ten years ago, I was asked to sit on the Notre Dame Arts and Letters Advisory Council (my mother, by then dead, would have been most proud), but I lasted only two years. I was always on the critical, if not cynical, edge. Who were these incredibly friendly—too friendly by the standards of the New Yorker I had become—people who seemed to have no edge or visible tattoos? What could I say to that many Republicans in one place? And when I heard and hear the issues that are up for debate at the university— Should the president of the United States be allowed to speak because he doesn't oppose abortion? Should the gay and lesbian organization be recognized by the university?—I feel like the place is in some kind of time warp.

But there's no denying that Notre Dame gave me some lifelong friendships, a good education, and a sense of the social gospel that has defined my Catholicity—a religion I continue to "practice" but usually feel as out of step with as I do with Notre Dame.

BILL HURD

(Class of 1969)

Bill Hurd came to Notre Dame in autumn 1965 from Memphis. He majored in electrical engineering and was a world-class sprinter on the track team and a jazz saxophone virtuoso. After graduation, he became a businessman and a physician. He and his wife, Rhynette, live in Memphis. They have two sons, one of whom, Ryan Hurd, was a member of the Notre Dame class of 2005.

BY THE TIME I WAS A SENIOR AT MEMPHIS'S ALL-BLACK Manassas High School in 1965, I had run the 100-yard dash in 9.3 seconds, then an unofficial national high school record. I had won consecutive citywide math contests, completed two advanced placement courses, been elected senior class president, and become the cadet lieutenant colonel/battalion commander of the National Defense Cadet Corps, similar to Junior ROTC.

I graduated fourth in a senior class of 367. The valedictorian and salutatorian positions were held by Carol and Cathryn Branham, the twin daughters of my dad's sister. Their story and mine made the cover of the popular *JET* magazine in 1965.

I had long had my mind set on MIT in Cambridge, Massachusetts, for college. My SAT scores were just average on the verbal section, but near perfect on the math section and on the Advanced Placement calculus test. So I was all set to attend MIT on a full academic scholarship.

However, because of my athletic performance, I had begun receiving recruitment letters from major universities. Ultimately, I received more than fifty such letters and was courted by the likes of West Point; UCLA, where alumnus and 1960 Olympic decathlon champion Rafer Johnson recruited me; and Villanova, a track and field powerhouse in the 1960s and 1970s that had Frank Budd, a former world-class sprinter, recruit me personally.

And then there was Notre Dame. The Notre Dame track coach was Alex Wilson, a 1928 Canadian Olympic silver medalist in the 4x400-meter relay. He was a very intelligent, soft-spoken, white-haired, tea-drinking gentleman, who knew all the nuances of coaching. And he personally came to Memphis to watch me run in a track meet and recruit me. I was very impressed that a head track coach would travel all the way from Notre Dame just to see me compete.

Ultimately the choice was easy. My two sisters and brother all had gone to college on my dad's salary from the US Post Office. By accepting a full athletic scholarship to Notre Dame, I knew that I would be lessening the financial burden on my family while getting the benefit of a university with a nice mixture of high academic standards and national athletic prominence.

As a Southern black kid, I had spent all my formative years in the segregated environment of Memphis, except for summers, which my siblings and I would spend in Kansas City, Missouri, at the home of my grandmother, Avar Pipkin. So at first, Notre Dame was somewhat of a culture shock.

Looking back, I concluded that the Notre Dame housing staff had purposely selected as my freshman roommate a student who had had limited dealings with black folk. Mike Holtzapfel was from Ironton, Ohio, a small town on the Kentucky-Ohio border, and was on the football team. Mike preferred to sleep with the window open in the dead of the winter and would have his radio blasting with what sounded to me like hillbilly music. By the end of the first semester, he was listening to Marvin Gaye and I, with the window still open, had become acclimated to the cold South Bend winters.

There were a couple of white student-athletes from Memphis who were upperclassmen and whom I perceived as not wanting to acknowledge me, even if our paths crossed on campus. Because I entered Notre Dame as a highly recruited athlete, there was a lot of fanfare and also a lot of expectation. I really felt like there was some degree of discomfort or resentment of all this among my fellow Memphians.

There were a dozen or so black students in my 1965 freshman class of 1,600. As we got to know each other, I became intrigued with the stories told by the black students who grew up in New York City, where their exposure to more worldly and sophisticated events and activities exceeded mine both in volume and variety. But coming from all-black Manassas, I had nothing to be ashamed of. I felt just as prepared to succeed at Notre Dame as anyone else—maybe more so. The first evidence of this was my being able to skip Calculus I, the content of which I had already covered in an AP course at Manassas.

I have many fond memories from my first two years at Notre Dame, and three black upperclassmen stand out in them. Frank Yates (Class of 1967) was a senior from Memphis's Father Bertrand High School who donated to me his notes from previous courses in differential equations and physics. Frank was always there to lend his support and encouragement. Upon graduation from Notre Dame with a near-perfect grade point average, he was selected a Fulbright Scholar. He subsequently received his doctorate in statistical psychology at the University of Michigan and became a tenured professor there.

Ron Homer (Class of 1968), who grew up in Brooklyn, New York, was the kind of guy you'd just love to hang out with. He was one of those New Yorkers who seemed to have all the answers. Ron started out as a pre-med major but transferred to psychology, got an MBA, and eventually became a bank president in Boston.

The third black upperclassman was Alan Page, an All-American defensive end at Notre Dame and my designated barber. He was one of the first black athletes to sport a shaven head. Alan graduated to NFL stardom with the Minnesota Vikings and, after his retirement, was elected to the NFL Hall of Fame. After law school he became the Honorable Alan Page, the first black justice of the Minnesota Supreme Court.

I started out as a math major but switched to electrical engineering. I managed to organize my study schedule, be an important part of the track team, and continue performing music. In 1965 the NCAA still prohibited freshmen from intercollegiate competition, so Coach Wilson scheduled me to run in a select number of high-profile Amateur Athletic Union invitational track meets. On one occasion, I placed second in the 60-yard dash in the Milrose Games at Madison Square Garden. It was my first trip ever to New York City.

I recall another trip that involved the entire Notre Dame track team. In the spring of 1967, the team was traveling by bus from South Bend to Williamsburg, Virginia, where the College of William & Mary hosted the William & Mary Relays, a meet where I eventually would receive the Most Outstanding Performer award.

Because of the lengthy bus ride, we stopped overnight in rural Virginia. I was the only black team member on this trip. The bus pulled up to a small motel and all fifteen or so of us gathered in the small lobby as Coach Wilson engaged the desk clerk. The clerk's eyes scanned our faces and his gaze seemed to focus on mine a bit longer than on any of the others. After a moment of silence, the clerk announced that "the Negro" couldn't stay there. Coach Wilson quickly replied, "If he cannot stay, no one will stay." In the end we went to another motel with no problems.

One of the great by-products of the college experience is lifelong friendships. Bob Cann, from the Bronx, New York, was the only other black electrical engineering major in my class and he is, to this day, one of my best friends. He also is the godfather of my older son, Bill Jr. In addition to getting our bachelor's degrees together from Notre Dame in 1969, Bill and I got our master's degrees from MIT's Sloan School of Management together in 1972. He and I both are physicians, but we each started medical school without knowing the other was going to apply.

I can proudly say that I played football at Notre Dame, even if for only one season. I hadn't played high school football because my dad was concerned about my safety. He figured that, because I was the city's fastest athlete, there would be competition to injure me. Similarly, at Notre Dame Coach Wilson was not thrilled at the thought of my suffering an injury just before the beginning of the indoor track season.

One evening, during a spring 1967 training workout in the Athletic and Convocation Center, where the track and football teams worked out in close proximity, football coach Ara Parseghian approached me. After introducing himself—as if I didn't already know who he was—he proceeded to ask me if I'd like to be a part of the Notre Dame football team. Without hesitation I said yes. He told me to enjoy an abbreviated summer and report early to campus before the fall semester.

It seemed like every guy on the team was six-feet, four-inches tall and 240 pounds, and the only advantage I had was my speed. My jersey number was 14, and I played wide receiver. I didn't get a lot of playing time because I was on the second team, behind the starting wide receiver, All-American Jim Seymour. Nevertheless, I thoroughly enjoyed being a small part of the mystical Notre Dame football history. It was an amazing feeling to run through the tunnel onto the Notre Dame Stadium playing field with my teammates amid the game-day atmosphere. Besides Seymour, other notable teammates were Bob "Rocky" Bleier, Terry Hanratty, and Bob Kuechenberg, all of whom went on to brilliant NFL careers.

Social life at Notre Dame for me was out of the ordinary. I was often treated like royalty, being a star athlete in a school where star athletes are worshiped and plentiful. Notre Dame did not become coed until I left, but Saint Mary's College provided opportunities to meet girls for those inclined. There were many unsuccessful attempts to be set up for blind dates with girls from Saint Mary's who wanted a date with a star athlete. I was not comfortable dating white girls because of the way I had grown up in segregated Memphis society, where interracial dating was viewed negatively. Besides, I would have more time to focus my studies, track and field, and music. But undoubtedly, all of this attention was a huge ego boost.

By my senior year, I had been selected Notre Dame Athlete of the Year 1968; become the track team captain; held the American record in the indoor 300-yard dash; held several Notre Dame track records, two of which still stand today (100 meters in 10.1 seconds and 200 meters in 20.3 seconds); and won the outstanding saxophone soloist award at the 1967 Notre Dame Collegiate Jazz Festival.

There were other honors as well. Notre Dame President Father Theodore Hesburgh nominated me to be a Rhodes Scholar. I recall going to meet him in his office in the Administration Building under the famous Golden Dome to get prepped for the national Rhodes Scholar selection process. I vividly recall flying home to Memphis and my dad driving me to Sewanee College in Sewanee, Tennessee, for the final interview.

About a year after graduating from Notre Dame, I ended up at the school I had dreamed of attending as a teenager. My wife, Rhynette, and I were married in June of 1970, and that fall I enrolled at the Sloan School of Management at MIT. By May 1972 I would earn my master's degree from MIT, Rhynette would receive her MAT from Harvard, and our first son, Bill Jr., would be born at St. Elizabeth Hospital in Brighton near Boston. We didn't have lots of money, but we were happy grad school grads and proud young new parents.

We wanted to move to a warmer climate, so I accepted a consulting job in Nashville, with a requirement that I teach management courses in the business department at Tennessee State University, and Rhynette accepted a position in the English department at Fisk University. I also got involved with the incubation of minority business ventures in Nashville. Many of my clients were in the healthcare field, including several black physicians. One outcome of this was the establishment of a minority–owned and operated medical center. I was a co-founder and investor in this venture, which eventually generated enough income to help finance my medical school education.

The idea of becoming a physician came from several motivations. I wanted to be my own boss and move at my own pace. I also had seen how physicians were able to use their training and skills to heal sick people and make them better. I was constantly searching for a discipline that could hold my interest but would still allow me to think analytically like the engineer that I was.

I entered Meharry Medical College in the fall of 1976 at age twenty-nine. Because of previous investments and business ventures I did not have to worry about income, so I could focus on med school. I also worked as an adjunct professor for Fisk University and had a steady income from frequent music gigs. Otherwise, med school consumed most of my waking hours. It was an exciting and fulfilling time in my life. There was a feeling of learning something new every day. I could see parallels between functions of the human body and specific engineering principles.

At med school graduation in 1980, I was matched with the University of Tennessee ophthalmology program in Memphis, becoming one of the first blacks admitted to that residency program. I had been to Notre Dame, MIT, and Meharry, but the University of Tennessee experience turned out to be the most difficult one, in part because of isolated efforts to make life hard for me. I was constantly dealing with racial issues, primarily generated by white, Southern physicians not accustomed to working with black physicians of equal education, training, and skills. Nevertheless, before completing my residency I was able to finish the design and construction of a device that measures certain inner parts of the human eye. I secured US and foreign patents on this device, the slit-lamp mountable intraocular biometer.

In 1982, while I was a resident physician under the guidance of the renowned Dr. Jerre Freeman, I began participating in medical missions to medically underserved countries. Our first trip, to Ometepec in southern Mexico, was the beginning of a long series of mission projects in Mexico, Brazil, China, South Africa, Senegal, and Madagascar. Over almost twenty years—until safety concerns following the 9/11 terror attacks brought them to a halt—I and my mission colleagues restored sight to thousands of patients, and shared and exchanged knowledge of surgical techniques and medical diagnostic and therapeutic procedures with foreign host physicians.

In 1982, our second son, Ryan, was born. In 2005, Ryan also became a Notre Dame alumnus, graduating with a double major in computer science and Japanese, with honors. Now thirty, he has secured his dream job as a visual effects artist and computer animator for Digital Domain in Los Angeles, after having worked in Bejing and Tokyo for four years. Most recently, Ryan received credit as a visual effects artist on the blockbuster film *Iron Man 3*.

In 2010, Rhynette, who not only earned a PhD in English literature at Vanderbilt but also a law degree at the University of Memphis and became a practicing lawyer, was appointed by the governor of Tennessee to replace the retiring D'Army Bailey on the Eighth Division circuit court. In 2012, she returned to the bench, replacing the ailing Judge Kay Robilio in the Fifth Division circuit court.

After twenty-seven years in private medical practice, I have recently considered retirement. But because I still enjoy practicing ophthalmology and my surgical skills have not diminished, I have compromised by working shorter hours. This allows more time for golf and for my favorite pastime, music.

DON WYCLIFF

(Class of 1969)

Don Wycliff came to Notre Dame in autumn 1965 from Terre Haute, Indiana. He majored in government and was involved in student government and efforts to recruit black students. After graduation he briefly attended graduate school and then became a journalist. After thirty-five years as a working journalist, he became a teacher of journalism at Loyola University Chicago. He has two sons. He and his wife, Pamela, live in South Bend.

VERY EARLY IN MY FRESHMAN YEAR, IN THE AUTUMN OF 1965, I went one Saturday night to a post–football game concert at Stepan Center. The featured performers were Little Anthony and the Imperials, a doo-wop group that had had a few big hits in the late 1950s, fell out of popularity, and were making a comeback in the mid-1960s.

Somehow I managed to get close enough to the stage that I actually could see the beads of sweat on the faces of Little Anthony and his partners as they worked out. And as I watched and listened to them, I found myself marveling at the fact that I was in the same room, breathing the same air as these famous performers who, until that night, had existed for me only within a little plastic box behind an AM radio dial. Surely, I thought, this place that I have come to, this University of Notre Dame, is over the rainbow.

By the time I graduated in June 1969, Little Anthony and the Imperials were the least of the marvels I had experienced at Notre Dame.

Thanks to teacher-guides with last names like Nicgorski, Goerner, Kromkowski, Silver, Smelser, Evans, Dunne, and O'Malley, I had encountered—and contended with—thinkers like Plato, Aristotle, Aquinas, Locke, Descartes, Ellison, Sartre, Baldwin, Thoreau, and dozens of others.

These contests were no contest, of course. Any of those great minds was better on his worst day than I was on my best. But thanks to my Notre Dame education, I had begun to gain a sense of my own intellectual potential, my capacity to appreciate big thoughts, and maybe, occasionally, even to *have* one. I had begun learning how to be a scholar.

All of this happened thanks to a host of good people—my high school algebra teacher, Sister Margaret Sullivan; my high school principal, Father Joseph Beechem; Patrick J. Fisher, an Indianapolis lawyer and Notre Dame alumnus who went out of his way to connect me with the university's admissions office; and Anonymous, a person whose identity I did not know then and still do not know, but who donated a four-year scholarship for me because Notre Dame thought I had promise.

I did not choose Notre Dame. Rather, Notre Dame *happened to me* as suddenly and unexpectedly as that Kansas cyclone happened to Dorothy Gale, the little heroine of *The Wizard of Oz* who found herself swept away from home and over the rainbow.

In April of my senior year of high school—Paul Schulte High in Terre Haute, Indiana—I was still uncertain what I was going to do when I graduated two months later. I wanted to go to college, but wasn't sure how to make that happen. My devout Catholic parents had nine children and not much money. I was the second oldest. My older brother, Francois, who later followed me to Notre Dame and graduated in 1972, had joined a religious order, the Brothers of the Poor of St. Francis, after his high school graduation in 1961. There was no way I was going to do that, but the Marine Corps had a certain appeal for me.

I had applied to one college: Xavier University in Cincinnati. I did so because Francois had gone there for two years before his order pulled him out and sent him to teach in one of the schools it staffed. Xavier was the only college I even vaguely knew anything about. Xavier admitted me and gave me a scholarship to cover my tuition. But that left room and board, and I didn't know how I would handle that.

To make a long story short: Father Beechem insisted I apply for and accept an interview for a scholarship being given for the first time that year to a black graduate of a high school in the archdiocese of Indianapolis. It turned out that I was, for technical reasons, ineligible for that scholarship. But about a week after the interview, Mr. Fisher called our home in Terre Haute and asked my mother whether I might be interested in going to Notre Dame. Less than a month later, I had been admitted to Notre Dame with a full scholarship. Thanks to Anonymous, I was headed over the rainbow.

I was one of eleven or twelve black students in a class of 1,600 who entered Notre Dame that fall. I used to be able to recite all the names, but age has weakened my memory. There were Bill Hurd, Bob Cann, Larry Smith, Ken Lay, Al Dean, Bob Whitmore, Dwight Murphy, Tony Brunson.

Hurd was a brilliant student, a world-class athlete, an accomplished jazz saxophonist—one of those people in whose presence I always felt inadequate. Smith and Lay were New Yorkers and that, in my mind, was synonymous with "sophisticated." Whitmore and Murphy were varsity basketball players and exhibits A and B for why I could never be a successful walk-on, as I had fancied I might. Brunson was a Chicagoan who left after the first year. He used to wear a little porkpie hat and had a jaunty style of walking and carrying himself that I always associated with the term "Negritude."

I was intensely unhappy for much of my freshman year. Homesickness was a big part of it. So was the fear I felt because of the requirement to maintain a 3.0 grade point average to retain my scholarship. I ran scared from day one.

But by far the biggest cause was Notre Dame's all-male character. Through grade and high schools, I had attended Catholic schools, and my brothers and sisters and I were always the only—or virtually the only—black students in our schools. As a result, I had no social life. Indeed, I had never had a date. College, I had thought, would be different. But it wasn't. At least not until Kay Scott appeared.

Sylvia Kay Scott was what we used to call a "townie." She was a junior at South Bend Central High School when I met her at an off-campus party given by someone—I'm not sure whom. We started dating, and even after we no longer dated I remained friends with Kay, her parents, and her sister Toni. Had it not been for Kay and her family, I might well have bailed out of Notre Dame that first year. Thanks to them, I didn't.

My freshman year roommate in Farley Hall was Steve Foss, of Albuquerque, New Mexico. Steve was a musician—a drummer—and a German major. We got along pretty well—after I made peace with the fact that I could not save Steve's immortal soul for him. The first couple of weeks of school, I literally dragged him out of his top bunk and down to the chapel for Sunday morning mass.

Next door to us were three other freshmen who became our friends: Jeff Davis from California, Joel Connelly from the state of Washington, and Dave White from the Boston area. In fact, the summer after our sophomore year, Dave and I exchanged home visits.

Around a corner from my room lived Michael Lehan, who became one of my best friends. Mike was a year ahead of me. He came from the little town of Dunlap in western Iowa, and he was a GP—General Program of Liberal Studies—major. It was to Mike that I often would scream when I was getting the worst of it in an argument with Aristotle or Descartes. We worked together for two summers as counselors in the Upward Bound program. And we even did some traveling together—driving like the fellows on the old *Route 66* TV show down to San Antonio once to visit a mutual friend.

I'll never forget the night—it actually was about 5 a.m.—we came upon a car stopped on a bridge outside of some small town in East Texas. The white woman in the car must have been terrified when she saw our car pull up behind her and a tall black guy and a short white guy get out. But we put her at ease, changed her tire for her, and then, declining her offer to stop and have breakfast at the hospital where she was going to work as a cook, got back in Mike's car and drove off.

Professor Walter Nicgorski was a young PhD from the University of Chicago in just his second year on the faculty when I took his course, "Political Order," in my first semester at Notre Dame. By the end of the course, my intention to major in political science was cemented, and Professor Nicgorski had become a mentor. He later hired me as a student assistant; he annually wrote letters of recommendation for me to the university scholarship committee, and he helped me choose graduate programs to which to apply.

Besides Professor Nicgorski, I benefitted from the teaching and mentoring of half a dozen other professors and staff members. There were Professor Edward Goerner, also in political science; John Kromkowski, a political scientist who directed Notre Dame's Upward Bound program; James Silver, an historian who came to Notre Dame after being run out of the state and the University of Mississippi for publishing a book that attacked the state's regime of racial terror; Marshall Smelser, also an historian; theologian John Dunne; philosopher Joseph Evans, and Notre Dame's legendary teacher of English literature, Frank O'Malley.

The first extracurricular activity in which I became involved at Notre Dame was the Committee on Negro Enrollment (CONE), a student government–created effort to boost the number of black students at the university. When I joined in freshman year, the group was being run by a sophomore from Rockford, Illinois, Steve Weeg. Later on—I think in my junior year—I became chairman of CONE.

It was my recruiting activities that led to one of my oldest and dearest Notre Dame friendships: with John Goldrick, a member of the admissions staff during my undergraduate years and, later, director of admissions for many years. I was in the wedding of John and his wife, Jackie, at the Log Chapel on the Notre Dame campus, and I am godfather of their older daughter, Shaheen.

After graduating from Notre Dame in 1969, I went to graduate school at the University of Chicago, intending to earn a doctorate and teach political science. But on December 4, 1969, an event occurred that took me in a different direction. The Chicago police raided the West Side headquarters of the Black Panther Party, killing two of the group's leaders. As I watched and read the news coverage of that story over the weeks and months that followed, I realized that journalism was what I really wanted to do with my life. So I left graduate school after a year, went back to my ancestral home in Texas, and got the first job in my thirty-five-year newspaper career.

In 2000, when I was a top news executive at the *Chicago Tribune* and making more money than I had ever expected to, I realized it was time to pay forward the debt to Notre Dame and Anonymous that I had incurred thirty-five years earlier. My youngest brother, Brian (Class of 1985), and I together endowed the Wilbert and Emily Wycliff Scholarship at Notre Dame, in honor of our parents. Four family members besides Brian and I have attended Notre Dame: my brothers Francois (Class of 1971) and Chris; my niece and goddaughter Lisa Robinson Honore (Class of 1992); and my younger son, Grant Wycliff (Class of 2010).

Our Wycliff hearts truly do "love thee, Notre Dame."

CHAPTER 3

The 1970s

It began with the killings of students at Kent State and Jackson State Universities in 1970. It ended with the Iran hostage crisis—fifty-two Americans, diplomats and ordinary citizens, taken captive in Tehran in November 1979 amid the fervor of an Islamic revolution.

Between those bookend events, the decade of the 1970s encompassed the impeachment and resignation of a president, Richard Nixon; the resignation of a vice president, Spiro Agnew; two assassination attempts on Nixon's successor, Gerald Ford; a murderous terrorist attack in the midst of an Olympic Games, the Munich games of 1972; an embargo of customers by oil-producing nations that sent energy prices soaring; a mass murder-suicide of more than nine hundred Americans in a South American jungle encampment called Jonestown; an accident at Three Mile Island that exposed the perils of nuclear electricity generation; the rise and fall of an African dictator, Idi Amin of Uganda, whose erratic and murderous behavior unnerved anyone who dealt with him; and a persistent inflation—"stagflation," it was called—that hobbled economic growth.

The 1970s were, on balance, more a worst-of-times period than a best-of-times. And yet, the decade did have its moments of joy and promise.

President Jimmy Carter, who had given the commencement address at Notre Dame in 1977, the first year of his presidency, presided the next year over the signing of the Camp David Accords at the White House by the leaders of Egypt and Israel. It was the first break in the long history of enmity between Israel and the Arab world.

Earlier in the decade, before his ignominious departure in the wake of the Watergate scandal, President Nixon finally concluded a peace deal with Vietnam and, in a move that has become almost a synonym for paradoxical political behavior, engineered an opening to China. The US and China had not had a relationship of almost any sort for a quarter of a century.

Nixon also began efforts to normalize relations with the Soviet Union, visiting Moscow in 1972, concluding trade deals, and signing the first agreements to limit arms and begin ratcheting down the level of nuclear terror between the two states. Talk of "mutual assured destruction" began to give way to talk of "détente" and "peaceful co-existence."

Beyond the world of geopolitics, developments were occurring whose effects we still feel today. In 1970, the first Earth Day was celebrated and "the environment" began to grow as a subject of social, political, and scientific concern. In 1971, the Twenty-sixth Amendment to the Constitution, setting a voting age of eighteen, was adopted. In 1973, the Supreme Court issued its still-controversial decision in the case of *Roe v. Wade*, declaring abortion a constitutional right. In 1978, Louise Brown, the first "test-tube baby," was born in England. In 1976, the Apple Computer Company was formed, and the following year it offered its first product for sale to the public. In 1978, Pope Paul VI died, fifteen years after ascending to the papacy and ten years after issuing *Humanae Vitae*, the encyclical that forbade Catholics to use artificial birth control. His successor, who took the name Pope John Paul, died after only thirty-three days in office. He was succeeded by Karol Wojtyla, the cardinal-archbishop of Krakow, Poland, who took the name John Paul II and proceeded to become a force in both the church and geopolitics for the next quarter century.

And then there were events that were simply cultural markers in our lives together as a people. Among them: the announcement in early 1970 of the breakup of the Beatles; the death in 1977 of Elvis Presley, the "King of Rock and Roll"; the bizarre kidnapping, radicalization, capture, prosecution, and imprisonment of newspaper heiress Patricia Hearst.

At Notre Dame the 1970s were an era of far-reaching and highly consequential change. The biggest change—and unquestionably one for the better—was the admission of women undergraduates for the first time in 1972. No more would the Irish be only the sons of Notre Dame, but her daughters, also.

For blacks on campus, it was an era of growth in numbers and of breakthroughs in their roles and status in the Notre Dame community. In 1970, David Krashna of Pittsburgh became the first black to be elected president of the student body. Until the election in 2016 of Corey Robinson, Krashna remained the only African-American to have held the position. Later in the decade, Joya De Foor of Atlanta became the first black cheerleader. In 1971, receiver Tom Gatewood became the first black captain of the Irish football team and Cliff Brown became Notre Dame's first black quarterback. In 1970, Joseph G. Bertrand, one of Notre Dame's first two black basketball players and a 1954 graduate, became the first black member of an advisory council, in the College of Business.

On the larger national stage, Father Ted Hesburgh's tenure as a member of the US Commission on Civil Rights came to an unceremonious but not inglorious end in 1972. President Nixon, who had prevailed upon Hesburgh in 1969 to accept the chairmanship of the commission, chafed at its criticisms of the government's laggardly pace on school desegregation and other civil rights initiatives. Armed with a new mandate after his resounding victory over George McGovern in the 1972 election, Nixon decided to rid himself of the thorn in his side. He demanded Hesburgh's resignation, which he got.

ARTHUR C. MCFARLAND

(Class of 1970)

Arthur McFarland came to Notre Dame in autumn 1966 from Charleston, South Carolina. He majored in government and was the first president of the Afro-American Society and a student representative on the university's board of trustees. After graduation he earned a law degree at the University of Virginia. He made his career practicing law and, for nearly thirty-four years, as a judge in Charleston. He and his wife, Elise Davis-McFarland, have two children.

IT WAS A BEAUTIFUL SUNNY MORNING IN SEPTEMBER 1966 when my cab turned onto Notre Dame Avenue and I first saw the glittering Golden Dome. I had just traveled for nearly twenty-four hours alone by train from Charleston, South Carolina. This was my first trip so far away from the city where I had spent the previous three years as an activist in the civil rights movement. In 1963 I was arrested with other students at sit-in demonstrations and attended the March on Washington. In 1964 I joined eight other African-Americans in desegregating the previously all-white Bishop England High School. In 1965, I was the only black player in the all-white high school basketball league in South Carolina. By 1966, I was looking for an integrated college environment outside South Carolina.

I received an invitation to apply for admission to Notre Dame. While I was Catholic, Notre Dame had not been on my radar before that letter. I was so impressed that I applied. When I received my acceptance letter, I was overjoyed. Although my guidance counselor was not encouraging, my parents, Thomasina and Joe McFarland, celebrated. My mother told me that if I did not succeed at Notre Dame, I had a home to return to. She helped pack my trunk with everything I needed to survive a world with which she had no familiarity. She rested on her faith that she and my father had prepared me for any uncertainty I would face. Her prayers would be answered four years later as she, my father, other family, and friends witnessed my graduation at the Athletic and Convocation Center. This would be their only visit to the campus.

I was assigned room 133 in Cavanaugh Hall. My roommate was Tom Davis, a white student. There were two other black students in Cavanaugh—Francis Taylor (Class of 1970) and Leon Jackson. We were among eleven blacks in the freshman class and twenty-eight blacks in the undergraduate student body. The freshman orientation program was designed to introduce us to the concept of the "Notre Dame man," interpreted by me as "a conservative Catholic white male." According to "The Satisfactions of Negro Students at the University of Notre Dame," a 1968 study by Freddy Williams, a black freshman, and sociology Professor Donald A. Barrett, 64 percent of Notre Dame blacks were Catholic compared to 97 percent of the student body generally. This cultural gap resulted in the development of a strong bond between the black freshmen and black upperclassmen.

My first year was like that of other freshmen who were experiencing independence for the first time. I adapted to the rigors of academia, which I initially found challenging. I engaged in intramural sports, including basketball behind the bookstore or at "the Rock." I joined in the excitement of the 1966 national championship football season. I relished the idea that I no longer had to wash or iron my clothes as I had been raised to do. What a privileged life! I rebelled against the requirement of a necktie at dinner. I found the meals "soulless" and drank too much milk. Fall merged into a seemingly unending winter of some of the worst weather South Bend had seen in nearly two decades.

As a child of the civil rights movement, I recognized that racial stereotyping was a problem at Notre Dame. An incident in Cavanaugh Hall confirmed my view. One night, Francis, Leon, and I engaged dozens of our Cavanaugh classmates in an impromptu discussion of civil rights and race. Our dormmates questioned the worthiness of "Negroes" to enjoy the same opportunities as whites. Their opinions were based on the negative stereotypes of blacks portrayed on television and in the media. Of course, the three of us were "the exception." Our efforts to dispel their racist notions seemed hopeless. I thought there was a clear disconnect between Father Hesburgh's work on the US Civil Rights Commission and racial sensitivity on the Notre Dame campus.

In 1967, I moved into Alumni Hall with Bill Hurd (Class of 1969). Bill was an outstanding student in engineering, a track star, and an accomplished jazz saxophonist. He introduced me to jazz greats including Charlie Parker, John Coltrane, and Pharaoh Sanders. This led me to host a jazz show on WSND radio in the summer of 1969. I also bonded with another dormmate, Walter Williams (Class of 1971). Bill, Walter, and several other Notre Dame and St. Mary's College students began discussions about organizing a black student union. By the spring of 1968, the Notre Dame Afro-American Society (AAS) was formed. I was elected president and Walter vice president. This was the beginning of the movement for inclusion of African-Americans in the total life of the university.

The first activity of the society was a "Big Brother" program for the thirty black freshmen entering Notre Dame in the fall of 1968. Walter assigned an upperclassman to each entering freshman and conducted a separate orientation program during the first week of school. I was assigned to Mike Sales of Columbus, Georgia. This was a successful undertaking.

The year 1968 was a transformational one for students and faculty at Notre Dame. Demands for change in university governance and student life, as well as the introduction of liberal ideas and ideology, took root. The rise in black consciousness on campus was fueled by off-campus events in the larger black community, including the assassination of Dr. Martin Luther King, Jr. In September 1968, the society protested a speech by US Senator Strom Thurmond, an avowed segregationist from my home state of South Carolina. We demonstrated outside Washington Hall carrying protest signs calling for the end of racism. This was followed by demonstrations at football games, where we raised issues addressing the quality of life for black students.

In October 1968 we delivered to Father Hesburgh a list of demands developed by the AAS. These included: establishing a black student scholarship fund; hiring full-time black recruiters; increasing black student enrollment to 10 percent; hiring black counselors; hiring blacks in supervisory positions; increasing black faculty; establishing a Black Studies Program; and providing remedial and tutorial programs. On the eve of a planned demonstration at the nationally televised UCLA–Notre Dame basketball game, Father Hesburgh agreed to establish a faculty-student University Committee for Afro-American Students to address our demands. The demonstration was cancelled. As AAS president, I appointed six black students to the committee, including David Krashna (Class of 1971), who later became the first black student body president at Notre Dame.

To its credit, the university kept its commitment to address our demands. In 1969, in order to fund the Black Studies and black scholarship programs, the university dropped its forty-five-year ban on playing in postseason bowl games. Other steps included hiring a black counselor and funding a Black Arts Festival, hosted by the Afro-American Society, in 1970. In less than two years, the society had improved the environment for blacks at Notre Dame. By removing barriers to racial diversity, the door was opened for the admission of women to the undergraduate college.

The accomplishments of the Afro-American Society would not have been possible without the unity of purpose and determination of black students to create a better experience for ourselves and future black Domers. However, the ability to achieve some of the society's goals was enhanced by a change in the campus social environment for black students. The black women of St. Mary's College, along with several black families of South Bend and Niles, Michigan, including the Taylor, Scott, and Marsh families, provided a social lifeline for black Domers. In addition, many of us established strong relationships with black students from several Catholic women's colleges, including Mary Grove in Detroit, Mundelein in Chicago, and Barat in Lake Forest, Illinois. The alternating weekend campus visits, telephone calls, cards, and letters through the week made campus life at Notre Dame more palatable.

My campus activities at Notre Dame were extensive and rewarding. In addition to my two-year tenure as Afro-American Society president, I was a student representative on the Notre Dame Board of Trustees Student Affairs Committee; represented the university at the National Student Association Convention in 1969; worked as a counselor in the Notre Dame summer Upward Bound program; and traveled on high school recruitment trips for the Office of Admissions.

I gained extensive public relations experience through regular interviews with the campus print media as well as radio and television appearances. Sometime during my time at Notre Dame, I was given the moniker "Chief." This was prescient because, during the ensuing decades, I have held positions where my official title included the word "chief."

Upon graduation in June 1970, I experienced mixed emotions about leaving Notre Dame. On the one hand, I would be freed from the cold, seemingly endless grey winter skies, or turning onto Notre Dame Avenue after an out-of-town weekend and experiencing a sinking feeling. On the other hand, I had come to Notre Dame as a boy and was departing as a mature adult, hopefully having made Notre Dame a better place. My collective experiences at the university prepared me for a rewarding life, including some lifelong friendships; attaining a law degree from the University of Virginia; a fellowship at the NAACP Legal Defense Fund in New York; a law practice in Charleston; appointment as chief judge of the Charleston Municipal Court for 34 years; election as Supreme Knight and chief executive officer of the Knights of Peter Claver, the largest black Catholic lay organization in America; marriage to a beautiful woman (Elise) who conducted my orientation session upon my entering UVA; raising two wonderful children (Kira and William); being a founding member of the Black Alumni of Notre Dame (BA of ND); being a charter member of the Notre Dame Club of Charleston; and countless hours of strategizing and negotiating sessions.

After four years at Notre Dame, I earned a degree in government. But more importantly, I learned how to serve others. For both, I thank the university.

FRANCIS X. TAYLOR

(Classes of 1970, 1974 MA)

Frank Taylor came to Notre Dame in autumn 1966 from Wash-
ington, D.C. He majored in government and international
studies and was in the Air Force ROTC program. After gradu-
ation he became a career US Air Force officer, retiring at the
rank of brigadier general. He was US Ambassador for Coun-
terterrorism and Security and later became a vice president for
security at General Electric Co. He and his wife, Constance,
live in Fort Washington, Maryland.

IN SEPTEMBER 1966 I ARRIVED IN DOWNTOWN SOUTH BEND
aboard the South Shore Railroad from Chicago, where I had spent the
summer living with my Aunt Inez and Uncle Benjamin and working
as an apprentice painter. I can still remember the train arriving in the
middle of Main Street in then-thriving downtown South Bend, and me
standing alone with all that I owned in a trunk that my Great-Aunt
Jenny had used to move to Chicago in the 1950s from our family home
in Vicksburg, Mississippi.

There were many Notre Dame students at the train station that
day, and one of them helped me get a taxi to campus and Cavanaugh
Hall, where I would live for the next two years. To my surprise I was
assigned to room 411, a single on the fourth floor of Cavanaugh. This
was both good and bad. On one hand, it made my adjustment easier
because I didn't have to get used to a roommate. On the other hand,
I'd have welcomed the opportunity to adjust to a roommate.

There were eleven other African-Americans in my class, and we almost doubled the number of African-Americans at Notre Dame to twenty-six, amid an undergraduate student population of about six thousand. Three of us were in Cavanaugh Hall, and the others were spread among the freshman dorms. I met Arthur McFarland of Charleston, South Carolina, and Leon Jackson of Jackson, Mississippi, on our first day, and from that point the adventure began for all of us. Arthur and I have been friends ever since. I was the best man when he married Elise in 1975, and he was my best man when I married Constance in 1983.

Leon, unfortunately, did not remain at Notre Dame and graduate. He joined the military at the end of the 1960s and we lost contact. In the end, eleven of the twelve African-American freshmen who entered Notre Dame in 1966 graduated in June 1970.

Most who attend Notre Dame seem to have very fond memories of their time as undergraduates. I was not one to tout my undergraduate experience as memorable. I grew personally as a man and a human being. I developed academically and became a fairly good scholar. I had experiences that I never would have had in a different university community, and graduated in four years to become a United States Air Force officer, which had been my goal all along.

As I reflect on my Notre Dame experience, it is clear to me that my attending Notre Dame was providential. As a senior at historic Dunbar High School in Washington, D.C., I was present when Don Wycliff came to speak about opportunities for black students at Notre Dame. I had never considered Notre Dame a possibility but applied on a lark. I also applied to several Ivy League Schools. As fate would have it, Notre Dame was the only one of six schools to accept me.

I knew little about the university and had no idea what I would experience. My only thought was that Notre Dame was the only chance for me to achieve my goal of attending a great school and pursuing my passion to become a military officer. I really did not think much about the demographics of the school or the fact that Notre Dame was a Catholic university. I must say that Notre Dame was the first time in my life that I had to live and work with white people on a daily basis. Washington in the mid-1960s was still very much a segregated city; I had attended an essentially all-black high school, and I lived in a segregated part of the city. While I did not feel overt racism when I arrived on the Notre Dame campus, the environment was clearly different from any I had experienced before.

Several years after I graduated, my mother, Virginia Morgan, told me that she had been very concerned about my attending Notre Dame because of the cost. She had shared her concerns with a Mr. Carley, a member of her church, St. Thomas More Catholic Church. Mr. Carley was an elderly, white, Irish Catholic widower who lived on our block. He told my mother that attending Notre Dame would open many great opportunities for me. After that conversation, she said, she determined that she would do all she could to make attending Notre Dame a reality for me.

While I was not aware of my mother's discussion with Mr. Carley, I was acutely aware throughout my time at Notre Dame that my being there resulted from the financial sacrifices endured by my single mother and her siblings in Chicago. Failure was not an option after all that my family had done to get me to Notre Dame, and that thought remained with me throughout. When I left Dunbar, I was awarded two $500 scholarships, one from the PTA and the other from an endowed scholarship of a former member of the Dunbar faculty. I did not receive a scholarship from Notre Dame. I had loans every semester and did work-study for three years to make ends meet. I was also a resident assistant in Stanford Hall for my last two years; that covered my room and board. For my senior year I earned an Air Force ROTC Scholarship, which covered tuition and significantly improved the financial picture for my extended family and me.

Over the course of our freshman year, Arthur McFarland, Leon Jackson, and I bonded. We played pluck (three-handed whist) almost every night, among other distractions. There were few African-American women at Saint Mary's and little opportunity for dating. Interracial dating was unspeakable at the time. The university tried its best to introduce us to African-American women from other Catholic colleges in the region from Chicago to Detroit. However, there were long periods when the social scene was pretty dim. My sense was that Notre Dame wanted to increase minority attendance and began that process without understanding the cultural challenge of introducing minorities to the campus, without understanding that fitting in was not automatic.

The Notre Dame athletic department had done some outreach into the South Bend black community to ease the social adjustment for the athletes. Those connections were often the only social outlets available on our all-male campus. Through this connection, I was introduced to the family of Tom and Mamie Taylor (no relation) in South Bend. The Taylors and their four daughters—Jackie, Sherry, Toni, and Leslie—and one son, Tommie, became my extended family. I do not know if they claimed me on their income tax, but they should have, given the amount of time that I spent at their home over my four years at Notre Dame! We remain in touch to this day.

Academics were a real challenge for me, coming from an inner-city high school. I went to classes where people were discussing material that I had never been exposed to, where standards and expectations were very demanding, and I did not find myself particularly well prepared for the challenge. The Freshman Year of Studies was a godsend that allowed me the time and support to survive. My first semester grade point average was 2.0; for the second semester it was 2.387. Each semester thereafter I got better and, by the time I graduated, I was very close to the coveted overall 3.0.

My professors were excellent and really strove to work with students. I needed all of the help that I could find. Of all my professors, the one who had the most profound impact on me was Dr. Peter Walshe, a white South African who had fled the apartheid regime and come to teach in America. He introduced me to Africa and kindled a lifelong academic and work interest in the continent. The South African situation fascinated me and, through Peter, I learned about the struggle for freedom against apartheid there as we were living the struggle for civil rights in the US. My study of Africa and my experiences in becoming an adult during the US civil rights movement have had the most profound impact on how I think about the world we live in and how we must work to improve it. Out of struggle come increased opportunities to change how people live and develop. That would be one of the principles that I would live by in life.

It was in the Air Force ROTC program that I found a real home. I came to the Notre Dame ROTC program with three years of high school ROTC experience. I joined the drill team, learning how to march and handle a rifle. Colonel Vic Ferrari, a veteran of World War II, and the ROTC cadre embraced me and my dream of becoming an Air Force officer from the first day. They afforded me numerous leadership opportunities in the Notre Dame unit and more broadly across the ROTC program in the country. If I was not in class, working, or playing cards with Arthur and Leon, I was at the ROTC building staying engaged in as many activities as I could. I finished the ROTC program as a distinguished graduate and with a commission as a second lieutenant in the Air Force.

Another lifesaver for me was Notre Dame athletics. An avid fan of all sports, I attended every football and basketball game on campus for the four years I was an undergraduate. In my freshman year, Alan Page was the only African-American on the football team, and there were two African-Americans, Bob Whitmore and Dwight Murphy, on the basketball team. Bill Hurd was the only African-American on the track team. Over the course of the next four years, recruitment of African-American athletes expanded significantly and enriched life on campus for all of the students. On the athletic field, we were the Irish and it did not matter the color of your skin—you felt part of something that was bigger than you. I still follow the Irish and, with my two sons, Jay and Justin, had the pleasure to join Arthur McFarland and his son Jose at the 2013 national championship game in Miami.

Since leaving the university, I have come to understand how those student experiences helped shape my development as a man and informed my approach to life. Notre Dame taught me that I could survive and prosper in any environment, that good people come in all shades, and that looking for the best in people normally finds the best. Finally, it taught me that a quality education is the best basis for success in America. I may not have understood it at the time, but Notre Dame has made me what I am today, and for that I will be forever grateful.

David Krashna

(Class of 1971)

David Krashna came to Notre Dame in the autumn of 1967 from Pittsburgh. He became the first black Notre Dame student body president. Upon graduation he obtained a Juris Doctor degree from the University of California at Berkeley School of Law, and practiced law in the San Francisco-Oakland Bay Area. He is a retired Alameda County, California, superior court judge who serves as a law professor.

THE IRISH NUNS, PRIESTS, AND LAY TEACHERS AT ST. PAUL'S Orphanage in Pittsburgh infected me for life with the love of Notre Dame. As a boy, when the sisters asked us on Friday evenings to pray on our knees in the dormitory for Notre Dame's success on the football field on Saturday, I had no problem with that. It sounded entirely reasonable. I built rudimentary transmitter radios at St. Paul's and spent countless hours listening to Notre Dame football games involving nothing but white players, a fact of which I was oblivious. At least then.

My social worker, George Wagner, who now resides in Pasadena, California, persuaded me in high school to diversify: to apply for admission to more colleges than Notre Dame. I went through the motions, but I was going to Notre Dame.

I believe it was in the spring of 1967 when I was accepted. I was elated. Sister Mary Brigid Moriarty, my kindergarten teacher at St. Paul's, and Anna Mae Sanford, my foster mother, were as proud as I was happy. Sister Mary Brigid had taught me the Irish jig, which I performed on the earliest television, and Mrs. Sanford had taken me and my brothers, James, Matthew, and Timothy, from the orphanage into her home in the housing projects in the Hill District of Pittsburgh.

I hitched a ride to Notre Dame with a Bishop Canevin High School classmate and his parents to start my freshman year in September 1967. I vividly recall turning left from Angela Avenue onto Notre Dame Avenue and seeing Our Lady atop the Golden Dome directly in front of me. I was home.

I struggled academically my first year but gradually caught on and ultimately achieved the dean's list during my Notre Dame tenure.

On my first day at Notre Dame I arrived in my Farley Hall room after my roommate, who had left on the upper bunk his duffel bag with the red lettering "Bessemer, Alabama." My mild terror was alleviated when later that day I met my roommate, Charles "Chick" Barranco, a fine southern white gentleman. In Farley Hall I also met the co-editor of this book, Don Wycliff, from Dayton, Texas. Don was very smart, black, and became my mentor, a mere two years older than me. I did not reconnect with Don until more than forty years after our graduations.

From the beginning, I always tried to push the cause of black students at Notre Dame. On November 16, 1968, at a dreary, cool Saturday afternoon football game, I along with more than a dozen other black Notre Dame students (my co-editor included) jumped over the retaining wall in Notre Dame Stadium during halftime of a game against Georgia Tech to protest with banners the lack of black Notre Dame football players. I have the vivid memory of a white lady on the Georgia Tech side applauding. I still wonder why.

Phil McKenna, the 1969–70 Notre Dame student body president, invited me to serve in his cabinet as human affairs commissioner, and we surmised that there was a compelling need to increase the number of black students at Notre Dame. Father Theodore M. Hesburgh, the president of the university, agreed and arranged to send me nationwide to recruit black students. He assigned to me faculty tutors—top professors on campus in theology, English literature, and economics—so that I could maintain my academic performance while I traveled to recruit. My theology tutor, the renowned Father Charles Sheedy, would become a lifelong mentor and friend.

To aid the recruiting process, I formed the Recruitment Action Program (RAP) and enlisted the help of Notre Dame students, black and white, including Arthur McFarland, president of the Afro-American Society. RAP was a hit. One evening in the spring of 1969, I visited Father Ted's office to report that our recruiting efforts had resulted in the then-largest contingent of admitted black students. Father Hesburgh exclaimed: "David, how can we pay for these students to attend Notre Dame?"

Father Hesburgh found a way. He persuaded the Notre Dame board of trustees to reverse its forty-five-year ban on postseason football bowl participation in order to fund minority student financial aid.

I was encouraged by many Notre Dame students to run for student body president in the spring of 1970. I was honored to be elected that March as the first black president of the Notre Dame student body! My running mate and good friend was Mark Winings from Elwood, Indiana, a Protestant—Notre Dame was 96 percent Roman Catholic at the time. On election eve, my campaign manager and still good friend, Robert E. Pohl III, and I walked across campus with a few supporters. Each member of the group lamented that there was no way the Notre Dame student body would elect a black student body president. I remained quiet.

As we watched the election results later, we were stunned: we won each residence hall, as well as the off-campus and overseas student votes. The student newspaper, The Observer, which did not endorse me, had predicted a close election. In the event, I won with what was then the largest plurality in the history of Notre Dame student body elections.

I remember that my supporters arranged during the evening of my election triumph for a radio hookup with my foster mother, Mrs. Sanford, back in Pittsburgh, who was able to partake in our festivities by listening to the speeches.

My office window as student body president faced Father Ted's office window in the Main Building. I tried to wait each evening until Father Ted turned off his office light before I turned mine off. Except for one night.

I often fielded phone calls from whoever called me in my student body president office. I enjoyed speaking, often arguing, with people about social issues of the times. Late one evening a male adult caller convinced me to get off the phone and head home immediately, even if Father Ted's light was still on. This call came after I had led a march calling for the first Notre Dame student strike of classes to protest the

US invasion of Cambodia during the Vietnam War and the shootings of students at Kent State and Jackson State Universities. The caller threatened me and mentioned in unmistakably explicit terms that my life and liberty were at stake.

My experience as Notre Dame student body president exceeds the capacity of this essay, but a few stories demand to be told. Eric Andrus, a member of my cabinet, organized an effort to ask Notre Dame students to give up one of their football game tickets during the 1970 season so that poor local youngsters could attend a Notre Dame home game. We received more student ticket donations than there were youths available to attend the game! I had the honor of presenting the colors before the game to two of the selected youngsters.

As student body president I was asked to support individual students in a variety of personal and academic matters and interacted with virtually every member of the university administration. I fondly recall working with the late Michael DeCicco to retain student-athletes at Notre Dame. Our student government administration was also active in the nascent movement towards coeducation, appearing before the university's board of trustees to support the cause.

But my favorite experiences as president were everyday conversations with fellow students of every race regarding the issues of our times: racism, sexism, the Vietnam War. While not an authority on any of these issues, I had an opinion on all of them and had plenty to say — at times, maybe too much.

Upon returning to campus in autumn after the raucous and exhilarating spring of 1970, student apathy on the major issues of the times prevailed nationwide. As student body president I called a Notre Dame "General Assembly of Students" (GAS) to revive what I thought were still pertinent issues — campus racism, sexism, coeducation, but the gas had dissipated. GAS was a failure.

One commentator on my Notre Dame times, Aaron Kreider, remarked that I was "the most radical Notre Dame SBP ever." Another commentator, Pete Peterson, a contemporary of mine, remarked: "Dave was no Malcolm X." I agree with Pete.

As a student I met often with Father Hesburgh. We did not often agree on issues, but we always respected each other. That respect endures to this day. I have a treasure chest of written correspondence from this remarkable public servant and Catholic priest. I also appreciated that he was concerned about me as a student, always asking me during my recruiting activities how my studies were coming along. And I think he likes my wife, Gina, more than me! Father Hesburgh and his personal secretary, Melanie Chapleau, are personal friends, and always will be.

Over the years I have tried to recruit black students to Notre Dame, including my twin sons, André and Omar, who chose instead St. Mary's College in Moraga, California, and UCLA, respectively. I am working now on my five grandchildren. In my longest assignment as a superior court judge in Alameda County, California, I served abused and neglected children as a juvenile dependency judge and decided such basic issues as with whom these children will live and where they go to school. I am always on the lookout for the youngster who might aspire to attend Notre Dame.

I keep my hands entwined in the Notre Dame admissions office process. I believe that Notre Dame should aggressively continue to re-cruit black students. To this end, the Notre Dame administration must expend and exert as much resources and energy as the university does to enroll black student-athletes.

Thank you, Frazier L. Thompson, for blazing the trail that many of us have followed, and for your courage.

Notre Dame helped me develop leadership skills, which have served me well throughout life. Notre Dame also reinforced and re-fined a core value I learned at St. Paul's Orphanage: I strive to love and respect every individual I encounter, no matter who they are.

My family and friends describe me as I am, a Notre Damer. There is no antidote for my condition in life. I am a black Domer.

JOHN BANKS-BROOKS

(Class of 1972)

John Banks-Brooks came to Notre Dame in autumn 1978 from Hastings, Nebraska. He majored in government and was a member of the Glee Glub. After graduation he earned a master's and a law degree and worked on Capitol Hill. He eventually became a public affairs and communications professional. He lives in Springfield, Illinois.

LBJ WAS PRESIDENT. THE GREAT SOCIETY SEEMED WITHIN REACH. *Suddenly Negroes were in vogue, at least at the nation's elite colleges and universities; these institutions pursued and then wore their new-found diversity as badges of honor. I did well (enough) on the SAT and a national achievement test targeting minority high school students. Dozens of letters arrived pleading for my interest. More than a few made it clear that forwarding a completed application was a mere formality for my acceptance.*

Notre Dame also expressed interest. Or, perhaps, "curiosity" is a better word. The then all-male school dared tell me, a devoted Cornhusker, that it seriously desired to know if I was worthy of being a Notre Dame Man. I considered such a challenge from that overrated football school as a quasi-insult. I also found it irresistible. I like to think that we both won.

Not all my lessons happened in class, nor were they limited to sharpening the intellect. My biggest lifelong lessons? Advancing civil rights was not just a matter of catching the six o'clock news, cheering heroic acts of civil disobedience from afar or praying from the sidelines.

Notre Dame taught me that it was as much a personal struggle as a political battle.

What else? That the most valuable gift is the strength to trust oneself, to take the leap of faith. Without that, strength, love, commitment, courage, and a sense of self-worth are unattainable goals.

IT WAS A TEN-DAY ROAD TRIP, MEANDERING BY BUS THROUGH the Deep South, my first venture below the Mason-Dixon Line. Rural Alabama, Mississippi, Georgia—even at the time I couldn't recall which state was which day. Made no difference to me. As a Nebraska boy, the very thought of the Deep South made me queasy; it was as foreign as Bangladesh or Pakistan. Grateful and proud to be a member of the Notre Dame Glee Club traveling squad even as an underclassman (unknown by me at the time, but only by virtue of Notre Dame President Father Theodore Hesburgh's command) I was nonetheless still nervous about traveling to and through "another country."

Peering out of the bus window, I suddenly understood where the term "heat wave" came from. It was so damn hot and humid that I actually saw wave after wave of mind-numbing heat submerging the land as far as the eye could see. I gazed, taken aback, at the sheer number of black folk working the fields. They appeared so still and silent, so resigned, not even bothering to glance up at our bus. It's for that reason that I recall them as faceless, drained of any curiosity. The more I took in the scene rolling by the harder it was to cope. I don't mean intellectually but viscerally—my throat tightened while my belly began to mimic wave after wave of that oppressive heat.

"Those are my people out there," I thought. "My people!"

This was a hard realization. My grandma, aka Grammo, had raised me to be "separate and apart." The small, orderly farm community where I was raised didn't so much accept as allow its tiny colored population. To be a Negro and violate community norms was ground for permanent expulsion, especially for us colored boys. So in addition to staying absurdly neat and clean, I needed to be on my best behavior at all times. There were certain things I was never, ever to do: disobey Grammo's unforgiving curfew, show anger in public, accept rides home from classmates if white girls were also in the car. It wasn't that Grammo taught me to distrust so much as to be extremely cautious. If she were a politician she would have been ahead of her time: "Trust but verify."

Unfortunately for me, the only white folk who met her standard for trust were regular churchgoing adults who had been "baptized in the blood of the Lamb." I not only grew to be unusually observant of my immediate surroundings, but also to be exquisitely, awkwardly, self-conscious.

As for the colored townsfolk clustered with us between the railroad tracks and the county fairgrounds, well, I was encouraged to be friendly with them but not to become friends. Not that they weren't in the main also good and decent people, but because Grammo was intent on letting this town, still laden with its heavy German heritage, know that we were especially "deserving."

Our modest, manicured lawn, fragrant flower beds, trimmed hedges, and broomswept sidewalks out-Germaned the Germans'. If Grammo thought well of her colored neighbors, she sent Gran'pa over to help with their lawns. She felt a special obligation to Mizz Sophie, who lived just a block away, but I'm sure that, at least in part, that sense of obligation was because of the immense girth that rendered Mizz Sophie largely immobile, and because of her inordinately skinny husband's decided preference for drinking and smoking over horticultural pursuits.

In my world, separate and apart meant spending hours in my room trading confidences with imaginary friends, reading and listening to AM radio. After sundown I could get KOMA out of Oklahoma City and, on a good night, WLS from Chicago. As much as I loved to read, I loved music even more. The Supremes, Marvin Gaye, Chad and Jeremy, Petula Clark, Martha Reeves and the Vandellas—these and other beloved artists transported me to glamorous locales—Los Angeles, Chicago, Detroit, New York, San Francisco. ("If you're goin' to San Francisco be sure to wear some flowers in your hair . . .") I was absolutely convinced of my million-dollar vocal talent because, by singing along with the radio, I just knew that I was as groovy as any big-city boy. When I sang with Marvin or Petula, we were one voice. Best of all, while indulging in those sacred Top 40 Pop moments, I was no longer separate and apart, no longer exquisitely and awkwardly self-conscious. I was too cool.

But now, here I was in the Deep South, very aware that on this miserably hot day, separate and apart meant being separated only by a window, some metal and a swiftly moving set of tires. I felt overwhelmed with guilt yet enormously relieved that I was able to glide past my people. I certainly didn't want to be out there laboring under that too-hot sun knowing that the next day meant only another swim in that dirty brown swelter. Right outside the window were guys who shared my birthday but had no future—unless spending a bleak dull eternity working the fields could be called a future. But for the grace of God . . .

Because it offered an occasion for me to become "one voice" on campus, the Glee Club served as an anchor; joining with others for a daily sing-along was the one time of day that I didn't feel isolated. Although the club's director impressed me as a bit scatterbrained and somewhat aloof with everyone, I had the distinct impression that he had a particular distaste for me. Maybe it was because I didn't have a million-dollar voice after all. Perhaps it was because there might have been a directive straight from the Golden Dome that any Afro-American trying out for the club was to be granted membership. Or it could have been that during my first couple of years in the club, I was the single black face in an otherwise lily-white group. Perhaps it was all in my head. Despite my powers of observation, it was sometimes difficult for me to figure out when it was a matter of "them as them," "me as me," or "me as an African-American."

Nonetheless, that night, dressed in tails, looking like high-class penguins, we were putting the finishing touches on a concert some-where in Mississippi. As a final encore, fellow second tenor Adrian D. (what an astounding voice!) had a moving solo in a Negro spiritual. The director shot Adrian an "it's-show-time" look and then, announcing the spiritual's name, remarked that it was about "some darkie" praying that God would take away his burdens.

You could have heard a pin drop after that intro. Unable to breathe, my teeth clenched, my hands now fists, shock somersaulted into fury. I partly whispered, partly lip-synced the chorus, every eye in the audience on me despite Adrian's moving solo. During that eternal moment—it still churns in my chest—I stood stark naked on that stage, pretending to sing.

Afterwards, back on the bus, two or three of the bolder clubbers assured me that the director "didn't mean it," but excusing him only made me angrier. No one challenged him about it. No one sat next to me on the bus that night. But I wanted just one, just one, clubber to murmur, "He's an asshole for saying that." I wanted someone, anyone, to acknowledge, "You know, that wasn't right." Judging by our maestro's indifferent demeanor, he hadn't given it or me a second thought (or even a first one for that matter).

Still painfully exposed, I kept staring out of the window into the dark futilely, praying for just one sympathetic voice, just one knowing look or a comforting arm around the shoulder. True, it wasn't merely my right but my obligation to speak up for myself, but I lacked the courage. Besides, that would have broken Grammo's rule to neither express hurt nor show anger in public. Nonetheless, boyhood training aside, if there was ever an occasion to display self-reliance, this was that time. But all those muted voices and averted looks fused with my unwanted seclusion to convert my indignation to dread. So I just sat there. Stone-faced. Silent. Alone. At a total loss.

Then I thought of my people working the fields that day and realized that I was never really separate and apart from them. For me as for them, it was after dark in Mississippi—but I was far from home.

RONALD J. IRVINE*

(Class of 1973)

Ron Irvine came to Notre Dame in autumn 1969 from Atlantic City, New Jersey. He majored in history, participated in intramural sports, and was active in student affairs. After graduation he held several sales and marketing positions with major pharmaceutical companies before establishing his own consulting firm in 1987. He and his wife, Jacqueline, have two grown sons and live in Lake Forest, Illinois.

IN JUNE 1969 I WAS ONE OF FOUR STUDENT-ATHLETES HONORED at the Atlantic City All-Sports Association annual awards night. Two were from my school, Atlantic City High, and two were from the local Catholic school, Holy Spirit High. A key point of the evening was when our college choices were announced. There seemed to be a palpable buzz in the banquet hall when it was announced that I, the only black person on the dais, was headed to Notre Dame, the campus of the Fighting Irish.

Only a few months earlier, Notre Dame hadn't even been on my radar, but I was now beginning to understand the magnitude of its reputation, both on and off the field. The only thing I knew about it previously was the weekly thirty-minute football highlight reel that ran on TV, and that it was located somewhere in the Midwest. As an inner-city New Jersey kid, I was pretty much looking at Rutgers or some other in-state school for college, with Princeton being my dream school. In either case, I'd have to get financial aid, because our family didn't have funds for college.

I had been accepted to Rutgers with a nice financial package and was waiting to get money from Princeton. Around this time, I had a girlfriend at home. Given that we were spending a lot of time together, somehow my parents got in their collective heads that maybe my going "farther away" to school might not be a bad idea. So when the Notre Dame opportunity presented itself, my folks were all in and there were no further discussions about going to school in the Garden State.

Richard Cordasco, president of the Eastern New Jersey Notre Dame Alumni Association, came to Atlantic City High School and introduced four black scholar-athletes—Bruce Brock, Robert Friday, George Nelson, and me—to the Notre Dame experience and encouraged us to apply. We all were eventually accepted, with Friday, Nelson, and me going on to South Bend. Brock went to Boston University.

Key to four black Atlantic City kids of modest means being accepted to Notre Dame was the interface of the alumni association with Joseph Bair, head of the Greater Atlantic City Youth Association. Mr. Bair spent time with us, encouraged us to be bold, to dream big dreams and be open to change. This was very important because some of us were the first or second person in our families ever to attend college. He was always reaffirming that we do well. Mr. Bair also was aware of our financial situations and worked diligently to help us secure decent financial packages. As we promised Mr. Bair, all three of us who went to Notre Dame graduated.

A few weeks before heading off to South Bend, I received information about campus housing choices. We had the option of living in a cluster of black students or living in the general student population. We could also request a black roommate.

Living in a black cluster—later to be called the "black concentration"—appealed to me at the time. I knew there weren't many black students. For some reason I had the number five hundred in my mind, in an undergraduate student population of about 6,400. So I was excited that the few black students wouldn't be so spread out, especially in those times of heightened racial consciousness ("I'm black and I'm proud!").

Arriving on campus with my parents wearing a shirt and tie, I quickly changed into a dashiki after surveying the landscape and noting in particular a striking upperclassman, Rick Gross, in his dark shades, black tam, and animal print shirt. I noticed the black students eagerly seeking out and greeting each other and welcoming the newbie black freshmen. I became aware of the Afro-American Society and learned there were thirty incoming freshmen and the total number of black undergrads was only sixty or so. That was a real stunner!

Given this small number, most of us connected pretty easily, especially the freshmen. We were also close with our Saint Mary's counterparts, who numbered about a dozen freshmen. Freshman year was memorable, given our new sense of freedom. Fortunately we had the guidance and direction of certain black upperclassmen who encouraged us to stay on track and avoid, or at least minimize, distractions. Arthur McFarland, a South Carolina native, would be an occasional visitor when the music and card-playing became excessive among the underclassmen in the dorm. Similarly, Ernie Jackson, a football player from Bartlesville, Oklahoma, was not bashful about coming into your room, closing the door behind him, and having a serious "Come to Jesus" talk with you about "focus." The takeaway from these encounters was that we should emulate the folks who were performing and doing well, not those who, unbeknown to us, were flunking out.

Over the next three years, the number of black students increased three- to fourfold. Though still not a significant number, these new students were a welcome sight. They came from many different backgrounds. Most fit right in, but some seemed to think they were on another planet. It became clear that in Notre Dame's eagerness to attract black students, it had accepted some who clearly weren't a good fit. Some folks didn't like the university and didn't stay long. Turnover was too high.

South Bend was like an oasis to many of us. We got to know the black folks who worked on campus. Mr. Ernest Rice, who manned the security entrance to the South Quad, was a father to us all. He was a dignified, principled man who tolerated no foolishness from anyone. His impact was so great that, for many years after his retirement and upon learning of his problems with diabetes and blindness, my classmate the late Ron Dallas and I would often leave football games at halftime to visit with him.

Others of importance were Granville Cleveland, the law school librarian, and, for me, Joy Jefferson, who worked in the School of Architecture. Joy was a Riley High School product who was taking classes at Indiana University South Bend while working at Notre

Dame. I recall what a treat it was to visit her at home and spend time with her folks for Sunday dinner and help her younger brother, Cedric, with his geometry homework.

Occasionally some of us would go to a local Baptist or Methodist church service, similar to what we had at home. Once we went to the Muslim mosque in South Bend to hear a young Minister Louis Farrakhan speak. His message struck a chord with some and at least one student, the well-respected, always principled South Bend resident Brian Paul Smith (now Brian Ali), ultimately converted.

Notre Dame, being all-male, did have scheduled events in which coeds, including black ones, visited campus for the weekends. These occasional visits were highlights of a social life that wasn't there on an ongoing basis. Notre Dame did turn coed my senior year, but the very few women on campus seemed more a novelty than a social outlet.

Looking back as a student, the weight of my four years at Notre Dame was such that I couldn't wait to get out. The warm fuzzy feelings I now have after forty years were clearly not there when I graduated. I never felt I quite fit in at Notre Dame. The handful of black students and the environment certainly weren't conducive to feeling like I was at home. The experience felt more like an experiment that perhaps could have been better thought out.

But after graduation, I did feel the Notre Dame acceptance because that is how you came to be identified, if you chose to be embraced as a part of the Notre Dame family. The Notre Dame name opened eyes, opened doors, gave you opportunities and exposure. Of course, you still had to deliver and perform, but you never had to repeat or expand on where you went to school.

As president of the Afro-American Society during the 1971–72 academic year, I was the organization's primary interface with the university president, Father Theodore Hesburgh. A particular learning and growth experience for me occurred when I was asked by some members of the football team to speak with Father Hesburgh on behalf of a black player, Larry Parker, who was involved in an altercation in which a white player suffered a broken jaw. Father Ted greeted me warmly in his office. He set aside a golf putter he had in his hand. I attempted to state my purpose for being there. However, he proceeded to escort me around his office, sharing his pictures, mementos, and experiences with world leaders, presidents, and other iconic figures such as the Reverend Martin Luther King Jr. He further intimated that he would be leaving the United States Civil Rights Commission because he was tiring of President Richard Nixon's behavior.

At this point, I again brought up the reason for my visit. Father Ted brought me close to him and, in a lovingly purposeful way, said, "Ron, there is nothing that either you or I can do about that." Consequently, Parker did have to leave school. And although he was allowed to return, he did not finish at Notre Dame.

My positive feelings toward Notre Dame likely influenced my older son, Philip, who also attended Notre Dame and graduated in 2002. My message to him was simple. Be a sponge, soak it in, and experience all that is Notre Dame. Looking back, I was not quite as open to new experiences as perhaps I could have been.

Most people who knew me growing up would not be surprised to see the person I have become. My values and foundation were developed early on from my family, my neighborhood, the public schools I attended, and, of course, the Methodist church. What Notre Dame did was keep me centered, strengthen my moral compass, and polish me up a bit.

*Ron Irvine died unexpectedly in November 2014.

Gail Antoinette King

(Class of 1975)

Gail King came to Notre Dame in autumn 1972 as a transfer student from Saint Mary's College. She majored in history and spent much of her free time assisting with events sponsored by the black studies office. After graduation she worked in the human resources field before earning a master's in library science at the University of South Carolina. She now is a media specialist at an elementary school and lives near three of her four daughters in Columbia, South Carolina.

WHEN DAN SARACINO, THEN AN ASSISTANT DIRECTOR IN THE admissions office, asked me if I would consider transferring from Saint Mary's to Notre Dame for the start of my sophomore year, I knew it was an opportunity that I could not pass up. Notre Dame was admitting women for the first time in history, and I would be among the first class of young females to attend. I distinctly remember Dan saying he thought I had the determination to make it. His words were encouraging, because that was just what I wanted to do: make it. I wanted to succeed for more than just myself; back in those days any door you went through you also opened for those of your race who would come behind you.

That type of responsibility was not a burden: it was just a fact. My parents had ten children. I am their fifth. My older sisters and brother always looked after me, and I always looked after the younger ones. It was how we were raised: to care about those who came after you. This obligation extended to my community. I remember my neighbors in

Piscataway, New Jersey, showing up at my house when I first prepared to leave for college. After wishing me well, they said that whatever I accomplished for myself I also accomplished for them. This duty, coupled with the significance of my attending Notre Dame, overshadowed any thoughts concerning any future difficulties I might have adjusting to life at the university. And there were some difficulties.

I had never traveled more than a few miles from home, and was quite homesick for some time. This new community I belonged to was made up of about eleven black girls and fewer than two hundred black males. We had our race in common, but we were from different parts of the country and had varying backgrounds and goals. Among those students I met, none was experienced enough to give advice or mentor me. However significant race was for me at home, I never felt prohibited from having non-black friends and acquaintances. At Notre Dame, race created an invisible boundary that both nestled and limited, sometimes hindering interaction with those outside our circle.

My biggest challenge was the coursework. I had never thought about "learning styles" when I enrolled, and was unprepared for the large, lecture-style classes and the rigorous coursework. My study skills were woefully deficient. I discovered that it would take much more than determination to make it through Notre Dame. I would have to learn to become organized and disciplined. Still, I erroneously believed that I was on my own. I fought for the grades I earned; and only once in those early years did I even think to get a tutor.

As time passed, life at Notre Dame was more than just meeting bleak responsibilities. I went to my first concert and professional play. I heard a live orchestra for the first time. I met famous writers, politicians, and activists, and I witnessed humility, charity, and selflessness from the not-so-famous students and adults who helped shape me into who I am today. I was also blessed with several mentors: kind Frances Hubbard, secretary in the black studies office, who extended a listening ear to many of us in the office and who opened up her heart and home to those of us who needed just a little mothering; dear professor Dr. Maben Herring, who gave me advice only when I asked her, and who was a model for what I could become; compassionate Father Jerry Wilson, vice president of business affairs, who became one of my few connections to Notre Dame after I left as we annually exchanged Christmas greetings for many years.

By my senior year at Notre Dame I felt more at ease. That does not mean I felt that I finally fit in, but I did finally find a place for myself there. I "knew the ropes" by then, enough to mentor younger students. I had weathered the growing-up years and was crossing over into adulthood. I had an idea about where my future was headed, and, when it was time to graduate, I was proud that I had made it through.

Initially I was grateful, because as a person I learned how to disregard perceived limitations and realize my full potential while embracing diversity. I have taught that to my students and to my daughters, who are far more courageous than I ever was. Only recently did my gratitude extend to a glimpse of the bigger picture that I finally realized I had been a part of.

I recently took my niece on a college tour to a small private university in the Southeast. Its enrollment is only 1,100 students, with a teacher-to-student ratio of thirteen to one. There are only slightly more males than females, and the culturally diverse student population was evident, including students from thirty-two countries. In physical appearance the campus reminded me of the beauty that is Notre Dame. Our young guide exchanged greetings with students along the way, and spoke of service and purpose. I was struck by a sense of community, warmth, and focus. An assistant director of admissions, who happened to be African-American, spoke of the importance of finding a school that "suits your learning style" and how the needs of the students are addressed in that university's core curriculum.

"Boy, if only my experience at Notre Dame had been like that," I thought.

Later, as I reflected in my hotel room, I realized that this southeastern university probably did not have that sense of warmth and community for its black students back in 1972. If black students are comfortable in colleges today, it is because students like me were uncomfortable yesterday. Somebody had to be first, to pave the way, to open the door for others. It made sense that I was among the first. I was raised to do just that.

I realized my attending Notre Dame was more destiny than opportunity. God placed me at Notre Dame to be a forerunner for young people like my niece. She is worth it, and I am good with that. I just wish I had been aware of His providential hand on my life back then. I could have relaxed in the knowledge that I did not have to rely on my own strength, that my journey was by His design and in His hands, and thus my destination was secure.

ANN CLAIRE WILLIAMS

(Class of 1975 Law)

Ann Claire Williams came to Notre Dame as a law student in autumn 1972. She had earned her bachelor's degree at Wayne State University and a master's at the University of Michigan. After earning her Notre Dame law degree, she became an assistant US attorney, a US district judge for the Northern District of Illinois, and then a member of the US Court of Appeals for the Seventh Circuit. She and her husband David have two children and live in Chicago.

MY FIRST MEMORIES OF NOTRE DAME HAVE TO DO WITH MY dad, Joshua Marcus Williams, who always rooted against the Irish because of the very small of number of African-American football players on the team. I had no actual connection to Notre Dame until my best friend's husband decided to go to law school and selected Notre Dame. I visited campus a few times just to attend football games and parties.

While completing my work for a master's degree at the University of Michigan, I took the LSAT, did well, and decided to apply to law school, but I was too late for the class entering in 1972. So I decided to return to teaching in an inner-city Detroit public school. To my shock, that summer I received a call from Phil Faccenda, Notre Dame general counsel and law school faculty member, asking to meet with me in Detroit. Someone had dropped out of the class, and after he met me, I was offered a full tuition academic scholarship.

How did he get my name? Willie Lipscomb, a fellow African-American Wayne State University graduate (who also went on to become a judge), had been attending a pre-law program on campus and heard about the cancellation. Willie, who was like a big brother to me, contacted Associate Law Librarian Granville Cleveland, the only African-American on the staff and also a member of the admission committee, and suggested that I get the spot. So my first official contact with Notre Dame Law School was extremely positive.

I arrived on campus the day before classes started and moved into Lewis Hall, the graduate dorm for women. Coming from Wayne State University, where the majority of the 35,000 students worked, and from the very liberal University of Michigan, where men were allowed in the women's dorms at all hours, Notre Dame and parietal hours were a culture shock. Also, there were very few African-American students on campus and even fewer African-American women. There were no African-American professors in the law school and in most undergraduate departments.

This was quite an adjustment for me. There were seven African-American law students in my class, and in total, African-Americans numbered eighteen out of five hundred. Although both law school deans who served during my three years on campus, Tom Shaffer and David Link, believed that diversity was important, some of the faculty did not. Many of my fellow students had not attended school in diverse environments, and the transition was very difficult for us African-American students. But as time progressed, the faculty and our classmates opened up and we were able to thrive and become leaders in the community.

Notre Dame's president, Father Ted Hesburgh, a champion for civil rights and the second chair of the United States Civil Rights Commission, spoke often and with deep conviction about the need for diversity at all levels on campus. He was our champion and a great mentor in so many ways. In fact, I was there in 1973 when Father Hesburgh started the Center for Human and Civil Rights, the first center of its kind attached to any law school. Professor Howard Glickstein, its first director, became my mentor, faculty advisor, and supervisor when I clerked in that office. As a result of this association, I was able to meet giants in the civil rights movement, including Vernon Jordan, William T. Coleman Jr., and Jack Greenberg. The training and exposure I received was critical to my development as a lawyer and jurist.

I have watched with pride as the center has evolved into a preeminent institution, educating hundreds of international human rights lawyers and judges from more than eighty countries.

Father Ted's support on other levels was also invaluable. After we black law students demanded a meeting with him, he agreed that forming a Black Law Student Association on campus was necessary and would be beneficial. And in 1973, we began our BLSA reunion weekends to provide alumni interaction with current students to nurture, inspire, and assist in their professional success. This year, the BLSA celebrated our forty-first reunion. Father Ted also blessed the formation of a university-wide alumni association for African-Americans, which led to Hispanic and Asian-American alumni associations as well. He understood our need to gather together to share our heritage and experiences, and recognized that the support we derived from our alumni associations enabled us to become more vital and active members of the larger Notre Dame family. Father Ted also introduced the lay board of trustees at Notre Dame, which continues to impact me because it set the stage for my appointment to the board, on which I still serve as secretary. Ultimately, I was blessed to receive an honorary degree and the Sorin Alumni Award from the university.

Unfortunately, Father Ted's progressive attitude did not trickle down to all aspects of the university. With the challenges we faced, we also became very close to many of the undergraduates facing similar challenges, especially the athletes. We celebrated Thanksgiving and other holidays together and formed a bond that has remained strong throughout the years.

But I also benefited from Father Ted's vision of coeducation when I was fortunate enough to become an assistant rector at Farley Hall during my second year of law school. With many civil rights posters adorning my walls, I became the first African-American assistant rector on campus. I served under the leadership of the beloved Sister Jean Lenz, who became an iconic leader on campus. We opened the third women's hall on campus. After surviving a chaotic but rewarding first week, we sat down on a bench outside Farley.

We both breathed big sighs of relief and Sister Jean said, "Annie, I am so glad we have survived this. I must confess I was quite nervous about working with a gung-ho black woman law student from Detroit and I wondered if I had prejudices that would surface and cause difficulties between us."

"Well," I said, "You should have seen me when I heard that I was going to be working with a nun from Joliet!" We laughed and we became sisters for life. And that was a big part of Notre Dame — developing lifelong friendships.

My first job as a law clerk on the United States Court of Appeals for the Seventh Circuit, the court on which I serve today, came as a result of the recommendation of then Dean David Link, one of those lifelong friends. Having been one of my professors, he believed I had the ability, dedication, and skill set to excel as a judicial law clerk. Dean Link gave my name to then Chief Judge Luther Swygert, a Notre Dame alum, who referred me to Judge Robert Sprecher, who hired me. This clerkship opportunity opened doors that have led to my spending my entire professional career in the Dirksen Federal Building in Chicago. After clerking, I became an assistant United States attorney and chief of a criminal division. Then I was honored and humbled to receive a presidential appointment to the United States District Court before assuming my second lifetime judicial position on the Court of Appeals. I often wonder where I would have been without Notre Dame. I doubt my path would have been the same, so I have much to thank Notre Dame for.

Father Ted once said, "You don't make decisions because they are easy, you don't make decisions because they are cheap, you don't make them because they're popular. You make them because they're right." Following his example, which reinforced the philosophy of my parents, I have tried to make decisions in my life because they are right, fair, and just.

When I look back on my path and those of my fellow African-American Notre Dame law alumni, it is clear that while our experiences were difficult at times, the education, intellectual rigor, and values instilled in us at Notre Dame prepared us for the world beyond campus. I have been blessed and able to serve as president of the Federal Judges Association; chair of a US Judicial Conference Committee; founder of the Black Women Lawyers Association of Chicago, Minority Legal Education Resources, and Just the Beginning — A Pipeline Organization; creator of the public interest fellowship program for Equal Justice Works; and leader of training delegations of lawyers and judges throughout Africa for Lawyers Without Borders.

I look at my fellow BLSA alumni and see them holding positions as judges and government officials, prosecutors and public defenders, law firm partners, corporate and business leaders, academics, and public interest attorneys. I see hundreds of BLSA alumni excelling in their careers and, equally important, dedicated to the community and world around them. We became different kinds of lawyers due to Notre Dame Law School's fundamental commitment to ethics, charity, and excellence. And we have become valuable members of the Notre Dame family and in our own communities, both local and national. And my dad, who had once cheered against the Irish, became a proud and loyal son of the Notre Dame family.

Father Ted's message of diversity and inclusion has long been a part of the university's core value system. Father Edward "Monk" Malloy and Father John Jenkins have enthusiastically embraced the importance of having diversity on campus at all levels and recognize that diversity and inclusion of African-Americans is important for all of us. Students of color now comprise roughly 20 percent of the student population, yet only 3 to 5 percent are African-American. And, unfortunately, faculty diversity statistics remain very low. As co-chair of the board of trustees' Social Values and Responsibilities Committee, we regularly grapple with this issue. Has progress been made? Surely it has. Is there much left to be done? Surely there is. Should we continue to press for a greater representation of African-Americans at all levels of the university? Surely we must.

BONITA BRADSHAW

(Class of 1977)

Bonita Bradshaw came to Notre Dame in autumn 1973 from Compton, California. She majored in fine arts (industrial design). After graduation she became a technical illustrator in the aerospace industry before becoming an educator. She has two daughters and lives in Rancho Dominguez, California.

IT WAS THE FALL OF 1972 WHEN I RECEIVED A LETTER FROM Notre Dame saying that, as part of the admission application process, I would be interviewed at my home in Compton, California, by Dr. Emil T. Hofman. The day of the interview my mom was up early, baking cookies and setting out good china. When Dr. Hofman arrived, mom invited him in and served tea and homemade cookies. We sat in our rarely used living room as he asked questions about my life and goals. About thirty minutes into the interview, Dr. Hofman said he didn't think that my education in Compton would make for academic success at Notre Dame. No sooner had he finished his sentence than my mom swooped in, scooped up his tea cup and saucer, and said, "Well, I guess this interview is over."

Despite Emil T.'s skepticism and that of my Dominguez High School counselor, I was admitted to Notre Dame. And my parents told me that, regardless of anyone's skepticism, they would support me wherever I went. I chose Notre Dame and became part of the second class of women admitted to the university. I was the first black woman from my two hometowns—Gary, Indiana, where I was born, and Compton, where we had moved when I was in elementary school—to be accepted to Notre Dame. I was one of twelve black women in the 1973 freshman class.

Since I had never seen the campus, I arrived at Notre Dame a couple of weeks early and had ample time to walk the campus by myself. I was overwhelmed by the architecture, the flowers, and the statues. I walked to the lakes and ran from the ducks. I came upon the Grotto and, as I walked up and lit a candle, it was as if something came over me and I had a feeling of belonging. It was at that moment I knew that Notre Dame was where I belonged. The Grotto became my solace and my favorite place while I was at Notre Dame. Since becoming an alumna I get that same feeling of belonging every time I visit the Grotto.

I had always shared a room growing up, so having roommates was nothing new and truly nothing I wanted to repeat. So I didn't spend a lot of time in my room or with my roommates during freshman year. By the end of the year, I had become friends with another black freshman, Andrea "Andi" Ransom. We both applied for singles in Lyons Hall, which was being converted to a women's dorm, for the following year, and we both were awarded singles!

I struggled academically freshman year after I severely sprained my ankle while trying out for the basketball team. I went through the winter on crutches in the snow. I considered myself an athlete and had great expectations of playing sports while at Notre Dame, but that didn't materialize my freshman year. When I wasn't in class I spent a good deal of my time, by choice, with other black students. I loved to dance so I started a dance-drill team that actually performed at the men's basketball games. I sang in the gospel choir, although I knew nothing about gospel music. I even sang Al Green songs on the north quad at all hours of the night with friends, while students trying to get their rest yelled "Shut up!" from their dorm windows. I occasionally went off campus with my assigned family through a program administered by Paula Dawning, a counselor for the black students, or with Frances Hubbard, the secretary who worked in the black studies program office. Sometimes I would rustle up as many friends as I could to get rib-tip sandwiches to split and eat until we were full! I still eat only rib-tip sandwiches to this day.

With the encouragement of Paula Dawning, I got involved in the Big Brothers Big Sisters program and mentored wonderful little brothers with whom I still communicate today. I took part in the creation of the first newsletter for the black community at Notre Dame, "The Ebony Side of the Dome," and created the original artwork for the logo. I was always present when the black cultural arts center brought guest speakers, such as Julian Bond, Angela Davis, and Stokely Carmichael, to campus.

The down side of life at the Dome was heart-wrenching at times for me. I remember as a freshman going into a store in South Bend to buy art supplies, and a woman screamed, "There's a n-word!" and she was pointing at me. Go figure! I called home that day and cried to my mother.

That same year in the South Dining Hall, I put my tray in the window on the conveyor and one of the workers pushed it back and yelled that he wasn't "busing no n-word's tray." I walked away in disbelief and called home yet again.

Over spring break in Howard Hall, someone's father, wearing a big, ten-gallon hat, tried to summon me, saying, "Hey gal, c'mon over here and empty my son's trash cans!" He thought I was a maid. I told him, "Just one moment," walked away, and didn't return.

One winter night my sophomore year, Andi and I had just pulled a chilled bottle of Manischewitz Cream White Concord out of the window when we were interrupted by a knock at the door. It was a girl who lived on our floor who wanted to ask us a question. "Sure," I said, "come on in." It turned out that she wanted to see our tails! She said that she had grown up learning that at night black people grew tails! Now that warranted a call home for sure!

I encountered behaviors like these far too often. When I walked to class students asked to touch my hair, or would call me the n-word from behind. Though frustrated often, my mom could always bring me back around and put me back on track. My first two years at Notre Dame were beyond challenging, and, needless to say, I made a lot of calls home.

There were a couple of individuals other than my mom who kept me sane and added benefit to my life while at Notre Dame. The first was Father Theodore Hesburgh. I met him shortly after joining the yearbook staff my first year. I had encountered so much overt and covert racism that I joined a sit-in on the steps of the Administration Building in protest. When asked who could help us, I suggested talking to Father Hesburgh. I was escorted to his office and there we talked about racism, the world, and my life at Notre Dame. He spoke about ignorance and expectation, and he listened to me. I felt somewhat relieved and totally respected. He told me his door was always open, and I used it. Some days I would run into him at the Grotto, and on other days he'd be walking about campus with his hands tucked behind his back. I appreciated our conversations, as I know they lessened the number of my phone calls home. On the day of my graduation, Father Hesburgh spent ample time with my parents talking about me, and I will always respect him for being honest and available.

An individual who first scared me to death but whom I later learned to love to death was Coach Richard "Digger" Phelps. Digger didn't appear to ever see color. He saw skill, ability, and potential, or the lack thereof. I saw Digger's job as molding individuals into prime athletes, and he took it more seriously than anyone I had ever seen before.

As a freshman and a sophomore I worked for Astrid Hotvedt in the women's athletic office. As a junior and a senior I worked for Digger in the men's basketball office. Watching him interact with his athletes and watching his practices gave me a bird's-eye view of what being a real coach was. He was passionate to a fault and never held anything back.

After graduating from Notre Dame and moving back to California, I began to coach basketball and I strove to be that kind of coach. And when I ended my very successful eighteen-year coaching career, I could only thank Digger for modeling the style of coach I became. I'm proud to say that I was well respected by most and had teams that were feared by many.

After graduation I realized I was deeply affected and personally angry about part of my experience at Notre Dame. Professionally I realized that I was hired and lauded because of my having graduated from Notre Dame. But because of what I had experienced, I preferred that my children not become legacies. As an alumna, I wanted to help with recruitment efforts but could not say, in my heart of hearts, that Notre Dame was the "best place" for a black student. I wanted to be proud of being part of the "ebony side of the Dome" but had to acknowledge that a good many other Domers didn't even want us there. I was part of the original Black Alumni of Notre Dame meetings and am even in a picture of the pioneers of the organization that hangs in the convocation center, but my name is not there.

Everything changed dramatically on May 4, 2003. That's when I had a conversation with Andrea Renee Ransom on her deathbed. In her pain—she was dying of breast cancer—and without hesitation, she was thinking of me. She whispered, "Stop being so mad. Stop remembering so much. I know what you went through. I know what *we* went through, but you got through it and you're still here. A lot happened to us . . . but you're still here. Do your artwork and stop being a closet artist. Help children learn because that's what you're passionate about . . . and stop being mad."

I made her a promise to stop being mad, and when she passed away shortly thereafter, I was done. Today, I am totally optimistic about the future of my relationship with Notre Dame. I am active in my alumni work. I have grown and changed, as I hope the racial climate of Notre Dame has grown and changed. I am finally embracing every moment and opportunity I have with Notre Dame and without. I do love Notre Dame and I am who I am, in Notre Dame and in life.

JOYA C. DE FOOR

(Class of 1977)

---

*Joya De Foor came to Notre Dame in autumn 1973 from At-
lanta. She majored in accounting and became Notre Dame's
first black cheerleader. After graduation she earned an MBA
from the University of Southern California and worked as a
finance executive, including serving as Los Angeles City treasurer. She and her husband, Thomas Klinger, live in Long
Beach, California.*

"IT WAS THE BEST OF TIMES; IT WAS THE WORST OF TIMES."
This Charles Dickens quote best describes my Notre Dame experience. For many years, I refused to face my true feelings about my
undergraduate time. Why? Because I have been conflicted!

In August 1973, almost thirty years after Frazier Thompson broke
the color barrier, I arrived at the university alone from Atlanta, Georgia, in just the second class of undergraduate women admitted to
Notre Dame. My parents had asked if I wanted Mom to accompany
me. Although I was afraid, I said no. I had received a partial scholarship, work-study, and a loan, but the package covered only about half
of the expenses. Being from a middle-class family, I understood the
sacrifices my parents made for me to attend the college of my choice
and for my younger sister to attend private school. There was also my
five-year old brother to consider.

I was comforted by the knowledge that, to assist in the transition,
I was assigned a South Bend family to serve as a source of support. I
was blessed with the Cleveland family. The late Granville Cleveland

was the law school librarian, and his wonderful family would become my shelter in the storm called Notre Dame.

Upon arrival, I easily found my room in Breen-Phillips Hall, but was apprehensive because I had always had my own bedroom. As I was changing clothes, my first roommate arrived with her entire family. When I asked for her brothers and father to leave while I changed, she told me that it was okay if her brothers stayed because they had sisters and they dressed in front of each other all the time. Needless to say, I quickly dressed and left. This roommate eventually requested a roommate change.

Later that day, I was getting familiar with the dorm when a man who identified himself as an alumnus approached me and asked me to take his daughter's luggage to her room. He seemed incredulous that I was actually a student, explaining to me that the only "Negro" women on campus when he attended worked in the dorms, the dining rooms, or the laundry.

This was my introduction to Notre Dame campus life. Over the next four years, I was:

- informed by a finance professor, who replaced one who had suffered a heart attack, that he had never had any "girlies" or "coloreds" in his class before; there were six women in the class and I was the only minority among approximately one hundred students;
- refused an excused absence for an approved university activity (the only student in the class so denied);
- called the "n-word" for only the second time in my life;
- asked to leave my dorm room for the weekend because my roommates' parents or boyfriends did not know that they had an African-American roommate;
- excluded, along with my African-American partner, from a cheerleading picture requested by a Notre Dame alumni group in North Carolina;
- told by a female cheerleader that she couldn't have an African-American partner because she "bruised" easily; and
- accused of stealing clothes from the laundry room.

At times, my parents sensed something was wrong, but I assured them that I was "fine." Dad shared two pieces of advice that not only buttressed me during my time at the university, but also have guided me throughout my professional life. He told me that "the playing field will never be equal," and "if you have to be three times better, that is what you have to do without complaint."

Make no mistake: there were good times that were just as impactful. I had long admired Father Theodore Hesburgh for his civil rights activities and national advocacy. I was humbled that this man took the time to meet with a lonely, frightened young woman late one evening and encouraged me to persevere. I was privileged to be one of the first gospel chorus members, even though I am Roman Catholic and, to this day, tone-deaf. I was a member of the cheerleading squad for two years, and one of my most enduring relationships is with one of my former squad members. As moving and impactful as my meeting with Father Hesburgh was an experience when, while visiting Chapel Hill, a group of Notre Dame alums wanted to take a picture with the cheerleaders, except for my partner and me. I was moved when some of the other squad members refused to be photographed if my partner and I were to be excluded.

When I tried out for the squad for my second year, I was not selected. At that time the practice generally was that, once selected, being re-selected was a virtual formality. I was shocked when my name was not announced as a member of the squad! Several who had observed the tryouts could not understand why I was not selected and publicly voiced their disbelief at the outcome. The ensuing public outcry resulted in a second tryout. With Coach Richard "Digger" Phelps and several members of the basketball team in vigorous support, I was selected to join the squad after the second tryout.

Coach Phelps remained supportive, encouraging, respectful, and kind throughout my remaining time on campus. Professors Adam Arnold of the College of Business, and Alex Cheponda and Jerome Thornton of the College of Arts and Letters challenged me to my fullest potential, were always available for guidance, and offered reassurance when I most needed it. I was honored to serve on the Senior Class Fellow Committee and to personally meet the cartoonist Garry Trudeau. No doubt the closest I will ever be to a president was when President Jimmy Carter spoke at my 1977 commencement. After graduation, I was honored to be one of the founding members of the Black Alumni of Notre Dame and was a Notre Dame Club of Los Angeles board member.

Would I make the decision to attend Notre Dame today? Absolutely! My ambivalence has long been resolved. Without the grace of God, my parents, and the university, I would not be the person I am today. I graduated from Notre Dame as a confident, secure, and capable woman. My grades were not great, but my education was excellent and provided the basis for my full-scholarship graduate degree, a very successful career in finance, and numerous leadership positions in trade organizations. More importantly, the Notre Dame experience has provided essential training in courage, character, integrity, and honesty. This training served me well in my last high-profile position, when I made the choice of doing the right thing instead of keeping my job.

I am in awe of Frazier Thompson and those who helped shape him as a person. Reflecting on my experience at the university decades later, I cannot imagine the isolation or fear that he experienced nor the courage, strength, faith, and perseverance that he embodied.

For his enduring example, I will forever remain in his debt.

MANNY GRACE

(Class of 1979)

---

*Manny Grace came to Notre Dame in autumn 1975 from Bur-
lington, Massachusetts. He majored in psychology and was a
member of the Notre Dame Marching Band. After graduation
he earned a law degree at Columbia University, clerked in the
Second Circuit Court of Appeals, and practiced law. Today he is
associate general counsel to the Walt Disney Company. He and
his wife, Karen Caffee, and their two children live in Pasadena,
California.*

IT WAS A SWELTERING EVENING IN MID-AUGUST OF 1977.
Four of us were huddled together in our dorm room in Cavanaugh
Hall. This was my assembled brain trust, my closest friends and room-
mates. Gathered with me were Rick Rihm, an accounting major from
Piqua, Ohio; Michael MacDonald, a physics major from Ormond
Beach, Florida; and Bob Lombardo, another accounting major from
Stamford, Connecticut.

"If we had time, we could mail-order high-heeled sneakers," said
Michael.

"Yeah, but we don't have time," I replied.

The final auditions for the Notre Dame Marching Band would
conclude that evening. Time was running out, and we were short on
ideas. Not only were we short on ideas, *I* was a little short. I was just
a hair under the six-feet, two-inch height requirement to audition for
the famed Irish Guard, the elite marching unit of the University of
Notre Dame Marching Band.

The Irish Guard has been part of the pageantry and fiber of the Notre Dame Marching Band since 1949. The Guard announces the presence of the Fighting Irish, and protects the ranks of the band by marching in an unwavering line at the head of the formation. They are the tall, non-smiling bodyguards of the band. Their attire alone attracts attention. The Irish Guard wear the bright red doublet of the Old Black Watch, a blue tartan kilt, hose and flashes, white leather cross belts, a leather-and-white horsehair sporran with black tassels and silver cantle (a dress pouch for a kilt), a tartan plaid sash slung over the left shoulder and fixed with a silver brooch, called a cairngorm, black shoes, white spats, and, on top of it all, a tall black bearskin shako helmet with a gold plume.

With the full uniform on, a guardsman stands about seven feet tall. It takes about thirty-five minutes to put on all this gear. And you'd better put it on correctly, because the Guard undergoes a full inspection in full view of thousands of fans and spectators before each football game, conducted by the Captain of the Guard and former members of the Guard. During the inspection, guardsmen must stand at attention without moving, speaking, or smiling. They are stoic and imperturbable as they practice the art of the "thousand-yard stare."

My brain trust was out of ideas and the final auditions were about to begin. In just a few short minutes I would compete against twenty other guys who also wanted desperately to become part of the storied tradition and lore of Notre Dame. And the competition would be intense, since there are only ten members of the Guard, and that year, due to few graduating seniors, there were only three available spots. Once you are selected to be a member of the Irish Guard, you retain that position until you graduate. I wanted one of those spots. So my roommates and I turned to a low-tech but time-tested solution to the height problem—we stuffed athletic socks into my sneakers and I joined the line of newbies hoping to be chosen.

Although my height was a potential issue, it wasn't my only concern. I am black, and if I were to be chosen, I would be the first black member of the Irish Guard. For over thirty years, the Irish Guard had been tall and exclusively white. There had never been a black member of the Irish Guard and, at Notre Dame, tradition means everything. I wasn't looking to be a rebel, or make some kind of statement. I just thought the Guard was an awesome sight and wanted to be a part of it. But I wasn't sure if I would be evaluated based on my marching skills, my attitude, and my military bearing, or if something else would determine whether I would be chosen to represent the university.

I wasn't concerned about my marching ability because marching was in my blood. I grew up on Army bases in Massachusetts and Alaska, and I watched from the stands when my father and his battalion paraded before audiences and "trooped the stands"—when division after division would march past the base commander and the military brass on the parade grounds. All I knew was that I wanted to be like my dad. I longed to be in uniform and to be part of a special marching unit that performed before crowds. When I was old enough, I marched for nine years for a succession of more accomplished drum and bugle corps in Massachusetts. In addition, my high school had an Air Force Junior Reserve Officer Training Corps (JROTC). I rose through the ranks and graduated from high school as a first lieutenant. Looking back, it may have been a little nerdy in high school, but I enjoyed marching and drilling before my classmates.

I loved marching. I loved the symmetry, camaraderie, and spectacle of performing before a stadium of fans with other members of a marching unit who are similarly enthused by the crowd. And on top of all the great marching, the Guard was flat-out cool. They were literally and figuratively "Big Men on Campus," and they generated a great deal of admiration and respect. I knew that if the selection was based solely on marching ability, I would have a good shot, but if the decision was based on anything other than merit, I would be out of luck. So I did the only thing that was in my control—I stuffed my shoes and practiced, practiced, practiced. I marched to my classes in O'Shaughnessy Hall, mimicking the distinctive, high-stepping march of the Irish Guard. While standing in line at the South Dining Hall, I danced the Damsha Bua, the victory clog step that the Irish Guard performs on game day when the Fighting Irish are victorious. I would go into a trance-like stare and challenge my roommates to try to distract me while I stood at attention in my dorm hallway. I was ready.

Guard auditions were conducted by the senior members of the Guard and band director Robert "O.B." O'Brien, associate director James Phillips, and assistant director Fr. George Wiskirchen, CSC. I knew O.B. and the other band directors because I was a returning member of the drum section of the band, having marched the previous year as the band member who pulled the rolling tympani, or "Thunder Drums," which were played by Kevin Pritchett, another black band member. I thought that the band directors liked me and was pretty sure they would evaluate me based on my marching skills alone.

But tradition is a difficult thing to overcome. I knew that everyone involved in the audition decision would be thinking about whether the university was ready for a black guardsman. How would it look? Would a lone black face disrupt the homogeneous look of the Irish Guard? Would a black guardsman distract from the desired "One Guard" effect?

The last night of the auditions, after the evaluations had been completed, but before the results were to be posted in the band office in Washington Hall, Jim Phillips saw me and asked me to join him and O.B. in his office. Jim said that no decisions had been made yet, but he wanted to know if I had considered the fact that, if chosen, I would be the first black member of the Irish Guard.

Before I could answer, O.B. chimed in and asked if I would be able to handle the pressure? What if some people weren't ready for a black Guard member? What if the other members of the Guard were unhappy to march with a black guardsman? Honestly, it was the first time that I had considered the question. I was so focused on the goal that I hadn't spent too much time thinking about what the Irish Guard might think about me trying out for the squad or the consequences of actually making it.

I told the band directors that I was pretty used to being the darkest man in the room, both in my hometown of Burlington, Massachusetts, and at Notre Dame. So if chosen, I would be okay being the first black member of the Guard as long as the other guardsmen respected me. Satisfied with my answer, the impromptu meeting ended and I left the band offices wondering what I had started.

The next day, I was ecstatic to learn that I had been selected to be one of the three new members of the Irish Guard. Whatever concerns I had about being accepted by the other guardsmen proved unfounded. It was simply never an issue with them. Surprisingly, or perhaps not so surprisingly, the only adverse reaction I received came from some of my fellow black students at Notre Dame. The majority of my black classmates (and there weren't that many of us at that time) thought it was cool, but a small minority of the black students didn't like the idea. Some of the more vocal black students asked me why I wanted to be in the Irish Guard. Wouldn't I feel silly wearing a kilt on football Saturdays? What the hell did the Irish Guard have to do with my culture—or with football for that matter? What was I hoping to accomplish?

I tried to explain that the Irish Guard represented the best of the marchers in the Notre Dame band and I simply wanted to be among the best. After all, there were lots of black players on the Fighting Irish football team, and I bet none of them were Irish, fighting or otherwise. The football players weren't being accused of falsely aspiring to be Irish. They were simply doing what they loved and playing for one of the best football teams in the country, which happened to be called the Fighting Irish. Luckily, my other black classmates understood what I was doing and always gave me a shout-out when the Guard and the band marched by.

That's what Notre Dame meant to me—it was a place where you could experiment and aspire to be whatever you wanted to be. Wherever your interest lay, there was a group there willing to welcome you with open arms. Sure, Notre Dame was sometimes a small place populated by people with small minds, or a place where some clung to a blind allegiance to traditions at the expense of experimentation. But on the whole, Notre Dame was a magical place for me.

I marched for two years as a member of the Irish Guard. I have great memories of the sometimes rough but always funny members of the Guard. I remember the secret traditions of the Guard (which, of course, I shall take to the grave), the camaraderie of a small group of *large* men united by the bracing sensation of the wind blowing up our kilts, and the surge of pride we felt as representatives of the University of Notre Dame.

Best of all, I remember the energy and excitement we generated on game day, when we entered the stadium to the resounding chants of "Here come the Irish!" I remember the sights and sounds of the Guard high-stepping at full speed onto the field behind the drum major, our heads turned to the right as we struggled to keep the line perfectly straight, kilts bouncing up and down, and then stopping on a dime—as one cohesive unit—just as the band struck up the opening notes of "Hike, Notre Dame." But mostly, I remember how cool it all was, how I hoped the day would never end, and how I hoped we would get a chance to dance the Damsha Bua.

RICHARD RYANS

(Class of 1979)

Richard Ryans came to Notre Dame in autumn 1975 from Memphis. He majored in accounting and participated in several organizations, including the Black Cultural Arts Council, League of Black Business Students, and the Notre Dame Gospel Choir. After graduation he returned to Memphis and worked as a staff accountant for Deloitte and Touche. He and his family live in Elkridge, Maryland.

"SO LET ME GET THIS STRAIGHT. YOU, A BLACK BAPTIST FROM the South, are going to a predominantly white, Catholic institution in the North? Who does that?" It was a question that friends and family alike asked when they heard the news: I was going to Notre Dame.

"Notre Dame? But why?"

And so it began . . .

In today's world, where African-American students are much more apt to choose from a variety of academic institutions, making such a decision isn't such a foreign concept. But in 1975, for the son of a Baptist preacher in Memphis, Tennessee, it was a big deal.

Maybe it was the fact that I didn't want to go to an Ivy League school like my brother Charles, who had gone to Princeton the year before. Maybe it's because I didn't want to attend a local college, as my parents had desired. And maybe there was some element of defiance attached to it. In any case, my mind was made up. I was headed to Notre Dame.

While I was an athlete and an avid sports fan, I had never really been a Notre Dame fan. In fact, I often found myself rooting against the Irish. I didn't care for the whole Catholic theology thing, either; maybe I could help them see the error of their ways. I mean, really, confessional? That would never work in our church.

But there I was, getting ready for my transition to South Bend, sight unseen. There were no spring visitation weekends for minority students back then, so my first sight of the campus was during orientation week.

How I made the decision to attend Notre Dame is a story in itself. A few friends and I had made a pact: we would all attend Harvard University upon high school graduation. Since we were all great students academically, we all received admission to Harvard. Yet I was the only one who chose not to go. I couldn't explain it at the time, but it just didn't feel right. Maybe it wasn't a part of God's plan.

Then I decided to attend the University of Tennessee because it had a great minority engineering program. Trouble was, Tennessee's financial aid package left a lot to be desired, so it, too, was kicked to the curb.

In the midst of my decision-making process, I received an invitation to attend a Notre Dame information session at the home of a local Notre Dame alumnus, Lee Piovarcy (Class of 1963). I remember he showed a slide presentation of the campus and had some local alums speak. Afterwards, I had conversations with several of them. I went home feeling like this could be the place. I later did more research, and decided to take the boldest step I had ever made: "Ticket from Memphis to South Bend, please. . . ."

Upon my arrival, I was immediately impressed with the beauty of the campus. I thought to myself, "This might work out well after all." And since Notre Dame was a religious institution, I figured that the attitudes of the students and professors would be at a "higher level" than at other universities that I had considered. That thought lasted about forty-five minutes. For you see, not long after I had settled in my room, my roommate showed up. Maybe it was my name. After all, Ryans could be a derivative of Ryan or O'Ryan. In either case, I must be a white, Irish Catholic who would work well with him.

Upon seeing me, my roommate and his family assumed that I was part of the dorm help staff, and that my reason for being in the room was to assist "Mr. Ryans" in bringing up his luggage. They then proceeded to ask me to do the same for them. When I introduced myself as Mr. Ryans, the look of shock and horror on their faces was priceless. They immediately proceeded downstairs to get a new roommate but were told that all the dorm rooms were full. Therefore, they were stuck with me.

And so it began . . .

As I quickly found out, my roommate had not had much personal interaction with black people. In fact, he mentioned that his only real knowledge of blacks was through television. I guess I was a test case for him. Needless to say, that freshman year was quite rocky between the two of us. We finally reached a tolerance level, but not a friendship. We didn't room together after that year; in fact, I didn't see much of him the remainder of my time on campus.

It was at that point that I decided that my best formula for success was to, first, concentrate on my studies as much as possible and, second, stay close to my black brothers and sisters on campus. While I associated with students of all races and religions, both academically and socially, my "comfort zone" remained with the black student body. But even then, it wasn't with the entire black population. While I knew—or, at least, knew of—every black student on campus, I found myself drawn to those in my freshman class, as well as to certain male upperclassmen who weren't hesitant to "show us the ropes" as to how to survive (and in some cases, manipulate) the Notre Dame system. I mean people like Lionel Phillips, Tom Hampton, Stan Towns, Reggie Reed, Theodore Slaughter, Keith Tobias. They showed us how to take advantage of what Notre Dame had to offer: classes and professors to choose; other black upperclassmen and faculty to know; black student organizations to become involved in. They mentored us. They even got us to the local barber shops and churches in town.

Several of us made a pact to make sure that we all succeeded, not only academically but emotionally, socially, and spiritually as well. This group included people like Tony Fitts, Don Hill, Carl Reid, Renard Gueringer, Henry Armstrong, and Byron Wilson. I found myself becoming actively involved in the black student organizations. I even helped establish a couple of them: the League of Black Business Students and the Notre Dame Gospel Choir, now known as Voices of Faith. I participated in a protest movement regarding treatment of minorities on campus, out of which grew the Office of Minority Student Affairs. And upon graduation, for those of us who had made it, there was such a sense of pride and accomplishment that we decided to hold our own "Black Graduation" ceremony just prior to commencement.

After graduation, I was one of many who held the opinion that the best sight of the Golden Dome was in your rear-view mirror. Adios, Notre Dame! Thanks for the memories!

I severed all ties with the university, even as I was learning that the Notre Dame name and degree opened a lot of doors and created opportunities that I might not have otherwise had. As I saw it, opening those doors and creating those opportunities were what my tuition money was spent for. So Notre Dame really wasn't doing me any favors, just fulfilling its part of the bargain. For many years I never returned to campus, rarely watched football games, and certainly didn't contribute any money. I ignored all those mailings and phone calls from the development office. Notre Dame has gotten enough of my money, I felt. It didn't need any more.

Then, in August 1985, another Notre Dame envelope arrived, and I was prepared to ignore it as well. But there was something different about this one. First of all, it wasn't from the development office, but from the alumni association. Secondly, it didn't have one of those stick-on address labels with my name on it; it was personally typed.

"What kind of trick is this?" I thought. I ignored the envelope at first, and didn't open it until a couple of days later. It turned out to be a letter written by Chuck Lennon, then executive director of the alumni association, and Father Ted Hesburgh, president of the university. It said that Notre Dame was having difficulty recruiting black students, retaining them, and getting black alumni involvement. It was soliciting assistance from black alums who had previously expressed an interest in working with the university on the role of blacks in the Notre Dame community (not sure how they got my name). The two men were requesting an on-campus meeting that October of black alumni and university officials to address these issues. After quite a bit of thought and consternation, I decided to attend.

And so it began . . .

My intent in attending this meeting was to hear what the university and the other black alums had to say, put in my two cents, and then head home. Instead I got drawn in by the plight of the current black student body and thought how I had wished that some black alum had cared about me like that when I was a student. One thing led to another, and I found myself knee-deep in the formulation, creation, and leadership of what is now known as the Black Alumni of Notre Dame. And almost thirty years later, I am still involved in its mission: to enhance the presence and experiences of African-Americans across the Notre Dame family—students, faculty, administration, and alumni. My involvement has been filled with challenges and triumphs, setbacks and victories, frustration and fulfillment. But at the end of the day, I would do it all over again.

For all the educational experiences afforded me, for all the lifelong friendships made, and most of all, for the opportunities to make a difference in the lives of our black students, I thank you Notre Dame. We don't know what the future holds for us, but I do know that whatever it is, it'll continue to be epic.

It's a phrase I wouldn't have uttered thirty-five years ago, but which I now sing proudly: "And our hearts forever, love thee Notre Dame!"

CHAPTER 4

The 1980s

In June 1987 Notre Dame experienced something it had not experienced for more than a third of a century: a president *not* named Hesburgh. After thirty-five years at the helm, Father Ted stood down and a new leader, Father Edward A. "Monk" Malloy, was piped aboard to take command. Then Hesburgh and his longtime second-in-command, Father Edmund "Ned" Joyce, boarded a motor home and drove away from the campus for a long vacation.

The transfer of power from Hesburgh to Malloy was radically different from the transfer to Hesburgh from his predecessor, Father John Cavanaugh, back in 1952. Describing the process in his autobiography, *God, Country, Notre Dame*, Hesburgh said his appointment was announced at the annual meeting where Holy Cross priests received their "obediences" — their assignments for the coming year — from the provincial. Then:

> As we walked out of the chapel, Cavanaugh reached into the pocket of his cassock and pulled out the key to his office and handed it to me. "By the way," he said, "I promised to give a talk tonight to the Christian Family Movement over at Veterans Hall. Now that you're the president, you have to do it. Good luck. I'm off to New York."
>
> Just like that, I was president of the University of Notre Dame.

Malloy's installation was substantially more formal and public. Indeed, his selection for the presidency the year before had made the

151

front page of the *New York Times*. There was a formal convocation, Malloy gave a formal inaugural address, and Hesburgh gave a formal valedictory address to a worldwide audience of alumni via satellite television.

That the change of presidents attracted such attention was a tribute to Notre Dame's growth in size and stature during the thirty-five Hesburgh years. Again, he sketched it well in his autobiography:

The student body had doubled, while the faculty had tripled. The annual operating budget had grown from $6 million to $230 million; the endowment from $6 million to more than a half billion. Since 1952 we had tripled or quadrupled the space available in classrooms, libraries, laboratories, offices, and public spaces. Almost everything that existed on the campus in 1952 had either been renewed or demolished. Faculty salaries had grown from among the worst to among the very best in the nation. Endowed and other scholarships had risen from $100,000 to more than $60 million annually.

The Malloy era would feature no less spectacular growth, and a continuation of the university's progress in fostering diversity in all aspects of the Notre Dame community. Two years before his departure, Hesburgh had planted a seed by encouraging the creation of the Black Alumni of Notre Dame, the first of the diversity organizations within the alumni association. Malloy both nurtured that seed and took initiatives of his own early on by adding more black trustees and advisory council members.

The black presence among the Fighting Irish was signaled and sealed definitively during the 1987 and 1988 football seasons. In 1987 Tim Brown became Notre Dame's first black Heisman Trophy winner, and its seventh overall. In 1988, the Irish captured college football's national championship with a black man, Tony Rice, at quarterback.

All of these Notre Dame events took place against a backdrop of often disconcerting world and national events.

To American baby boomers, who grew up fearing the Soviet Union and living under the constant threat of nuclear holocaust, the notion that there might someday not be a Soviet Union or a Cold War was about as unthinkable as that the sun might not rise in the east. Confrontation with the Soviets was an immutable fact of their lives.

Then, at some point in the late 1980s, that started to change. After the rapid deaths of a series of old apparatchiks—Brezhnev, Andropov, Chernenko—a new, younger Soviet leader took over. Mikhail Gorbachev was articulate. He actually allowed himself to be seen smiling in public. And he wore suits that didn't look as if they came from a rummage sale in Vladivostok.

It was Britain's redoubtable prime minister Margaret Thatcher who, after a meeting with the Soviet leader-in-waiting in late 1984, first broached the notion that Gorbachev was someone she—and, by implication, other Western leaders—could "do business" with.

Thatcher's friend, US president Ronald Reagan, picked up the ball and ran with it. In 1986, he and Gorbachev, who by then had succeeded Chernenko as his nation's leader, held a summit meeting in Reykjavik, Iceland, where they came close to agreeing to scrap their nuclear arsenals. Close, but not quite.

Still, a momentum had been created, and it was propelling the two nations, the US and the USSR, toward an end to confrontation. That momentum derived from events in addition to Gorbachev's initiatives. In Poland, the seed planted by Pope John Paul II's 1979 visit bloomed into worker rebellions against the communist government's economic and other policies. The most notable rebellion was the Gdansk shipyard strike, which began on August 14, 1980, led by Lech Walesa, an electrician who was later to be a Nobel Peace Prize winner and, after free elections in 1989, Poland's president.

In Czechoslovakia, similar resistance to the government blossomed into what came to be known as the Velvet Revolution, and the downfall of the communist regime.

But the decisive blow to the communist system came in East Germany. There, protests against the hardline government forced it in late 1989 to announce that, for the first time since the start of construction of the Berlin Wall in 1961, East Germans would be allowed to pass freely from East Berlin to West Berlin and vice versa. This action in effect marked the end of the Cold War. Elated Germans quickly began breaking off pieces of the despised wall as souvenirs.

Reagan, with his odd mixture of martial aggressiveness and idealistic peace overtures, was largely responsible for forcing Gorbachev and the Soviet Union to confront the economically ruinous implications of continued confrontation with the West.

On the domestic side of things, however, Reagan was less impressive, his win-one-for-the-Gipper bonhomie and "morning in America" rhetorical tropes notwithstanding. African-Americans, in particular, had difficulty warming to him, especially after the speech he gave during his 1980 campaign at the Neshoba County Fairgrounds in Mississippi. It was but a few miles from Philadelphia, Mississippi, where three civil rights workers were kidnapped and murdered by white supremacists during the Freedom Summer campaign of 1964. Employing the dog-whistle rhetoric of the GOP Southern strategists, he expressed support for "states' rights"—the code for Southern resistance to desegregation and black equality—and contempt for the federal government he sought to lead and which black Americans saw as the only reliable guarantor of their rights and opportunity.

Beyond the political, the 1980s featured a bumper crop of fascinating cultural, environmental, and social developments: Mount St. Helens erupted in Washington State in 1980; Ted Turner created CNN, the first cable news network; John Wayne Gacy was sentenced to death in Illinois for the murders of thirty-three men and boys; former Beatle John Lennon was shot to death in New York City; Pope John Paul II was shot at Vatican City (and later forgave his attacker in a prison meeting); Egyptian president Anwar Sadat was assassinated; Diana Spencer and Prince Charles were wed in London; the Space Shuttle Challenger exploded, killing all aboard; Barney Clark received the first artificial heart and lived 112 days with it; Sally Ride became the first American woman in space; the Coca-Cola Company, ignoring the principle "if it ain't broke don't fix it," introduced "New Coke" and quickly backpedalled to "Coca-Cola Classic"; the Soviet nuclear power plant at Chernobyl in Ukraine exploded in the largest nuclear accident in history; "crack," a new form of cocaine, appeared on US streets and gave added impetus to the "war on drugs"; the Exxon *Valdez* ran aground in Prince William Sound, Alaska, spilling hundreds of thousands of gallons of crude oil and creating an environmental disaster of unprecedented proportions.

One other deeply worrisome trend developed in the 1980s, a trend that would reach its apogee only after the turn of the new century. It was terrorism. With depressing frequency there were airplane hijackings; a cruise ship hijacking (the *Achille Lauro*); an airliner bombing (Pan Am Flight 103 over Lockerbie, Scotland); kidnappings from the streets of war-torn Beirut and other cities. Such events became a veritable obbligato, an ominous background theme behind the more prominent sound track of our lives.

PHYLLIS WASHINGTON STONE

(Class of 1980)

Phyllis Washington came to Notre Dame in autumn 1976 from Chicago. She majored in American Studies and was a cheerleader. After graduation she worked as a Notre Dame admissions counselor for five years, then spent almost thirty years in marketing with Merck Sharp & Dohme. She now is a corporate executive coach and leadership consultant. She and her husband, Jim Stone (Class of 1981), live in Somerset, New Jersey.

Lead me, guide me, along the way.
For if you lead me, I cannot stray.
Lord, let me walk each day with thee.
Lead me, O Lord, lead me.

(Doris Akers)

I'VE ALWAYS FELT THAT GOD HAS BEEN LEADING ME ON A journey; thus I have no regrets about anything that happens along the way. So how could I have not chosen Notre Dame? Besides, by choosing Notre Dame I became more deeply connected to the greatest woman ever to walk this earth—Mary, the Mother of God. So I would, without a doubt, make the same choice again.

I have been Catholic since birth, and my roots in Catholicism go back further than I know. One grandmother was educated by the Sisters of the Blessed Sacrament, founded by Saint Katherine Drexel, a pioneer of civil rights and social activism. St. Katherine and her sisters courageously stood in the service of black and Native American children. Granny Grace—"GG"—was one of those children. GG was forever grateful to Katherine Drexel. My other grandmother, Caribel, was African Methodist Episcopal (AME), but had my father raised Catholic because of something she saw in the faith.

For a short time in my life, my parents were also active as Unitarians, so much of what I learned about whites growing up on the South Side of Chicago was through our membership in the Unitarian church, my parents' white friends and co-workers, and the brief period when a white couple lived with us. Notre Dame changed that.

I almost missed the Notre Dame experience. If it hadn't been for Mom and Dad, who said, "What about Notre Dame?" the university would never have come to my mind. Religion was not a factor in my selection, yet the aspect of faith turned out to be most critical to my learning. My response to Mom and Dad's question was, "Where's that?" As it turned out, just ninety miles down the road. And had it not been for Deborah Childs, a classmate from Clarksville, Tennessee, I might not have ended up at Notre Dame. Deb and I visited the campus the same day, and as a result of our meeting, I said, "Why not?" The fact that the university was nearly all-white did not deter me. All the schools I was considering were predominantly white anyway.

Little did I know that there would be only nine black women in the 1976 entering class. (Yikes!) But I felt almost immediately that I fit in, especially with those nine women. So deep in my heart and early on, I knew that I was in the right place. I don't recall ever doubting that.

There were white friends who gravitated towards us and we to them. Separately, each of us nine also had a circle of white friends. How could we not? The majority of the nine were housed in Lewis Hall, where it was rumored most black girls were housed. And after the first year, I was able to room with Ramona Payne from Cincinnati, Ohio, one of the nine. In hindsight, I was grateful for that because it allowed us to form connections close enough to have lasted even to today.

Dorm life was a blast—and I have pictures to prove it. There are photos of us climbing the large trees near the statue of Father Sorin when autumn arrived; photos of us gathering outside of South Dining

Hall with other black students, rocking to New York beats from Stan Wilcox's boom box. While getting a great education, we made the most of our Notre Dame experience, and most of us graduated with gratitude for what we gained from the university as well as what we contributed.

In my world in Chicago, I had never known football, except that the men in my family gathered on autumn Sundays to watch "Da Bears." Participative sports in general were not that big in our family. We were, by and large, writers, readers, dancers, singers, eaters, and talkers. In high school I ventured into cheerleading for Hales Franciscan, the black Catholic boys' school nearest to St. Thomas Apostle, my black Catholic girls' school, and was selected as captain of the squad. One year Hales won the city championship in basketball. So while I knew nothing about Fighting Irish football and national championships, I did know something about being a cheerleader and about cheering for a winning team. That drew me to try out for cheerleading at Notre Dame.

The tryout my freshman year, although daunting, felt like a good fit. Cheerleading was familiar territory, and I enjoyed the dancing and the calisthenics. But it turned out to be one of my earliest run-ins with racism at the university. I had a little fan club of blacks *and* whites from Lewis Hall cheering me on. Notre Dame was in its fifth year of coeducation, but my fear wasn't about being on display as a woman among many males. For me it was about being on display as a black among many whites. There had been a black cheerleader before me and, thanks to her and others, I learned that some of the judges, all of them white, had given me zeros before I even began my routines. Once out in the open, this undeniable racism didn't sit well with the black student community. And there were other racially suspect practices causing unrest—the overall lack of black student representation, the noticeably absent photos of black students in campus publications, campus security stereotyping and hassling black males unnecessarily, students assuming that every black male was there to play some sport, and others. So we protested on the stairs of the Administration Building until Father Hesburgh agreed to meet with us. In addition to hearing our demands, Father Hesburgh "appointed" my black male cheerleading partner and me to the squad. This, of course, jarred the campus, but there I was. At the end of that season I tried out again for the following year. In that second round, not only did I achieve the highest final score of all women participating in the tryouts, my cheer mates looked beyond color to "elect" me as captain.

Another negative experience for me included having to go all the way up to the provost to obtain a grade I legitimately earned—in theology, of all courses. One engineering professor cared enough to sit me down to tell me that I could not be an engineer *and* a cheerleader. I chose cheerleading and American Studies. It could be a lonely life as a black female engineering student at Notre Dame, and I wanted to be able to look back and say, "I was happy at Notre Dame." There were many experiences like this—of blacks having a harder time proving themselves and prevailing in the end. It's the way of our world.

Most importantly, I cherished the deep faith connection that, for me as for many black students, Catholic and not, grew ever stronger. This aspect of my experience supports that I made the right college decision. I am who I am today in part because my adult journey began at Notre Dame.

I got it in my mind early that I had just as much right to be there as anyone. We all felt the same way. And Notre Dame is just as much my alma mater as any alumnus's. There may have been times early on when I felt academically inferior because I was coming from an educational background that was certainly inferior to that of most Notre Dame students. Although my high school was Catholic, it was inner-city and black, with many girls from the projects. So we were short-changed in many ways. My high school didn't even offer a senior math or science class, so I attended a local junior college to take calculus and got a tutor for physics. So while I struggled early at Notre Dame, I graduated with a pretty decent grade point average and have done pretty well for myself.

Notre Dame was never a consideration until my parents brought it to my attention. I had no family affiliation as so many white students do. I still don't. But my husband, Jim Stone (Class of 1981), established a legacy. Two of his four brothers (Dan and Chris) are Notre Dame graduates, as is a first cousin (Mel Tardy) and most recently a distant cousin, Holden Lombard, the first black in twenty years to graduate with a degree in physics. And there are two other relatives of Jim's who attend Notre Dame as current students. My son, Alex Stone, and daughter-in-law, Fatimah, now work at the university. So our family connections are growing, and I hope that Alex and Fatimah have a good enough experience that they won't someday leave with regrets, as so many black faculty, staff, and students do. I want them to have the love for the place that Jim and I have.

There are lots of great things that Notre Dame has become, and I don't have to call them out—they're obvious. I encountered and still encounter some of the finest people in the world there. But I also do not have to point out that racial and ethnic inclusiveness is *not* among those great advancements. In this day and age, I'm not sure why it should still be such a hard thing. As *the* premier Catholic university in the world, we should be at the forefront of what it means to be inclusive and welcoming. Instead, we still put up too many barriers, obstacles, and restraints that make it almost impossible to even remotely reflect the face of the real world. We have many miles to go before we can say that it's a good fit for most black students. I'm not sure we'll ever get there.

I believe first and foremost that Notre Dame needs to define what inclusion means for a school like ours, given our mission. We also need a shared vision of what that looks like in terms of student make-up and environment, and then develop a real strategy to move to a place where we admittedly feel comfortable. Maybe in the end that level of comfort turns out to be right where we are, but at least we'll know.

With all its faults, I consider myself blessed to have attended Notre Dame and will be eternally grateful to my parents. I proudly claim Notre Dame as my own, and I give back what I can because I choose to help the university advance to the extent that it can. I am black Irish, like it or not. (Literally. I completed one of those DNA tests and I am 20 percent of Irish ancestry. Who knew?) That has *got* to be divine guidance for my journey.

RAMONA MARIE PAYNE

(Class of 1980)

---

*Ramona Marie Payne came to Notre Dame in autumn 1976
from Cincinnati. After graduation she spent more than twenty
years in corporate and nonprofit leadership and now has turned
her focus toward writing creative nonfiction. She and her husband, Tony Fitts (Class of 1979), divide their time between
South Bend and Cincinnati.*

THE FIRST STEP IN MY NOTRE DAME JOURNEY WAS TAKEN LONG
before I began my freshman year in August 1976. I keep a photo near
my desk at home. In the photo, there are four girls standing on the
sidewalk between the South Dining Hall and Howard Hall. Three of
them are white. The fourth young woman is black, dressed in a light
blouse and flared skirt, and is holding her purse in front of her. The
photo was taken in 1953, and this young woman is my mother.

This photo reminds me of what I have found to be the two truths
of my Notre Dame experience. One truth is that to be part of Notre
Dame is to be part of a family, with its blessings and challenges. The
second truth is that God's hand was guiding me every step of the way;
He had a plan long before I understood how it would all work out.

My brother Reggie and I visited Notre Dame while we were in
high school. I had a meeting with Dan Saracino in admissions, and he
arranged for a few students to meet with me, even though most were
on break. We walked around the campus and, by the end of the day, I
knew I would apply because of the warm reception I received and the

academic reputation of the university. Notre Dame also made an impression on Reggie; he entered in the freshman class of 1977.

I felt academically and socially prepared for college. I was the only black student in my high school two out of my four years there, so unlike some of my other black Notre Dame classmates, I was immediately grateful to see more brown faces and did not complain about the lack of diversity. I knew there was room for improvement, but it was a more diverse situation than I had had in high school.

Racial diversity was not the only challenge facing Notre Dame during this time. The university was in the fifth year of coeducation and it was grappling with how to address gender issues on campus. In the years since, some of the first alumnae have expressed frustration with what they perceived to be an environment that was not ready for their presence. I did not fully recognize the significance of being in the early coed classes until decades later, because although attending classes with men was not a huge shift for me, it probably explained some of the dynamics I experienced in some of my classes. Most of the mentoring I experienced took place outside of the classroom and not from my professors. In fact, many years after graduation, I had a conversation with a Notre Dame dean who was shocked at my response to his question about which professors had been my mentors.

"No one," I said without hesitation. "The people who encouraged me at Notre Dame were largely staff."

The lack of mentoring by professors had been so counter to my experience in high school that this aspect of Notre Dame surprised me. I had gone to Ursuline Academy in Cincinnati, where both the nuns and the lay faculty were very encouraging and expected that, as women, we would make significant contributions when we embarked on our careers. There were some professors at Notre Dame who provided guidance, but overall my limited interaction with faculty was part of the reason I encouraged my daughter Helena to reach out to faculty when she enrolled at Notre Dame more than twenty years later.

I can thank others on campus, such as Angie Chamblee in Freshman Year of Studies or Barb Hoover, the security guard in my dorm, Lewis Hall, for keeping an eye out for me or being available if I needed to talk. That may not have been mentoring in the traditional sense of the word, but it gave me what I needed.

My primary support came from the friends I made while I was at Notre Dame. I remember the first few weeks of my freshman year so clearly. Most of the black freshmen—men and women—formed a tight bond, and we wandered about the campus together, as if there was strength in staying close to the herd. I remember the walk from Lewis Hall to South Dining Hall, where we ate our meals despite the fact that North Dining Hall was closer. Our dorm rooms even became beauty salons; I had come to campus with two hot combs and a small oven, something that I had to explain to my curious white roommate from New England, who had straight, thick, brown hair.

I also made friends through the meetings and dances in the Black Cultural Arts Center (BCAC) office in LaFortune, in a space that now houses administrative offices. The BCAC sponsored one picnic on a grassy spot near St. Joseph's Lake, another on the Carroll Hall lawn. Some of the white students could not help but stare, watching the group of black students laughing and eating as the sound of Lionel Ritchie singing "Easy [like Sunday morning]" wafted over the trees and the lakes.

Notre Dame gave me a group of women who have been part of my life since my days as a student. I grew up with four brothers and having girlfriends nearby was new for me. From late-night sessions evaluating the social situation or commiserating on the choice of a major or a boyfriend, we have been through some of the best and most difficult of times together. I finally understand what other women mean when they refer to sister-friends, for that is what these women have been for me. We made it through those developmental years of college into the workforce, have been in each other's weddings, seen the births of our babies, and attended our children's baptisms and graduations.

Notre Dame friendships are long-lasting, and when I speak to current students I share with them how close I have remained to my classmates, both the men and the women. But I also let them know that forgiveness and understanding will help in forming relationships while at Notre Dame. The behavior that students display when they are nineteen or twenty should be considered in context. Some came to the university with tough problems from home; others had problems handed to them on campus.

Understanding and compassion, even forgiveness, are traits that God has helped me to develop as part of my Christian walk; I also know that people had to use them with me. When I had this conversation recently with two sophomores, one nodded her head knowingly and said, "I'll remember that."

At Notre Dame I was confident enough to explore a path other than the one on which I originally set out, and the journey has been enlightening. I planned to study biology, possibly pre-med, but found my home in liberal arts—social sciences, art, and literature. After graduation, I worked many years in corporate positions and earned an MBA, but it has only been in the last fourteen years that I found my calling in nonprofit work and the arts.

I recall feeling bad about a test score that was much lower than I had expected and moping around before heading to LaFortune to meet friends. Before I reached the LaFortune stairs the cloudy gray sky had cleared, the sun was shining, and I felt God had given me the gift of a gorgeous day to lift my spirits. Often I would sense that God was encouraging me not to give up, to keep trying. During my time at Notre Dame, I began to know God in a deeper way. Amused at my immature mishaps, proud of my accomplishments and growth, and providing solace during my disappointments—He was always there.

THESE MEMORIES BRING ME BACK TO THAT PHOTO OF MY MOTHER. When I was a student at Notre Dame, I did not know my mother had been to the campus before I enrolled. She gave me that picture thirty years later, when I went back to Notre Dame to work as a development officer. She explained that the photo had been taken when she went to the university for the Catholic Students' Mission Crusade (CSMC), a student group dedicated to prayer, education, and service.

I found out later that my father had also visited Notre Dame twice with the CSMC while he was in high school. They were not dating at the time; that would happen later, when they were in their twenties.

I am amazed that decades before women came to Notre Dame as undergraduate students, and only six years after the first African-American student, Frazier Thompson, had graduated, God already knew these two young black students, my parents, would have two children; a granddaughter, Helena Payne Chauvenet (Class of 2003); a daughter-in-law, Sandra Cole (Class of 1981); and a son-in-law Tony Fitts (Class of 1979) become graduates of Notre Dame. His hand has been guiding our family all along—a nudge here, holding our hands there—and Notre Dame has been a significant part of that walk.

JOLI COOPER-NELSON
(Class of 1981)

Joli Cooper came to Notre Dame in autumn 1977 from Mobile, Alabama. She majored in finance and was an RA in Lewis Hall and president of the League of Black Business Students. After graduation she earned an MBA at the University of Pennsylvania's Wharton School. A founding member of a private equity firm, she has three children. One of them, Ashley Cooke (Class of 2011) is the third generation of the Cooper family to graduate from Notre Dame.

AS I SIT HERE ON THE FIFTH DAY OF NOVEMBER 2013 AND watch my beautiful mother transition to a better place with Our Lord, it's an opportune time to reflect on what the University of Notre Dame has meant to my family and me, because my mother so enjoyed hosting my Notre Dame friends.

The University of Notre Dame literally gave me life, since my parents met while my father (Gary Cooper, Class of 1958) was an undergraduate at the university. I fondly recall his colorful stories about riding in the back of the train from the segregated South to Notre Dame and how all the African-American students on campus could fit into one dorm room!

Fast forward seventeen years and I found myself following closely in his footsteps, arriving on campus in white knee socks and Earth Shoes from my days in Catholic high school in Mobile, Alabama. As the child of a Notre Dame alum, I was very aware of the wonders of the university, but I was eager to experience life under the Golden Dome for myself.

Lewis Hall was my home for all four years and, having gone to a predominantly white high school, my transition to college life was pretty uneventful. I was very involved in extracurricular activities and enjoyed working with Professor Adam Arnold in my leadership role as president of the League of Black Business Students. I traveled abroad to France, Germany, and Amsterdam, enjoyed great summer internships, and mentored young women as a resident assistant during my senior year. For the most part, I found Notre Dame to be a friendly and welcoming environment. The African-American students were an extraordinarily close-knit group due to our small numbers—fewer than twenty-five students in my graduating class— and although cliques existed, my friendships were authentic and key to shaping my positive Notre Dame experience.

I have fond memories of my time at Notre Dame, including many firsts: my first college football game, my first bagel, and my first love. I remember the conversation like it was yesterday, my father bellowing through the phone, "I didn't send you up there to find love—get back to studying!"

But the most wonderful thing that happened while I was at Notre Dame was that I found the love of lifelong friends and the love of service to others. Our Lady's university laid the foundation for my family's legacy of service and love. In terms of creating a legacy of service, I believe Notre Dame was instrumental in helping me define what is good and right in our world and my responsibility for making it a better place. I have always been outgoing, but don't recall being overly involved in community service until I arrived at Notre Dame. I enjoyed being a Big Sister and working with at-risk teenagers. The experience filled me with a sense of gratitude for the opportunities afforded me and, as a result, I have volunteered to serve at every opportunity throughout my life.

I was humbled to be acknowledged for my professional accomplishments and community service as the recipient of the 2002 Wharton Alumnae of the Year award and have served my community as a director on a host of nonprofit boards. My favorite boards include those focused on improving the lives of children, including Academy Prep of Tampa; The Children's Home; Junior Achievement; and Jack and Jill of America, Inc. In addition, I am honored to serve as the University of Notre Dame's alumni schools coordinator and to chair the ND Women Connect initiative.

When I reflect on the meaning of a legacy of love, I think about my family. I treasure the special bond the university has given my family—my father, Gary Cooper; my son, Ashley Cooke III (Class of 2011); and my uncles, William "Billy" Cooper (Class of 1963) and A. J. "Jay" Cooper (Class of 1966). All are Notre Dame alumni and, more importantly, humble servant-leaders, loving African-American men, and great role models. Although we have each followed our individual paths in life, I believe Notre Dame gave us a unified vision on the value of serving a higher purpose. The University of Notre Dame has truly blessed the Cooper family with a legacy of service and love.

Finally, I found the most wonderful friends at the University of Notre Dame. Friendships forged as a young student at Notre Dame have withstood the test of time, spanning decades of life's ups and downs, including marriages, divorces, births, and deaths. I'm blessed to say we have remained loyal friends to one another and to Our Lady's university. What more could I ask for? An immutable faith, loving family, and forever friends. And for these reasons, I truly love the University of Notre Dame.

KEVIN HAWKINS

(Class of 1981)

Kevin Hawkins came to Notre Dame in autumn 1977 from Los Angeles. He majored in psychology and was a member of the basketball team for three years. Since graduation he has worked in Los Angeles, Chicago, and Las Vegas. He currently is a mediation commissioner for the Federal Mediation and Conciliation Service. He and his wife, Karen, have two children and live in Boulder City, Nevada.

TO BEGIN, I TELL YOU WITH ALL SINCERITY THAT I LOVE THE University of Notre Dame. It's funny now, as I reflect upon my lifelong relationship with her, that our relationship is almost like an arranged marriage. From a young age, I and my siblings were imbued by my father, Tommy Hawkins, with his passion for Notre Dame. Our parents dressed my siblings and me in Notre Dame regalia, we learned the "Victory March," and we attended the USC game at the LA Coliseum every other year. We even visited campus and frolicked in the shadow of "Touchdown Jesus." Intended or not, the table was truly set for the love affair.

All this notwithstanding, I can point to one definitive day when the spark in my heart was truly kindled. It was an October afternoon in 1973. I was with my dad watching the Irish play USC on television. Notre Dame had not beaten USC since 1966, the tension was high in a tight game, and the Irish had the ball on their own fifteen-yard line. On the first play from scrimmage in the third quarter, Eric Penick broke off an eighty-five-yard run for a touchdown and the Notre Dame Stadium crowd erupted!

As Chris Schenkel excitedly described the play, the camera panned the roaring, jubilant crowd. Toilet paper was streaming through the stands and the Irish squad was mobbing and celebrating with Penick in the end zone. I was elated and turned to my dad to share the joy. There he was, standing at attention, his hands tight to his sides, chest heaving, tears silently streaming down his face. Confused, I asked him, "Why are you crying? We just scored a touchdown!"

My father just looked at me and said, "Son, it's Notre Dame. I can't explain it to you, it's just Notre Dame."

That moment will always remain a poignant memory, but I did not truly understand what it meant until years after my graduation.

Nearly four years later, in August of 1977, I strode onto the Notre Dame campus with my parents. Not a heralded athlete like my sire, but just another wet-behind-the-ears freshman. I was a member of the first group of students to move into Carroll Hall. Our group was ninety-nine percent freshmen, and quite an assortment of characters. We were a ragtag bunch from all over the country. It was an awesome collection of many different backgrounds, cultures, experiences, and interests. And Notre Dame, in its infinite wisdom, placed an African-American kid from Southern California with a white kid from tiny Whitney Point, a small town in upstate New York. In the months that followed, Bob Hogan and I built up a lasting friendship that remains close to this day. Along with Bob, each of my fellow residents at Carroll Hall touched my life and enhanced my experience at the Golden Dome. We grew up together as young men. We were a family. If there is one word that summarizes my time at Notre Dame, it is "family."

I am glad that I had the opportunity to simply be a Notre Dame student my first year before becoming an intercollegiate athlete. Being a regular guy with everyone else was really special. Believe me: joining the Notre Dame basketball team in 1978 is something I deeply treasure, but I truly believe the friendships and camaraderie I built as a freshman would not have been the same if I had come to campus on an athletic scholarship. People treat you differently as a Notre Dame athlete, and your focus shifts to relationships with your teammates and activities involved with your sport. I believe that not being an athlete my first year afforded me a richer encounter.

You see, I never felt like a "black kid at Notre Dame." I was just a kid at Notre Dame who had brown skin. We were all brothers and sisters; we were all "Irish." For that reason I was not active in the Black Cultural Arts Council (BCAC) and its activities. I felt that separated me from the other students by emphasizing our differences. To be sure, I am proud of the African ancestry in my heritage, but it does not define who I am as Kevin Hawkins. That is one of the things for which I am forever grateful to my parents. They encouraged me to be my own person and walk my own path; they emphasized that I should distinguish myself by the quality of my character, not the pigment of my skin.

This is not to say I did not have some challenging experiences with regard to my ethnicity. After I became a member of the basketball team, I heard some of the local people in South Bend refer to us as "Digger's N-----s." And in my senior year, I was dating a Caucasian underclassman who told me that she needed to stop seeing me because she was getting heat from some of our fellow students, and she was afraid of being branded and ostracized after I graduated and she had to continue on at the university. However, none of that diminishes my esteem for Notre Dame.

Perhaps the most significant experience I had in this regard was on the flip side of that coin. It was with my dear friend and teammate, the late Orlando Woolridge. We were leaving the South Dining Hall one sunny afternoon and heading toward his room in Fisher Hall. Someone was blasting a song by either The Who or Led Zeppelin out of their dorm room window onto the South Quad, and I began to sing along. "O" stopped, touched me on the shoulder and said: "Hawk, I have never really liked brothers who listen to that kind of music, but there's something about you, man." He smiled at me with that magnetic smile of his and we kept walking.

I cannot tell you how much that touched my heart. And I must share how the Notre Dame family stepped up after Orlando's death. Many, many people sent cards expressing love and condolences. There were also generous monetary donations forwarded to his family to help cover medical and funeral expenses. That, ladies and gentlemen, is the soul of Notre Dame.

Academically, I loved that we were all held accountable as students. Performance standards in the classroom were the same for everyone. A special memory I hold as a student is having former university president Father Monk Malloy as one of my instructors.

Because of his special relationship with my dad, Father Ted Hesburgh made time to have an extended personal meeting with me. However, other than that discussion, he did not afford me any other exceptional attentions. In later years I found out that he kept an eye on my progress. But during my matriculation he gave me the space to stand or fall on my own, so I could create my own Notre Dame legacy, outside of the shadow cast by my father. As he touched Tommy Hawkins, so Father Hesburgh touched me.

These recollections are just the tip of the iceberg. There is so much more about my time at Notre Dame that lies below the surface: a lovely birthday party for my brother David hosted by the dear ladies in Breen-Phillips; playing in games and the esprit de corps I continue to share with my teammates, other former players, and my father; being enthusiastically greeted by Keith, a wheelchair-bound fan who greeted, loved, and encouraged us in the tunnel outside the locker room after every home game in the Athletic and Convocation Center; my first fan letter; the Cooks, a South Bend family who made me feel special and welcomed me into their home; connecting and reconnecting with classmates via social media—the list goes on. Truly, for me, Notre Dame is "the gift that keeps on giving."

I thank Father Hesburgh for honoring me with the opportunity to become a Notre Dame man. I thank Digger Phelps for affording me the opportunity to be a collegiate athlete, which allowed me access to the Notre Dame basketball brotherhood. I thank all of my acquaintances, fellow Carroll Hall "vermin," classmates, fans, friends, teachers, and teammates for their warmth and kindness. I am truly humbled by the love they have shown me since 1977.

In September 1987 I was at a friend's house and we were settling in to watch the Irish play Michigan State. He is from Pittsburgh and a big Notre Dame "subway alumnus."

During the pregame show the network began to show clips of Heisman Trophy hopeful Tim Brown and a montage of the proud heritage of Notre Dame football, with the "Victory March" playing in the background. As the intro progressed, all of these memories, people, and experiences welled up and flowed over me like a tidal wave. I began to weep; tears fell like rain. My friend, startled and unsettled, asked, "What's wrong? The game hasn't even started yet!"

I turned to him and, echoing my father's words to me so many years before, said, "I can't explain it to you man. It's Notre Dame, it's just Notre Dame."

JAN SANDERS MCWILLIAMS

(Class of 1983)

Jan Sanders came to Notre Dame in August 1979 from Chica-
go. She majored in biology and was a member of several clubs,
including the Black Cultural Arts Council. After graduation
she earned her medical degree at the University of Illinois. In
1990, she joined the South Bend Clinic pediatric department
and has been a partner there for twenty-three years. She and
her husband, Leo McWilliams, a quadruple Domer, have two
sons and live in South Bend.

THE YEAR 1978 WAS ONE OF THE MOST WONDERFUL OF MY LIFE.
I was a junior honors student at Lindblom Technical High School in
Chicago. As a junior, I was starting the process of deciding the next
phase of my educational career. My parents, Joan and Earl Sanders,
were very influential in this process. They provided sage advice on
how to choose a college. They emphasized making a choice that fit my
personality, my field of study, and school location. We kept it simple
and stress-free and eventually narrowed the list to two: the University
of Illinois and the University of Notre Dame.

I had family and friends who attended these universities. My
sister, Holly, attended the University of Illinois, and close family
friends Daphne and Myrtle Perkins attended Notre Dame. Daphne
Perkins Berry (Class of 1980) and Myrtle Perkins Bell (Class of 1981)
strongly encouraged me to apply to Notre Dame. They mailed the application to me and I immediately filled it out. I placed it on top of our

piano and forgot about it for about six months. It was less than twenty-four hours before the deadline when I mailed it, and I thought all hope was lost. I was pleasantly surprised and very grateful when, several weeks later, I received my letter of acceptance from Notre Dame. I was later invited to visit the campus for spring visitation. It was during this visit that I decided to make Notre Dame my collegiate home.

My decision was based on several factors: the size of the undergraduate student body, the fact that I already had friends in attendance, and the academic reputation of the university. I was particularly attracted to the small class sizes that Notre Dame offered. I did not view the Catholic character of the university or the lack of diversity as a negative. I felt that as a Protestant African-American female, I would have the opportunity to add to the Notre Dame community.

I arrived in August 1979 and moved into Lewis Hall as a seventeen-year-old freshman biology major. I had an excellent experience in the dormitory despite the community bathroom, the slow-moving elevator, and the money-eating washing machines. Lewis provided a great sense of community and camaraderie. There was always a buddy to walk with to class or eat with at the dining hall. It was wonderful to be able to interact with other young women of varying cultures, ethnicities, socioeconomic backgrounds, and religions. Lewis Hall did provide me with many memorable experiences. Pizza sales, screw-your-roommate dances, and post-game parties in the basement were just a few. However, winning the An Tostal mud pit chariot race in 1983 was my highlight and crowning achievement.

The enjoyment of dormitory life, however, was always interrupted by the daily reality of class work and study. I attended Notre Dame with the desire to study biology and the hope of attending medical school. I knew the work would be challenging, but I wasn't intimidated. Rather, I was excited. I accepted the class work as a stepping-stone to my dream profession. I was confident that Lindblom had prepared me well, and I had an excellent group of friends and family supporting me at each step.

Registering for class each semester was one of the most anxiety-ridden exercises I've ever performed or been a part of. What was the nature of the class? How many papers did I have to write? How approachable was the professor? Is there a curve? These were just a few of the questions that were very influential when deciding whether to choose a class or not. Despite this difficult process, I managed to choose several stimulating, thought-provoking, intriguing classes. For instance, my junior theology class, "Women in the Bible," was taught by Professor Elisabeth Schussler Fiorenza. It was an in-depth look from a feminist perspective at the strengths and significant roles women had in the Old and New Testaments. The class was powerful and empowering, and I appreciated Notre Dame for allowing her to express what I viewed as nontraditional opinions. Another note-worthy course was general chemistry, taught by the legendary Professor Emil T. Hofman. His weekly Friday morning seven-question chemistry quizzes were intense, and I quickly understood the meaning behind the phrase "deliver us from Emil."

My freshman seminar and Spanish classes were both taught by the late Professor William Richardson. He was extremely passionate, enthusiastic, and knowledgeable about Latin American culture. I regret that he was the only African-American professor I had during my four years at Notre Dame.

Ironically, my favorite class of my undergraduate experience was perhaps my hardest: organic chemistry. My first organic test was the first that I had truly failed in college. I soon found myself in Professor Jeremiah Freeman's office weekly for tutoring. He was one of the most patient, kind, and encouraging professors I ever had. He saw my determination and helped me become successful in his class. Professor Freeman wrote an outstanding letter of recommendation for my medical school application, and for that I am eternally grateful.

The students in my classes were great, and it was during these classes that I made some wonderful, long-lasting friendships. The most important relationship, perhaps, was the one I formed with my now husband, Leo McWilliams (Classes of 1981, 1982, 1985, 1993)! I don't ever remember feeling intimidated, ostracized, or not accepted by the student body. I felt very comfortable, due to the diverse upbringing I had had in Chicago.

Perhaps my biggest surprise at Notre Dame was realizing that many of my classmates had had no previous contact with African-Americans. I was astonished that I was the first African-American many of them ever met or conversed with. These encounters were not offensive, but I found them amusing and perplexing at the same time. The African-American community during my time at Notre Dame was very small and close-knit. I believe that there were fewer than thirty African-American students in my freshman class. Each of us, I think, felt blessed to be a part of the Notre Dame family.

I graduated from Notre Dame in May 1983 with a bachelor of science degree. I continued my education at the University of Illinois medical school and, after graduation, completed an internship and a residency in pediatrics at Cook County Hospital in Chicago. My Notre Dame education more than adequately prepared me for my training after graduation. In fact, I felt that my first year of medical school was a review of all that I had learned at Notre Dame.

I returned to South Bend in July 1990 after accepting a partnership position at the South Bend Clinic. I could not wait to reconnect with the university. My husband and I decided to become involved in African-American student life and be a support structure in whatever way we could. He became a Black Alumni of Notre Dame board member, and I mentored several pre-med students and had them shadow me in the office. Our involvement over the years with the students has continued to evolve and has become more personal. Many of these students have become our "children." We have supported them by attending their extracurricular events and, among other things, taking them to church, to the dentist, the doctor, the grocery store, the airport, the movies, and out to eat. We have hosted and continue to host students for Thanksgiving and Easter dinners, and sometimes their families as well. Being able to provide encouragement and nonacademic support has really been a blessing for all of us.

In March 1992 and February 1995 I gave birth to my sons, Cheyney and Quinlan. For their entire lives they have participated in and attended various events around campus such as spring visitation luncheons, BA of ND reunions, class reunions, engineering open houses, sporting events, and graduations. They developed a love for the campus and the desire to attend the university beginning in their preschool years. Needless to say, my husband and I were very proud and excited when both of our sons were accepted as undergraduates, Cheyney in 2010 and Quinlan in 2013.

Many people would ask, "If you had to do it all over again, would you choose Notre Dame?" My answer is a resounding "Yes!" I have had the opportunity to witness how the Notre Dame family takes care of its own. I'm extremely grateful and appreciative of all the opportunities that have been given to me as a result of my affiliation with

Notre Dame. I am thankful for the success I've had in my professional life, which is a direct result of my association with Notre Dame. Through God's grace, I've been blessed to take care of not only many children of Notre Dame families, staff, faculty, and alumni, but also those of the general Michiana area as well. It has truly been a privilege to have been associated with such a wonderful community over the past thirty-plus years.

GINA V. SHROPSHIRE

(Class of 1983)

Gina V. Shropshire came to Notre Dame in autumn 1978 from Gary, Indiana. She majored in American studies and French, and studied abroad for one year in Angers, France. After graduation she worked briefly in the corporate world and then became an educator. She currently is an academic advisor in the Mendoza College of Business. She lives in South Bend.

NOTRE DAME FIRST ENTERED MY CONSCIOUSNESS DURING MY French IV class at Andrean High School in Merrillville, Indiana. One of my classmates was passionate about Notre Dame and his buddies would serenade him daily with the fight song. Ultimately this classmate did not attend Notre Dame—his son does—but that experience opened my eyes to an excellent university choice for me.

I entered Notre Dame in the fall of 1978. Our class was about 1,700 students: 25 percent women and maybe 2.5 percent African-American. I came for a good education and I received one. I studied abroad for one year in Angers, France. This was the most pivotal year in my life. I was able to see the United States from the outside in, and I was able to be an "unknown" for one year. Because I did not look like a typical American, the French had no idea who or what I was. The fact that I spoke French fluently baffled them even further. I went "raceless" for one year, an experience that actually taught me more about myself than most would imagine.

I returned to Notre Dame and majored in American studies and French; I was confident that I could go into corporate America with an arts and letters degree. I landed my first job with Philip Morris USA. This was a great start to my career, providing me with solid business experiences. However, after a few years with the company I realized that I did not want to work in corporate sales for the rest of my life. I left Philip Morris in 1986, and returned home to Gary to look for another job.

I started teaching French in August 1986 by complete luck. My mother learned that they needed a French teacher at Andrean High School, and, since I needed a job, I applied, thinking that I would substitute-teach for a few weeks. A few weeks turned into four years in a job that I ended up loving. Teaching ultimately led me to graduate school to study French; I knew I needed to learn more to be a better teacher.

I started my graduate work at Purdue University initially planning to complete only a master's degree in French language and literature. My professors however, were very supportive and encouraged me to stay and complete my doctorate. I did not want to write a dissertation on French literature, so I followed my interests, choosing to study foreign language education and higher education administration for my PhD. I went to Purdue expecting to work hard academically but left with a wealth of experiences in education, which included teaching, serving on Purdue's board of trustees, and filling several administrative positions.

Towards the end of my dissertation, I received a call about a position at Notre Dame as an academic advisor in the Mendoza College of Business. Being practical, I was open to educational administration in addition to tenure-track jobs. This job at Notre Dame worked well for my experiences, and it placed me logistically close to my family in Gary and Chicago. The timing was right, and so I returned to Notre Dame in the fall of 1998.

How does a French teacher relate to undergraduate business majors? Very well, it turns out. Some things about students are consistent and eternal. They wonder: What will I do with my life? I don't know what I want to major in. Can I change my major?

More than simply guiding students through the maze of classes and requirements, this job at Notre Dame allows me to encourage, excite, and expand students' personal and professional views. It puts me in the path of brilliant, dynamic students who often walk into my office knowing exactly what they will study and where they will go after Notre Dame. More importantly, it puts me in the path of brilliant, dynamic students who are struggling to find their own confidence to guide them through Notre Dame. They are all smart; my job is to convince them that they are more than their grade point averages indicate.

Recently, during a meeting with a young lady about her future goals, I thought, "There I am, many, many years ago, with the same doubts and fears." I cannot always tell them why, but I can assure these students that there is a great future waiting for them after Notre Dame.

Notre Dame creates a circle of giving through its network of alumni. I've relished the opportunities to meet my pioneers, especially the African-American men and women who preceded me at Notre Dame. Early in my career at Notre Dame, Alan Pinado Sr. walked into my office. He had seen my photo and name in the atrium of the Mendoza College of Business and came in to ask if I was related to the Atlanta Shropshires. Yes, I replied, and thus, Mr. Pinado and I were connected as friends. Alan was the first African-American to graduate in the Notre Dame MBA program, in 1958.

While visiting from Atlanta, Alan introduced me to Lemuel Joyner and his wife, Barbara, who have become my South Bend family. Lem graduated in 1957 with a bachelor of fine arts, then again in 1969 with a master of fine arts. He has had a long, distinguished career in art, art therapy, higher education administration, and spiritual guidance.

When I listen to Lem's stories about his time here at Notre Dame, I am listening to a devoted alumnus who loves his university. At the end of his senior year at Notre Dame, Lem joined his classmates who went to the Grotto and dedicated their lives to serving the Blessed Mother. And of course, in full-circle fashion, he reminds me that I am also serving the Blessed Mother by helping my students.

As I've met many of the African-American men who truly were our pioneers at Notre Dame, I've tried to collect their stories. I realized their voices had never been heard, and deserved much more attention. Where I would have thought the early African-American students would have been disengaged and bitter about Notre Dame, I have found many like Lem, alumni who remain devoted to Notre Dame. I recognize that there are many angry alumni who have never returned to campus, and their experiences are equally a part of Notre Dame's history. Initially, I plan to write about the men who came to

Notre Dame early and how many of them remain devoted Irish fans! I already know that their voices are coming through; one of my students reminded me of this recently.

A young lady who has struggled in the past with her academics is now joyfully completing her senior courses in her new major: management. She loves the classes and her professors and came in one day to tell me about a presentation she had given. She said, "Dr. Shropshire, I was nervous but I remembered what you told me: 'Just breathe!' That's just what I did—I just breathed and the presentation went well!"

I congratulated her and smiled, because I had told her "Just breathe," just as Lem has told me "Just breathe"—and remember that God works through you. Each day gives me a wonderful opportunity to be back, to reach back, and to give back. Thanks to Our Lady, and Go Irish!

MARGRET LaCHAPELLE SONNIER

(Class of 1984)

Margret LaChapelle came to Notre Dame in autumn 1980 from Houston. She majored in finance and Latin. She was active in the Black Cultural Arts Council, interhall sports, and community and volunteer events. After graduating she earned a law degree and has worked as an attorney and legal consultant for major corporations. She and her husband, Clayton, have two children, one of whom, Dylan, is a 2014 Notre Dame graduate.

I WEAR MY LOVE FOR NOTRE DAME ON MY SLEEVE, MY CHEST, my back, and even on my feet from time to time. Some might say the love affair began before I was born, when my grandfather was first asked to pray for the Notre Dame football team by the Irish priest at the local Catholic church in Louisiana. Yes, I am proud to say that I come from a long line of "church pulpit" or "subway" alums. And as much as I loved the Fighting Irish, my true infatuation with Our Lady's university did not begin until I met Sister Mark Edward Holm in high school.

Sister Mark taught me Latin, but after class we spoke of her time at Notre Dame. She had received her master's degree there. She shared memories of sitting beside the lake to read Emily Dickinson or Thoreau. She spoke of the Grotto as though it was her own private place of meditation and prayer, and of her classes and how brilliant the students and faculty were. She spoke of Father Theodore Hesburgh as a great leader and a good man. She even described the dining hall and how regal it made her feel. I told her simply, "I have to go there."

In August 1980 my parents and I packed the family car full of my most treasured belongings: photos of family and friends; my rosary; my guitar; a cowboy belt with my name on it; my books (works by Langston Hughes, Dr. Martin Luther King Jr., and, of course, Emily Dickinson and Thoreau); and my music albums (Handel's *Water Music*, Switch, Stevie Wonder, Dan Fogelberg, Conway Twitty and Loretta Lynn, Bob Dylan, Joan Baez, Carol King, and Nina Simone).

For years, I had dreamed of the day I would see the Golden Dome with my own eyes. I'd take that step to touch my toe on that holy ground and I would suddenly be transformed into this great intellectual, bobbing along the sidewalks of the campus feeling as though anything were possible. I'd find myself amid students excitedly engaged in debate, their arms moving up and down and their thumbs touching their index fingers as they discussed life, literature, art, and philosophy. What I actually felt was the worst kind of fear imaginable.

I was placed initially in temporary housing at Lyons Hall. There I met two roommates with whom I was to share one small room. It was hot and there was no air-conditioning. In Houston, people just did not live without AC. I wondered how I would survive. I could see my mom's makeup melting as my dad quickly reached for my fan and placed it in the window. Uhhh. Still hot. After the last item was unloaded from the car, I told my parents goodbye. Hug. Take care. I love you. I just remember wanting that painful time to be over quickly. We all managed to get through it without crying. That was a real achievement for my dad. I guess he had cried enough when I received my acceptance letter.

After several hours on campus I had yet to see another black person. I tried not to think about it. I mean, surely I wasn't the only one. Late that afternoon I gathered with other freshmen in the Lyons Hall chapel. There, sitting on the floor, I looked around at the other students. Some were looking back at me. Then I spotted another black student. I couldn't contain my relief. I smiled at her and waved. She looked behind herself to see at whom I was waving. She didn't seem to be as excited to see me as I was to see her. Continuing to scan the room, I noticed yet another black woman. There were at least three of us. Again, I smiled. She smiled back, but quickly set her glance elsewhere. It was then that I realized I might have another problem. These students did not recognize me as black—at least that's what I was thinking at the time. Terror set in. I'd never even thought about how I would be perceived by others at Notre Dame. You see, I grew up as part of a community of people of Louisiana Creole descent. We were every skin color you could imagine, but we were all black. At least that's how we identified ourselves. That's how the South identified us as well. Everyone at home and at high school knew I was black, although it was not unusual for strangers to ask me if I was Mexican, Jewish, or Italian. But just then I felt ambiguous, racially and otherwise. I wondered if there was any way I could fit in on campus. I felt like an odd stranger to absolutely everyone there. But what happened in the hours, days, and years that followed would forever cement my relationship with Notre Dame.

[F]or I was ... a stranger and you welcomed me. (Matthew 25:35)

The people of Notre Dame lived the gospel. Simply put, I was embraced. I was loved. I was valued. I was nurtured. I was accepted. I was included, and we became one. All of us strangers were united in our pursuit of learning about ourselves and others so that we could go out into the world and contribute to the betterment of society.

After that first dorm meeting, I met Joyce Jordan, my big sister from the Black Cultural Arts Council (BCAC). She took me to Lewis Hall, where I met Myrtle Perkins, a resident assistant. Together they introduced me to the virtual UN of denizens at Lewis. Myrt arranged for me to move into a permanent room at Lewis my fourth week of school. But it was hard leaving Lyons after three weeks. I'd already made great friends there. We remained friends even though we were no longer just down the hall from each other. I spent Thanksgiving that fall with my Lyons friends in Bowling Green, Ohio, where they managed to short sheet my bed. One of them spent spring break in Houston with me and my family. As for the friends I met in Lewis and through the BCAC, they became sisters to me. Three of them stood in my wedding. The men became my brothers, looking out for me and protecting me.

Everyone at Notre Dame was so accessible to me as a student. During any given week, I could attend mass with the legendary Father

Hesburgh or schedule a meeting to speak with him. The same was true of Father Joe Carey in student affairs and financial aid; Angie Chamblee, my freshman year counselor; and Father Leonard Banas. Father Banas was my Latin teacher. I loved his voice and the way he pronounced his words, especially Latin words. When he said my last name that first day in class, it sounded like poetry. I adored him. Latin may have been a dead language, but it was resurrected through Father Banas. He brought the Roman writers to life. I'll never forget that, while reading a work of satire by Lucillius in Latin, I translated an ancient criminal punishment as placing burning hot walnuts in a cave. Father Banas roared with laughter. Think of something even more painful than burning your hands, he said. Cave. Opening. Hole. Everyone has one. Oh, my goodness! Why, yes, that would be much more painful.

But most of our classes and the wine (cider) and cheese parties we attended outside of class were filled with an appreciation for the beauty and wisdom of the classical Greek and Roman writers and philosophers. I also remember gathering faithfully to watch the *I, Claudius* series with fellow Latin students each week in one of the small theatres. Such precious and glorious times.

But my life at Notre Dame wasn't all about Latin. There were the football, basketball, and ice hockey games, live concerts, dances, and so many lectures during any given week it was difficult to choose. Through various groups on campus, I was able to meet actors Cicely Tyson, James Earl Jones, Vincent Price, and John Amos, as well as the writer Alex Haley. Yet one of the most interesting people I met while a student was a homeless man by the name of Tom. Through Notre Dame, I participated in a program called Urban Plunge that allowed us to work and live at a homeless shelter for a week or so. Tom introduced himself by saying I could shake any one of his three hands. I was a bit alarmed at first. Suddenly, he lifted his shirt to reveal what appeared to be an extra set of fingers protruding from his side. I told him I preferred to do hugs, and I thought he would squeeze the life out of me. We laughed and, from then on, he took every opportunity he could to tease me during our stay.

At and through Notre Dame, I met and grew to love people with varied interests and of different faiths, beliefs, cultures, identities, economic groups, ethnicities, and orientations. I think they grew to love me, too. One of my friends at Notre Dame had never met a black person before me. We became family almost immediately and we still are. Our love for each other surpassed all socially constructed notions of race or identity. Notre Dame created the environment and opportunity for us to achieve that unity of spirit. I wish the world were more like Notre Dame. One family. United.

ELEANOR M. WALKER

(Class of 1984)

Eleanor M. Walker came to Notre Dame in autumn 1980 from Brooklyn, New York. She majored in biology with a minor in microbiology and sang with the Notre Dame Chorale and Voices of Faith Gospel Choir. After graduation she studied medicine at Washington University in St. Louis and became a radiation oncologist. She currently is director of breast radiation oncology at Henry Ford Hospital in Detroit. She lives in Troy, Michigan.

I AM A FIRST-GENERATION, NON-CATHOLIC, BLACK AMERICAN of Caribbean descent who grew up in a predominantly Caribbean neighborhood in Brooklyn, New York. Attending Notre Dame was somewhat unexpected given that most of the people who were in the science program in my high school attended Ivy League colleges. In fact, Notre Dame was not even on my radar until it was suggested by my college advisor. I knew of Notre Dame only as a college football powerhouse. As a result, when I finally decided to attend, one of my high school classmates asked whether I didn't think that Notre Dame was "beneath" me.

After taking the SAT, I was overwhelmed by the number of letters from colleges and universities suggesting that I apply. So one day in the fall of 1979, I took two shopping bags full of letters to my college advisor's office, poured them out onto his desk and asked *him* to choose the ones I should apply to. Notre Dame ended up among them.

I was admitted to many schools, but my decision came down to Notre Dame and Brown University. I visited both, but I felt very special when Notre Dame called my high school to talk with me about flying out for spring visitation weekend.

I remember getting there on a Thursday evening in April, during what would be An Tostal weekend. It had snowed earlier in the week but was in the 70s when I arrived. As we drove through campus the cab passed the Grotto. It was one of the most beautiful sights I had ever seen. There was snow on the top and all the candles were lit.

The people I met at Notre Dame that weekend were very nice, and many I still call "friend" to this day. My host, Jackie Rucker, was a freshman, and she showed me around campus. Gina Shropshire and Darlene Sowell were sophomores who took me under their wings that weekend. I met many students from New Orleans, many from St. Augustine's High School.

Ultimately it was a matter of money that made the final decision about my attending Notre Dame, but the university's academic reputation didn't hurt. Brown was my first choice because it had a seven-year medical program that I was interested in. But Brown did not follow up on its promise to put me into the program, so I decided on Notre Dame.

Initially I had some concerns about attending Notre Dame and not being Catholic, but I found the religious atmosphere to be a benefit. It blended well with my spirituality, and I felt accepted regardless of my religious belief. I was not uncomfortable at Notre Dame because I had gone to a predominantly white high school. My best friends today, like Sonya (Jones) Penn (Class of 1984), Valerie Walker (Class of 1984), and Lynley Donovan (Class of 1984), are from Notre Dame and are of all ethnic backgrounds.

The most difficult part of going to Notre Dame for me was the transition from the big city of New York to small-town life on campus and in South Bend. Mass transportation as I knew it was nonexistent, and I didn't like the food at Notre Dame. People there didn't even know what a bagel was at that time!

I remember meeting with Dean Emil Hofman in his office for a get-to-know-you conversation. He asked me what I wanted to drink. I told him that he probably didn't have it. He insisted that he did. Well, when I asked for Canada Dry Ginger Ale, he had to admit that he did not have it.

At Notre Dame, I lost the "freshman fifteen" instead of gaining it.

Members of the admissions office staff who were instrumental in recruiting me to ND continued to be supportive throughout my time there. Dean Emil T. Hofman was wonderful to me and supportive throughout my time at Notre Dame. These people believed in me and were invested in my success. Although there was an assistant dean who was very negative with black students who wanted to attend medical school, he did not take that approach with me and actually suggested Washington University in St. Louis, an option I otherwise would not have considered but ended up choosing. I was focused on getting back to the East Coast, but again I ended up at an excellent Midwestern institution.

Because there were very few black pre-med students, my interactions with other blacks in the classroom were limited. But outside of classes I spent time with the black students on campus and also with some of the white students from my classes and dorm. The women in my dorm, the "Lewis Ladies," as we like to refer to ourselves, were very supportive and friendly. We continue to be friends today.

Because of this relationship I didn't miss not being part of a sorority, although it would have been nice to have that option. To me, however, as a pre-med major, it was good not to have to go thru the sorority "line" experience. I was concerned that it might have affected my grades, and I was determined to go to med school.

Given that the university did not have the semester option of abroad studies at that time without losing a year, I also was not able to experience studying abroad, which was something that other students were able to take part in.

The major social issue for a black woman at Notre Dame was dating. Dating options for a black woman were very limited, and not many white men were brave enough to ask a black woman out at that time. Also, the brothers put the "fear of God" into any white guys who showed interest in black women. In fact, in my freshman year I was warned not to encourage a white guy in my class who was very interested in me. Of course, the message was given by one of the few brothers who dated the black women on campus. I actually wasn't very interested in the white guy, but on general principles I went out with him a few times. I couldn't accept that someone had the nerve to tell me not to date a white guy while it was okay for them to date white women!

I do feel that, because of the low numbers of black men on campus, I did not have many choices for a future spouse, given that college is where most people meet their partners for life. I don't think Notre Dame has a done great job of increasing the number of black students on campus. As an alumna I strongly believe that it is part of my job to help in that endeavor and to make life better for the students on campus now.

In general I think that the Notre Dame experience was great for me. I developed lifelong friendships and have had access to a diverse number of people who have helped me as I go through life. It is really as a graduate of the university that you realize what a great influence Notre Dame alums have throughout the country and how that influence can be advantageous in your professional life. I developed a great ability to network well because of Notre Dame. I enjoyed the spiritual aspect of Notre Dame and the fact that the majority of students believed in service. Those things have continued to extend into my life even now. Thru my work with the alumni club in Detroit, the Black Alumni Board, and the College of Science Advisory Council, I have been able to help influence changes at the university.

Would I choose Notre Dame again if I had to do it over? Given the same circumstances, then probably yes.

PHOTO GALLERY

The Black Alumni of Notre Dame black shamrock pin

Notre Dame's starting basketball lineup, 1951–52 (*top to bottom*): Leroy Leslie (F), Don Strasser (G), Joe Bertrand (F), Entee Shine (G), Norb Lewinski (C)

Joseph G. Bertrand on graduation day, 1954

Wayne Edmonds, Class of 1956, first
black football player to earn
a monogram

Wayne Edmonds,
Strong Of Heart honoree,
2012

Lem Joyner in
1957 yearbook

Lem Joyner, artist, presents
his artwork to Notre Dame
president Fr. John Jenkins,
CSC, 2014. Photo courtesy
of Gina Shropshire.

Booker Rice, Class of 1958, Notre Dame
track star (*second from left*)

Tommy Hawkins,
All-American basketball player,
above the crowd

Tommy Hawkins, Class of 1959, receiving his degree from Fr. Theodore M. Hesburgh, CSC

Don Wycliff with his parents on graduation day, 1969

Bespectacled Francis X. Taylor, Classes of 1970 and 1974 MA, at a residence hall birthday party, October 18, 1966

Brigadier General Francis X. Taylor, 2004 Corby Award winner, honored at a 2005 Notre Dame football game

Student Body President David Krashna calling 1970 student strike

Student Body President David Krashna in the president's office

Arthur McFarland, president of the African American Society, on the quad

Ron Irvine, Class of 1973

Manny Grace, Class of 1979, first black Irish Guard

Kevin Hawkins, Class of 1981 (middle, with arms extended upwards), at final home game, 1981

Piper Griffin, Class of 1984; Marguerite (Hazelwood) Keys, Class of 1981; Joli Cooper, Class of 1981; Gina Shropshire, Class of 1983 (*left to right*). Photo by Cheryl Stultz '81.

Yulette George, Christa Singleton, Lisa Boykin (*back row, left to right*), Valerie Waller and Charmaine Phillips (*front row, left to right*), in Walsh Hall, 1987

Opposite top:
Co-captain Byron Spruell (*right*) with co-captain Chuck Lanza and Coach Lou Holtz, 1987

Opposite bottom:
Byron Spruell with wife, Sedra, both Classes of 1987 and 1989 MBA, son Devyn, and daughter Aleah

Opposite, top:
Joli Cooper, Class of 1981
(*second from right*), with
(*from left*) her father, Jerome
Gary Cooper, Class of 1958;
Fr. Theodore M. Hesburgh,
CSC; and her son Ashley H.
Cooke III, Class of 2011

Opposite, bottom:
Jubba Seyyid, Class of 1992,
All-American fencer

Top:
Lisa Honoré, Class of 1992
(*second from left*),
with Notre Dame friends

Bottom:
Bonita Bradshaw,
Class of 1997, with former
basketball coach Digger Phelps

Basketball star Danielle Green, on Senior Night with her grandmother and father

American war hero Danielle Green, with Notre Dame Presidents Frs. Theodore M. Hesburgh, CSC, and Edward A. Malloy, CSC

Carol D. Anderson, Class of 2000 MBA, with her parents at graduation

Lauran and Justin Tuck contributing to the community

Black Domers Jan Sanders, MD, and Eleanor Walker, MD, with MD-to-be
Katie Washington (middle), the first black Notre Dame valedictorian

Football tri-captain Tai-ler Jones (*middle*)

Opposite:
Fiftieth wedding anniversary celebration of Percy and Olga Pierre, August 8, 2015, Washington, DC. *Left to right,* James O. Goodwin, Class of 1961; Jessie Christian, Class of 2014; Ben F. Finley Jr., Class of 1960; Percy Pierre, Class of 1961; Ben L. Finley, Class of 1992; Alphonso Christian II, Class of 1965; Kristin Pierre, Class of 1991

Corey Robinson,
student body president,
2016–17

The only two African-American
Notre Dame student body
presidents, Corey Robinson
(left), 2016–17, and David
Krashna, 1970–71. Photo
courtesy of Gina Coronel
Krashna.

Don and Pamela Wycliff with Notre Dame President Fr. John I. Jenkins, CSC, at a university dinner for Notre Dame scholarship benefactors

Pamela Wycliff, Melanie Chapleau, office assistant to Father Ted, and Gina Coronel Krashna (*from left*)

Don Wycliff, Father Hesburgh, and David Krashna. Photo courtesy of Gina Coronel Krashna.

ROSALIND GAFFNEY

(Class of 1985)

Rosalind Gaffney came to Notre Dame in autumn 1981 from North Babylon, New York. She majored in accounting and played clarinet in the marching band. After graduation, she worked for the accounting firm KPMG in New York City. She and her husband, Eddie, have three children and live in Huntington, New York.

IT WAS A COOL DAY IN APRIL. MY PARENTS DROVE ME TO THE airport for my very first flight. They were nervous, I was excited. I was off to South Bend, Indiana, to spring visitation at the University of Notre Dame. I am a New Yorker, and I had gotten into Cornell University, the Ivy League. I was thinking to myself, "I am just visiting because they offered me a free trip."

I got to the Notre Dame campus late and was staying with a friend from high school. The next day it snowed, rained, and reached seventy degrees. The joke was, "If you don't like the weather, just wait a minute." Long story short, I had the best weekend of my life.

I put down Lewis, Pasquerilla, and Breen-Phillips as my dorms of choice. I was put into Badin Hall. I could not remember where it was. I had spent most of my spring visit on North Quad, where most of the black people stayed. But I am flexible. My parents and I walked up to Badin and it merely looked *old*. I have an older brother and sister who attended state colleges in New York. The dorms were much nicer. This is Notre Dame—what's up with that?

I was in a quad with three other women, two from Illinois and one from Minnesota. Not only was I the only black one in the room, I was the only black freshman in the dorm. Matter of fact, I was the only black freshman female on South Quad! I wondered: Could this be possible? Well, my first plan was to transfer to Lewis Hall, the dorm the black girls were in, as soon as I could. Once again, long story short, I graduated out of the best dorm at Notre Dame: *Badin Hall*!

My roommates were all pre-med, but I was a business major. They gave me the sense that my classes were not as important and as difficult as theirs, that I was not quite as smart. Also, since I was from New York it was assumed I was from the inner-city and was toting a gun or a knife. One day, after a few weeks, I walked into our room and they were all sitting in the front room waiting for me. This did not look pretty.

The conversation began with the proverbial, "We need to talk." They were on one side of the room; I was alone on the other. My defenses immediately went up. They began, "We understand that you are in the band"—I'll get into that in a minute—"and your classes begin earlier than ours, but we need to know where you are. As much as Notre Dame is a safe campus, we should really know where you are during the day and night."

Well, I do not remember much of what was said next because all I could think of was how I was going to tell them to "stay out of my business." Who did they think they were? Last I checked my *parents* lived in New York. But at that moment, I heard one of my roommates say, "Rosalind, what if your father called and we had to tell him we did not know where you were. That we had not seen you all day." Wow! If that ever happened my dad would be in the car and would not stop driving until he arrived in South Bend.

Once I caught my breath, I politely got up and erased what was on the whiteboard above my desk. I put our names on it and began to write out my schedule. I suggested we try to have lunch together every day just so we could catch up. In that moment, I realized these women, whom I had known for only a few weeks, cared about me. Bad things happen everywhere and they wanted to insure those things did not happen to me.

I grew up that day. I am in contact with all three of those women to this day.

I played the clarinet and decided more as an afterthought than anything else to try out for the marching band. Ignorance truly is bliss. If I had realized practices were going to be five to six days a week, I probably would never have done it. Plus I had not played my senior year of high school—I took on extra classes so I could get into Cornell—so I was a bit rusty. But lo and behold, I made the cut. Then it was explained that practices were five days a week and the weeks of home games there would be an early Saturday morning practice. It did not matter if it was ninety degrees out, raining or snowing. Yes, back then, we would practice outside in the *snow*.

I was at Notre Dame from 1981 to1985, so college football fans know those were not Notre Dame's glory years. In my four years, we made it to one bowl game—the Liberty Bowl—and the stadium froze over. The grounds people chipped the ice off the seats onto the ground, so our feet were on ice the entire game. I made it through the Notre Dame winters unscathed. Yet I got frostbite at the Liberty Bowl in Memphis, Tennessee. Sadly, we also lost the game.

But I loved band, and I loved my experience with the band. Since practices were Monday through Friday, it helped me to better organize my days. I traveled to the University of Pittsburgh, Penn State, the University of Missouri, and the infamous University of Michigan. Michigan is a big, scary place if you are a Notre Dame fan. It was especially scary when an overzealous Michigan fan came up to me on my way to the stadium, touched the scarf of my uniform and said, "Eww, Notre Dame." My clarinet section bandmates quickly closed ranks around me and we moved peacefully into the stadium.

I never felt so proud to be a Domer as on Saturday mornings when I put on my uniform and walked to the Administration Building, aka Main Building, for the "Concert on the Steps." Some days I felt like a rock star, with people asking if they could take pictures with me or wishing me luck on our performance.

Once marching band was over, I participated in varsity band (for basketball games). But since the band was split in three for that purpose, I had to play only every third home game. That freed me up for other things, mainly the Black Cultural Arts Festival Fashion Show. My first year trying out, I did it more to support a friend than for my own enjoyment. She did not make it; I did. And I had a blast.

Unbeknownst to me, I had developed a reputation my freshman year as a "no hang." That meant that I did not hang out with black people. I had not realized I had this reputation—I was just busy with band. But after my first fashion show, the rep quickly changed. By my senior year I was president of the black business club and extremely active in planning the Black Cultural Arts Festival. I won the Frazier Thompson Scholarship my junior and senior years. I so cherish those days.

All in all, my four years at Notre Dame were some of the best days of my life. But it only got better. I just knew upon graduation that I would be back for football weekends in the fall and the fashion show in the spring. But life happened. A heavy work schedule, marriage, and kids did not allow me the time to do that. My daughter Genette now denies it, but she made it clear that *she* would not be attending Notre Dame, that Cornell was her top choice. Not wanting to be one of "those" parents, I did and said nothing. However, my mom went to work on my daughter. "What harm can one visit make?" she asked.

My daughter flew out with the intention of telling her grandmother, "I tried." It was Blue/Gold weekend. Two days later I got a phone call. "Mommy, I do not want to leave," Genette said. "I want to see the unveiling of The Shirt!"

Notre Dame certainly knows how to recruit.

For the next four years, with my parents in tow, I went to football games in the fall—yes, Genette also was a clarinet player in the band—and saw the fashion show in the spring—yes, she, too, was in it. She also had the pleasure of spending a semester in Japan (spring semester of course; cannot miss football season). And she became an avid Notre Dame basketball fan, boys and girls.

She wasn't in the best women's dorm on campus, but I suppose Walsh Hall (still South Quad) is a close second. In my four years at Notre Dame, I knew of only one black girl who was in Walsh, and she had transferred there from Lewis in her senior year.

My daughter is currently in law school at George Washington University in Washington, D.C., but she does not miss a Notre Dame football game and is tuned in one way or another to all the Notre Dame girls' basketball games. She even paid to get cable coverage of WNBA basketball, so she could watch the women she graduated with in 2013.

Both of us are disappointed with the rate at which blacks have been accepted at Notre Dame over the past twenty-five years. While the percentage of women has increased, the percentage of blacks has not increased as much. But we both enjoyed our Notre Dame experiences and are reaping the benefits of a quality education.

Oh, by the way, none of my roommates graduated pre-med, but I did graduate with a bachelor of business administration in accounting and got offers from six of the then Big Eight accounting firms. I guess all I have left to say is, "Sorry, Cornell. Go Irish!"

MELVIN TARDY

(Classes of 1986, 1990 MBA)

---

*Melvin Tardy came to Notre Dame in autumn 1982 from Mil-
waukee. He majored in studio art. After graduation, he taught
math and was a freelance artist/musician for two years. He
then returned to Notre Dame and earned an MBA. Since then
he has served as an admissions counselor and first-year academic advisor at Notre Dame. In 2011 he was ordained a
permanent deacon of the Catholic Church. He and his wife,
Annie, live in South Bend.*

ONE OF MY FONDEST NOTRE DAME MOMENTS CAME—NOT
surprisingly—at my first Notre Dame football game. The setting was
surreal—the first night game in Notre Dame Stadium history, September 18, 1982. The marching band featured its first trumpets (including
me) in Aaron Copland's "Fanfare for the Common Man" at halftime,
playing to a crowd of thousands and a national TV audience.

With the Notre Dame crowd chanting "Anthonyyyy, come out
and play-aay" (referring to Anthony Carter, the University of Michigan's star receiver) and "We—Are—N—D," Gerry Faust kicked off
his second year as head coach with an inspiring victory over the
Michigan Wolverines. Our band concluded the evening with a post-
game march through campus to the Golden Dome. Suddenly I was
hoisted high into the air and onto the shoulders of my madly cheering freshman roommate, Billy Mitchell, and other friends. In that unexpected moment of camaraderie, I finally felt that I might belong at
Notre Dame.

Nine months earlier I was so sure I *didn't* belong that I missed the admission application deadline—on purpose. My parents persisted, calling admissions for an extension. I spent Christmas break applying to a school in which I had no interest.

Being in the top 2 percent of my senior class at Brown Deer High School in suburban Milwaukee, I had high aspirations. Although my cousin Jim Stone had been a star running back on Notre Dame's football team and we had attended his Notre Dame commencement the previous year (1981), I wrongly assumed that a university could not excel in both football *and* academics. I even told my parents: "I don't want to go to Notre Dame; I want to go to a *good* school!" My discernment was further tainted by memories of overly strict disciplinarians and overt racism at Catholic elementary and middle schools that I'd attended in my native home, New Orleans.

I didn't want Notre Dame, but it apparently wanted me. Once I applied, Notre Dame invited me to visit at the university's expense—the only university to do so. That stoked my interest. In February, a friendly, bearded admissions counselor named Pat Leonardo met me at the bus station and brought me to Grace Hall. My overnight hosts were from St. Augustine, the well-known black Catholic high school in New Orleans. Admissions probably assumed they would be the perfect hosts. It probably *didn't* anticipate their saying, "Don't come here; we hate it. Go somewhere else!" At least they added that Notre Dame was a great place to be *from*, if not *at*. Oddly, such candor was a draw—I felt that they at least cared about me as a person. I was becoming more intrigued.

I appreciated the warmth of my hosts and their clique of black friends. During the visit, whites were ever-present, but anonymous. In my suburban high school, the opposite was true. Blacks were present, yet anonymous—bused in from a different world: inner-city Milwaukee.

Notre Dame's acceptance letter finally arrived, filling my family with pride. Yet, despite a generous financial aid package, I broke their hearts: I decided to pursue engineering with my friends at the University of Wisconsin–Madison. My mother looked me in the eyes and made one final pitch: "Why don't you try Notre Dame for a year? You can always transfer if you don't like it."

So I enrolled, fully intending to transfer after one year. Notre Dame was, in effect, on probation.

Marching band tryouts were held a week before orientation. I braced for competition, but instead found encouragement. Everyone— my dorm rector, band section leaders, even fellow trumpeters— welcomed me with phrases like "Notre Dame family." I even wound up in Grace Hall, the dorm familiar from my visit. As in high school, whites were main stage and blacks were anonymous; that is, until the night I met my quad mate: John Simmons.

On paper we were a perfect match: two black engineering intents who had run cross country at Midwestern high schools. Yet one awkward handshake was enough to expose differences. I was a Catholic introvert from a white Milwaukee suburb, raised by opera-singing parents from New Orleans. He was an extrovert, a dark-skinned Baptist raised by his mom on the rough South Side of Chicago. I was a gifted trumpeter, he a gifted basketball player. Beyond family, I felt more comfortable around whites than blacks; John, however, was unashamedly proud of his black identity.

When I made the band, the band made me. It served as my orientation to Notre Dame tradition: the sense of community, the musical traditions, and, of course, pep rallies and Notre Dame football weekends. Band members ate together, we hung out together, and some folks were lucky enough to develop romantic relationships. The band also exposed me to pre-rallies: drinking parties that preceded pep rallies. Like many blacks, I didn't drink—not to get drunk, anyway. My white bandmates's vulgar drinking songs, European in origin and tinged with subtle racism, soured my taste for band as the year progressed. (Maybe band directors drank, too. During one visit to the band office, the beloved jazz director, who rarely spoke directly to me, suddenly exclaimed, "That's *your* kind of music, isn't it!" In my hand I held a Haydn concerto, but then I heard it: gospel music was on the radio. Feeling uncomfortable, I tried to ignore him. "That's *your* kind of music, isn't it!" he repeated.)

Despite our differences, John and I quickly bonded. John felt obliged to orient me to the "ebony side" of Notre Dame. He dragged me to dinner at South Dining Hall, where many from our record-setting class of seventy-three black frosh were eating. It was my first experience at "the black table." Similarly, we attended a "welcome back" barbecue for black students. Friendly faces from February's visit smiled and said: "Oh, you made it here, huh!"

In essence, I was oriented to two Notre Dames—the visible white one and a hidden black one. I learned of white traditions like An Tostal (including togas, chariot races in the mud, and keg tosses) and black traditions like the Black Cultural Arts Festival (a week of black history activity, culminating in *the* black social event of the year: the BCAF Fashion Show). I learned that white parties promoted binge drinking, but black parties emphasized dancing. Unfortunately, I didn't drink and I couldn't dance!

John's presence made the visible invisible and the invisible visible. Where two or more of us blacks gathered, whether walking across campus or at the black table, even my closest white bandmates no longer noticed or acknowledged me. To them, I suddenly became invisible, anonymous. Conversely, John helped make me and mine visible to myself. Through John, I became more aware and appreciative of my race—of our diversity, creativity, and struggles. I began to appreciate the quick nod or "wassup" to fellow blacks in passing—confusing to whites, but to me a sign that I was no longer anonymous and distant to my own community. Though awkward and confused, I belonged; I had joined the struggle.

This is not to say that whites didn't struggle to fit in or to succeed academically, but there were unique qualities to the black struggle. All black folks were regularly obliged to step in and out of the two Notre Dames, often without realizing it. No matter our background or how we perceived our identity, blacks could never stay comfortably hidden in the white world of Notre Dame. Whites wouldn't allow it. Every day, someone would do or say something that would remind you of your blackness, of your differentness.

For example, Notre Dame security racially profiled me, asking for my ID to prove I was a Notre Dame student, or demanding that I lock and unlock my bike chain to prove the bike was mine because "we've had a lot of reports of bikes being stolen." Halos of empty chairs surrounded me in classrooms as people hesitated to sit next to me. One sunny warm day, I coaxed a handful of white section mates to join me outside for ultimate Frisbee. Once outside, they instead lay coldly on the grass to suntan for an hour, never warming up to the idea that I had been left out of the "communal" activity to which I had invited them. You see, the privilege of being white is that they never had to step out of their world, from the moment they set foot on campus until they graduated, unless they chose to do so.

Blacks, however, had no choice. When I struggled academically and tried to join tutoring or study sessions, white students questioned my SAT scores and white faculty and advisors encouraged me to switch out of engineering. When I confided in a seemingly compassionate rector or resident assistant about racism, their hearts sided with the perpetrators, insinuating that perhaps I was "misreading" or "exaggerating" the situations. Eventually, even my Catholic faith suffered. I rarely encountered black peers at mass—many were not Catholic and some even chastised my "white" faith. Meanwhile, I became disenchanted by the hypocrisy of white students *and* priests. To have a white peer profess their Catholic faith on Sunday, only to refer to your black roommate as a "nigger" on Monday, is enough to make you question that faith.

In truth, Notre Dame merely reflected the social order of the times. The civil rights movement—and in its wake integration, affirmative action, busing, and other social initiatives—had awakened black consciousness and opened the doors of opportunity, but they also had led to "white flight" away from all of this and the creation of the suburbs. Many blacks were first- or second-generation college students, "movin' on up" like television's *The Jeffersons*—not just to the Brown Deers and Notre Dames of the world, but also to our first real experiences of life as a "minority."

We were trailblazers. My parents had their first-generation college experience at Xavier, a fine, Catholic, historically black institution, and they did what they could to encourage and support me, but Notre Dame was different. There were virtually no visible African-American administrators, advisors, advocates, alumni, clergy, faculty, rectors, or other people in authority to call upon for advice. The black adults I saw—cooks, janitors, the elderly doorman at the Morris Inn—they always had a smile and a word of encouragement. Beyond that, however, as "minority" students, all we had were each other.

But even so, there were casualities. John and I, like many blacks, did not survive tech programs like engineering. Far too many of us didn't survive Notre Dame at all. John himself left after sophomore year. As for me, I began the year by putting Notre Dame on probation, but the year ended with me on probation—academic probation. My goal to transfer? I couldn't—no prestigious college would accept my low grade point average. I felt like a failure—academically, socially, and spiritually. I felt like I had let my family down—parents, grandparents, aunts. I even felt like I had let my people—my race—down. Oddly enough, it never occurred to me that perhaps Notre Dame had failed *me*.

Ultimately learning how to survive, I graduated with my class in four years, in 1986. Two years later, I returned to Notre Dame and earned an MBA in international finance. Notre Dame was indeed a great place to be from, so I joined, first, the admissions office, to recruit more African-American students, and later, the First Year of Studies, to help those students in that critical first year. I tried to provide the things I had longed for during my own Notre Dame journey: someone to help them understand and negotiate the journey; someone to help them stay true to their faith and values; someone to believe in their lofty goals; someone to help Notre Dame become a special place to be *at*, not just from—a place to *thrive*, not just survive.

In truth, many small, insensitive acts marred my Notre Dame experience; so, too, did small gestures accumulate to redeem it over time. The summer after my first year, I earned my first "A" at Notre Dame—in calculus, my toughest subject. My professor, Alan Howard, gave me hope—that I could succeed academically at Notre Dame, that Notre Dame had professors who actually cared about my success.

In his class I met a white kid from London named Andy Beaulieu. He seemed subtly different—humble, encouraging—and we could even study together. We became close friends. One day, while we walked along US 31 to a Roseland movie theater to see *War Games*, a cold chill gripped my spine as someone in a passing vehicle suddenly yelled "NIGGERRRR!"

Before I knew it, Andy went ballistic, retaliating with choice words of his own as the car sped off. I'd experienced such things since childhood, but it was new to this white kid from London. In a way, it became funny, because I spent the next twenty minutes calming Andy down!

For a brief moment, Andy was in the struggle; he was a common man like me. And it felt so very good to have someone to walk with on the journey.

Byron O. Spruell

(Classes of 1987, 1989 MBA)

Byron Spruell came to Notre Dame in autumn 1983 from Cleveland, Ohio. He majored in mechanical engineering and was a co-captain of the football team in 1987. He also earned an MBA at Notre Dame in 1989. After a long career in consulting, he recently became president of league operations for the National Basketball Association. He and his wife, Sedra, Classes of 1987 and 1989, live in Chicago with their two children.

SEEMS SIMPLE NOW, BUT LIFE'S JOURNEY IS NOTHING MORE than the collection of experiences, influences, events, and relationships that are put in your path and impact who you are. As an eighteen-year-old student setting foot on Notre Dame's campus to begin my collegiate experience, I had no idea it was that simple. But I certainly know now that all of this was meant to be—my destiny, so to speak.

I was born in Cleveland, Ohio, to wonderful, role-model, working-class parents, Walter and Eva Ray Spruell. My two older siblings and I were brought up very middle class (not poor, not rich, simply middle-class Americans) with the family motto of "Always do your best" with your God-given talents and abilities. Beyond that, all my folks ever wanted for us was to do better than they did. They were proud, hard-working, intelligent people without college degrees, which at the time wasn't a setback but instead a key driver of their desire for their children to get a college education.

My older sister, Toni, was the first in our family to earn a college degree and was a trendsetter from that perspective. She remains another great role model for me. My older brother, Selwyn, "dabbled" in higher education but never completed the mission.

Being blessed with academic *and* athletic abilities, I excelled in the classroom and in sports. (I even was a gymnast in my early days). My first love in sports, growing up in Cleveland, was actually basketball. But being six-feet, five on my high school team in those days equated to playing the center position with my back to the basket; today, being six-feet, five means being a tall guard. From a Division I scholarship perspective, it became very clear that I was best positioned on the gridiron, and I was groomed as such by my high school coach and mentor, Mr. Jeff Black.

As it turned out, I was recruited across the country. But I wanted to stay relatively close to home so my folks could see me play. I also wanted to pursue an engineering degree, given my love for math and science (and thanks to a sixth-grade teacher who had put into my mind that that's what I should be one day). Exploring many options, including Ivy League schools, I narrowed my choices to Notre Dame, Ohio State, Michigan, West Virginia, and Vanderbilt. Following my official visits, the choice was clear not only for me but also for my mother, whose only concern was that I would convert to Catholicism after being raised Baptist.

Graduating from high school as a co-valedictorian, I ultimately chose the University of Notre Dame because of the excellence and balance in academics and athletics, the tradition, the environment (which was similar to my high school experience), the spiritual mission, and the "stretch." Notre Dame was the place that would challenge or stretch me the most both on and off the field, and it would have been the biggest stretch for my family to afford, but for the athletic scholarship.

For me, ND was the best of all worlds and I felt very prepared for what was to come, even though I had no connection to the university beyond my family's recognition of the brand, Coach Black's diligence, an influential visit from Coach Gerry Faust, a short recruiting trip, and a talk with the Golics and a couple other Notre Dame–connected families from the Greater Cleveland area.

From freshman year (when I was redshirted due to a knee injury) to graduation, I never felt like an outsider and I completely enjoyed and still cherish my ND experience. I have maintained relationships with my teammates, coaches, classmates, professors, faculty, and staff. I am a proud "Double Domer" with a bachelor of science in mechanical engineering (thanks, Ms. DeBerry) and a master of business administration. On the field I learned many life lessons, including how to work through adversity with a nagging high-school knee injury. That early setback turned out to be a true blessing in disguise, as I moved from defensive line to offensive line the spring of my sophomore year and would later start at offensive line for Coach Lou Holtz during my last two years of eligibility and serve as co-captain with Chuck Lanza in my final year.

Playing for Coach Holtz was an amazing experience, and he is still a mentor and a "coach for life" to this day. He is committed to his players and has always lent an ear to help me focus on What's Important Now (WIN) in life's journey and the Trust, Love, and Commitment (TLC) you should have for and expect from any organization you are part of. He certainly instilled these key principles in his players on the gridiron and invested in us as productive citizens in society beyond.

My Notre Dame experience came with a bonus—a major one, indeed—as it was there that I met my best friend, partner, fiancée, and future wife. Sedra Walton and I met during our freshman year. We dated throughout our collegiate days, doing both undergraduate and graduate work. She also is a Double Domer, with a BS and MS in aerospace engineering. We were inseparable then, and over twenty-six years of marriage have so much to be thankful for, including two wonderful kids: Devyn, who is pursuing his business degree and playing football at ND, and Aleah, who is exploring future collegiate opportunities and playing basketball at St. Ignatius College Prep in Chicago.

Notre Dame played a big part in our development as individuals, as a couple, parents, and productive citizens. The only "dispute" we chuckle about—and a close colleague continues to point out—is that Sedra is listed on the ND Alumni site as the most notable alumnus in our family despite great achievements in both of our careers!

Sedra now directs "mission control" in the Spruell household following an outstanding career at United Space Alliance as a guidance, navigation, and control Space Shuttle flight controller at Johnson Space Center in Houston. Yes, I married a rocket scientist!

As for me, I always desired to utilize my engineering and business skills in some form or capacity. Despite dreams of being a design engineer at an automotive company or a professional athlete at some level, I started my career in consulting at Peterson Consulting, which is now a part of Navigant Consulting, headquartered in Chicago. For seven years Peterson provided me with a great opportunity to grow, develop, and contribute as a litigation-support practitioner and to apply my technical and business skills.

My consultative, business development, managerial, and leadership skills were further enhanced at the multifaceted, global brand of Deloitte. During a transformational twenty-year journey at Deloitte, I learned about myself as a leader and about organizational dynamics, including leadership, tone at the top, global business, apprenticeship, operations, and innovation, in a fast-paced, inclusive environment. In this model, I learned so much from my mentor and colleague, Barry Salzberg, who, among others, shaped and groomed me for success. It was Barry who "took a shot" on me and provided more stretch opportunities to make me the best leader I was capable of being. His care, diligence, focus, tenacity, intelligence, and preparation are characteristics I emulate every day to make an impact.

My professional coach, Dennis Perkins, often says, "Byron, you've been the beneficiary of incredible sponsors and catalytic moments. All you need to do is continue bringing the best of Byron to any situation and you will continue to succeed and contribute greatly to any organization."

I am grateful for Barry and Dennis and hope that at my newest employer, the National Basketball Association, this next chapter lines up for a storybook ending. Talk about a real and true dream job— this is it! As president of league operations with a focus on the integrity and future of the game, I'll be employing my skills, experience, and passions for sport and excellence. Given what I have experienced already, I expect to be adding Commissioner Adam Silver, Deputy Commissioner Mark Tatum, and other new colleagues to that growing list of sponsors, mentors, coaches, and influencers on my career journey.

So let me end where I started: with a simple "thank you" to my parents; my siblings; my coaches, sponsors, mentors, and colleagues;

and to my wife and kids. They have been the influences who have shaped the catalytic moments, events, and experiences in my life.

Notre Dame has been a huge part of my life's journey, from the time I first stepped foot on its beautiful campus as an aspiring freshman to today when I walk the campus as a graduate, former student-athlete, and member of the Notre Dame board of trustees. I look forward to leveraging my ND experience and being a positive influence and mentor to others who choose to walk a similar path.

LISA MARIE BOYKIN

(Class of 1988)

---

*Lisa Marie Boykin arrived at Notre Dame in autumn 1984
from Sumter, South Carolina. She majored in government and
philosophy and was the president of the Black Cultural Arts
Council (BCAC) her sophomore year. After graduation, she
lived in Paris, France, where she obtained a master's degree in
international relations and then went on to earn a law degree
from NYU School of Law. Today she's an attorney at Disney/
ABC Networks Group in Burbank, California.*

THE HEADLIGHTS FROM A PASSING CAR BRIEFLY ILLUMINATED
my driveway as I approached my house on Otsego Street. I had just
returned from the Notre Dame law library, where I had spent a long
day studying for what would be my last undergraduate final exam. I
knew I wanted to be a lawyer one day, and studying in the law library
made me feel one step closer to my dream. It was at the law library
where I met Granville Cleveland, the black law librarian, who knew
of my aspirations and always greeted me with a smile and an encouraging word.

That night, I felt awash with a sense of pride. The end was in sight.
Suddenly, out of the darkness came one ugly, angry word — "Nigger!"
My mouth dropped open in disbelief. I stared blankly into the distance until the car disappeared. This is my most vivid memory of the
events surrounding my graduation from Notre Dame.

In the days that followed and frankly in the years since then, I
struggled to reconcile my feelings about Notre Dame. There were

moments when I felt incredibly proud to be a Domer and moments when the racial indignities and misogyny I experienced on campus made me deeply resent Notre Dame.

Born in Philadelphia and raised by my grandparents in the suburban Main Line area, I moved to South Carolina at the beginning of my freshman year of high school when my grandparents retired. The first college application that landed on my grandparents' dining room table was from Notre Dame. I applied early admission and found out in December of my senior year that I had been admitted. I was sixteen. To say that my grandparents were elated would be an understatement. Born in the rural and segregated South in 1911 and 1916, respectively, earning a college degree from a school like Notre Dame was unimaginable for them. My gaining admission to Notre Dame was an answered prayer, and my grandmother, as black folks would say, was a "praying woman."

I had never been to South Bend and did not know anyone who attended Notre Dame. At the urging of my high school guidance counselor, I also applied to Spelman College. That way, she reasoned, I would have options in case I changed my mind about going to this school that was no more real to me than a beautiful brochure filled with pictures of happy white students. I've often thought how different my experiences might have been had I chosen an all-black women's college like Spelman instead of an overwhelmingly white and male university like Notre Dame, but that was not to be.

A few months later, the Admissions Office invited me to visit Notre Dame during An Tostal, one of the biggest celebrations on campus. Phyllis Washington Stone, who was then working in admissions, warmly greeted me on campus and showed me to Lewis Hall, where I stayed with seniors Piper Griffin and Hester Agudosi. Lewis Hall was where most of the black girls lived and I quickly made a lot of friends. I met Valerie Waller and Charmaine Davis, both freshmen at the time, who showed me around campus and took me to my first BCAC party in LaFortune. After a few days on campus and seeing what became my favorite place—the Grotto—I was hooked.

I met Marty Rodgers that weekend and he seemed to get a good laugh out of my enthusiasm for Notre Dame. His father and siblings were Domers, so being on campus was nothing new to him. He could see that I had just drunk the proverbial Kool-Aid. In large volumes.

That fall, my grandparents loaded me into our green station wagon with wood paneling and drove me from Sumter to South Bend. I ended up in Walsh Hall instead of Lewis. By the time I unpacked my Tina Turner, Wham!, and Culture Club albums, I realized that I was the only black woman in the dorm. Notre Dame was a tough environment. I was one of ten black women in a class of about two thousand.

A few days in, I met Christy Conklin. The first time I saw her, she was sitting on the floor near the entrance of Walsh Hall. She was smoking a cigarette. I thought this was the most epic display of courage and badassery. Nobody smoked in Walsh, or at Notre Dame for that matter (at least not openly). She did not care. I could go on about her progressive views, how she bucked tradition and challenged authority. It takes a lot of courage to be your own person and to resist the temptation to conform.

I thought instantly when I saw her that she was someone I should know. I introduced myself that day. We've been friends ever since. Knowing Christy at Notre Dame gave me the courage to be myself and to not shrink because I was different. I might not have expected to learn that lesson from a white girl whose privilege and family background easily shielded her from being an outsider, but that is one of many great ironies about my experiences at Notre Dame.

When I walked into my first class, English literature, I was the only woman. It was twenty-five white guys and me. Back then, no one thought how daunting it might be for a seventeen-year-old black girl to be the only female and person of color in a classroom. The student body was probably one-third female. I still remember my professor's name: Katie Conboy. She had long dark hair, and she was brilliant. I might have had three female professors during my four years at Notre Dame. Katie was daring just like Christy, and with unspoken solidarity, we supported each other in what was a challenging environment for a woman.

At the end of my sophomore year, tired of being the only black woman in the dorm, I asked to pull in four other black women: Valerie Waller, Charmaine Davis, Christa Singleton, and Yulette George. Sister Jo, the rector, cited a rule against pulling in more than one roommate. The five of us wrote a passionate appeal about the need for diversity and inclusion in Walsh and why we would not only be exemplary additions to the dorm but would also be role models for the other students. Later, Sister Jo called a meeting with us and her four RAs, who methodically refuted each point in our appeal letter, making us feel very unwelcome.

That's when we took our case to the highest authority, Father Ted Hesburgh. He immediately intervened and reversed Sister Jo's decision. He understood exactly why having other black women in the dorm was important. I will always be grateful to Father Ted for his kindness and for standing up for us in that situation. Somewhere in my garage, I still have the letters sent to me and my roommates (anonymously, of course) at 103 Walsh Hall addressed to "The Black Family." Undeterred, we thought that was funny.

During my senior year, I met Professor Derrick Bell, the first black tenured professor at Harvard Law School. Along with Thurgood Marshall, Constance Baker Motley, and Robert L. Carter, Derrick had worked at the NAACP Legal Defense Fund in the 1960s, arguing over three hundred school desegregation cases in the South. Father Ted invited Derrick to speak at a civil rights conference at Notre Dame. My government professor, Dr. Luis Fraga, handed me a copy of Derrick's book, *And We Are Not Saved*, and told me to show up for a luncheon the next week. I was seated next to Derrick who, by the time lunch was over, was encouraging me to go to law school.

By then, I already had plans to attend graduate school in France. We kept in touch, and when I left Paris to return to the United States, Derrick was at NYU School of Law. I would not have gone to NYU Law or become a lawyer had I not met Derrick Bell. We remained close until his passing in 2011, and to this day, his widow, Janet Dewart Bell, is like a mother to me.

My sophomore year, I had the good fortune of meeting Rev. Charles Kannengiesser, a French Jesuit priest who was my CORE literature instructor. Charles was my guardian angel both at Notre Dame and during the two years after graduation when I moved to Paris with his help to pursue a master's degree in international relations. Charles took me under his wing (literally) during my senior year. He invited me to live in an apartment in the lower level of his comfortable home on Otsego Street, where I thrived despite the strangers who, under cover of darkness and in ignorance, hurled ugly words from passing cars.

Although I've been conflicted about my feelings for Notre Dame, two things are for sure: I received an outstanding education and made lifelong friendships that shaped who I am today. I met Ben Finley my sophomore year in 1985 when he came to campus for those early meetings that led to the formation of the Black Alumni of Notre Dame. He's been like family ever since. In 2014 I went to Christy Conklin's wedding in Ireland, bringing our Notre Dame friendship full circle. I'm the godmother to Valerie and Steve Waller's oldest daughter—what a blessing. I'm also privileged to work at Disney with Manny Grace, whose goodness makes me smile. Father Ted, a tireless fighter for social justice, inspired my activism, as did Monk Malloy, whose open door and kind heart endears him to everyone. Living in Paris changed my worldview and that's because of Charles Kannegiesser. I would not be a lawyer had Father Ted not introduced me to Derrick Bell, and that would not have happened had I not gone to Notre Dame.

All roads lead back to Notre Dame, and I am the better for it. It may at times feel alien, but it's home.

MARTIN RODGERS

(Class of 1988)

Martin Rodgers came to Notre Dame in 1984 from Blue Bell, Pennsylvania. He majored in economics and was active in numerous initiatives aimed at fostering campus diversity. Since graduation he has worked in business, government, and the nonprofit sector. He currently is a managing director of Accenture and is a Notre Dame trustee. He and his wife, Monette, live with their three children in Falls Church, Virginia.

LEGACY.

I am one.

It is a gift inherited through no action of one's own. It is knowing that I am the result of those who came before, those who endured so that I might endeavor.

My father, Dr. William H. Rodgers III, was one of the first African-Americans to graduate from the University of Notre Dame, in 1955. We still do not know exactly why Dad chose ND over Yale. But if I had to guess, I believe it was because of the sense of place and because of the rituals and discipline and values embodied in the university's Catholic character that reminded him of the many Catholic boarding schools and summer camps he was shipped off to as a result of coming from a broken family.

My brother John graduated in 1978 and my sister Cheryl in 1980, in one of the earliest classes of women. She would say to this day that the gender challenges then were even greater than the racial challenges.

My father always loved Notre Dame. It was while there that he and the other handful of African-American students were warmly welcomed into the home of Lafayette "Dusty" Riddle and his wife Sedocia, on nearby St. Peter's Street. "Dusty" was his nickname because of the cloud of dust that arose as he stole second base. He was well known in South Bend as a player-coach-manager of at least a couple of different local and traveling Negro League baseball teams, including the Studebaker Coloreds. Family legend has it that Coach Frank Leahy saw him play and dropped him a letter saying he was saddened that the Majors were segregated and he could not play professionally. With only a fourth-grade education but a whiz at math, he became the first African-American uniformed police officer walking a beat in South Bend. He would later go on to work in city administration, and was said to be the only person in town who could fix the voting machines of the day.

Besides his own gregarious nature, Dusty's home was popular with the young African-American Notre Dame students, including my dad, because he also happened to have three beautiful daughters, the youngest of whom, named Charlotte, Pop would fall in love with and marry. So I am a legacy not only of Notre Dame but also of the wonderful townspeople of South Bend, who rose up to support those early African-American students. To this day, Mom still has an old *Ebony* magazine article featuring early African-Americans attending Notre Dame and how the community helped them.

My own Notre Dame experience and that of my siblings would be part of "coming home," not just to Notre Dame but also to South Bend and our beloved grandmother Sedocia and our aunts and uncles and cousins. Said another way, I am as much a product of St. Augustine's Catholic Church in South Bend, where so many of the priests aided African-American students and supported the long and hard fight for racial equality, poverty alleviation, and social justice in South Bend that still continues today, as I am of the Basilica of the Sacred Heart and of my dorm Fisher Hall's chapel. St. Augustine's is where my parents got married and my relatives still attend each Sunday.

Legacy.

It is the very small mark I hope to have left behind as a student and now as an alum.

After my first semester, I wanted to transfer from Notre Dame. I was miserable. My class was simply awful in terms of diversity, with, if memory serves, thirty-two black students out of some 1,800. I had been on campus dozens of times, but I suddenly didn't feel I fit. My dad asked me to stick with it a while longer and admonished me with the cliché that you are either part of the solution or part of the problem.

So I did some research, put pen to paper, and, after attending the Black Cultural Arts Festival (BCAF) Fashion Show, wrote an opinion piece in the *Observer* constructively criticizing Father Hesburgh and the university in regards to diversity and inclusion in general, and in terms of admissions in particular. My mother and father revered Father Ted. I had received countless blessings from him growing up, as we stood in receiving lines at the university's Science Advisory Council, on which my father was honored to serve for over two decades.

My father was worried about the piece when I told him I was writing it, and then I became worried when I saw people in the cafeteria actually reading it under the headline, if I recall correctly, "Father Hesburgh's Commitment to Civil Rights Has Waned." I remember thinking that title was way too strident, that "waned" was not a word I used regularly, and that my parents would disown me and I would be kicked out of school.

Instead, it turned out to be a lifelong lesson about what real leaders must do in terms of responding to constructive criticism. Father Ted, along with John Butkovich and Kevin Rooney, listened and took me up on my challenge and created in the Admissions Office the first student counselor position designed to focus on diversity recruiting.

And so it began. Admissions became a movement and a cause and the full-time counselors there really treated me as a colleague and an equal, even though I was just a student. We changed everything: where we recruited, our brochures, our videos, our messaging, our approach. We engaged students of color in admissions throughout the whole life-cycle, with thousands of calls made and handwritten notes sent over pizza and soda encouraging applications or acceptance of an admissions offer. We entirely revamped the tired old "sell weekend" that others in this book and I myself attended. Financial aid dramatically improved and Admissions and Financial Aid worked more closely and better together to advance diversity than ever before.

I worked crazy hours, studying in my office only after I had gotten done whatever needed to get done for Admissions. I went on recruiting trips all over Philadelphia, my hometown, and Indiana and Chicago during breaks and encouraged and coordinated other students of color and alumni doing so en masse. We covered college nights everywhere, including many new schools and neighborhoods that had never heard from ND before. It was all-consuming.

Over time our numbers began to dramatically improve, and the last class I was part of recruiting reached 21 percent traditionally underrepresented minority, if I recall correctly. One of the greatest thrills for me at school was to see on campus fellow students of color whom I had recruited as a student counselor.

This experience led to many others, in part because we quickly learned that through focused and committed effort in Admissions we would change our numbers faster than other facets of the university (the faculty, the curriculum, the hall staff, the student programming, even the hair care products inventory in the bookstore) could keep up with and adapt to. Diversity, while very hard, came more quickly and easily than inclusion. There are too many memories and highlights of those efforts around inclusion to go into in detail, but here are some that I was honored to be a part of:

- Black Alumni of Notre Dame (BA of ND) proposed and formed. As co-president of the Black Cultural Arts Council (BCAC) with my classmate and lifelong friend Lisa Boykin, I remember very clearly the experience of nervously presenting to all the assembled, distinguished African-American alums, including my father, and fielding questions.
- Celebrating President Rev. Edward "Monk" Malloy's brilliant "Year of Cultural Diversity."
- Creating the amazingly powerful and successful Multicultural Fall Festival with Adele Lanan from Student Activities and an amazing group of fellow students, including the second student counselor in Admissions and lifelong friend Mari Fuentes. I got the money for the festival directly from Father Malloy, who backed us students all the way.
- Planning minority self-development and other leadership development workshops with Ken Durgans, who was the head of Minority Affairs.
- Protesting apartheid in South Africa on the steps of the Administration Building and writing op-eds in the *Observer* about that policy.

- With nine other incredible, diverse campus leaders, including Esther Ivory, Carlton West, and Dennis Tillman, we launched the Notre Dame chapter of the NAACP.

These experiences all helped shape me and forged how I try to lead and what I value and fight for today. I am glad I stayed at Notre Dame and did not transfer. My life and who I am would likely be very different.

Legacy.

It is also a haunting question, one that we all have to have the courage to ask ourselves each and every day. What will our legacy be? What will we leave behind? What will they say at our funerals? Will we have left our families, our communities, Notre Dame, our companies, our country, and the world better than how we found it?

What is our unique legacy as black Domers?

I believe the great African-American educator Mary McLeod Bethune said it best and most succinctly: "we must lift as we climb." Our Mother, the beautiful Lady of the Lakes sitting on top of the Dome, expects nothing less.

CHAPTER 5

The 1990s

It was a great way to begin a decade. On the afternoon of February 11, 1990, Nelson Mandela emerged through the front gates of Victor Ver-ster Prison near Cape Town, South Africa. After twenty-seven years in captivity, he suddenly was a free man. And four years later, after the disestablishment of apartheid and the institution of a new non-racial democracy, he would be president of South Africa.

Along with the reunification of the two Germanys later in the year and the dissolution of the Soviet Union at year's end, Mandela's release had about it an air of unreality, as if it were a dream. The world, it seemed, had been turned upside down.

It didn't take long, however, for ugly reality to assert itself. On August 2, 1990, Saddam Hussein's Iraq invaded neighboring Kuwait. United States President George H. W. Bush declared that Iraq's brazen violation of international law "will not stand," and preparations began for the Persian Gulf War, America's first major military excursion in the Middle East.

Much of the 1990s the United States and the rest of the world spent trying to establish a new architecture of international relations, a new paradigm to replace the one lost when the Soviet Union col-lapsed and dissolved at the end of 1991.

Just how diabolically difficult this would be became apparent when President Bush, at the request of the United Nations and in concert with "the international community," sent troops in De-cember 1992 into the East African nation of Somalia. They were to create a safe space among warring militias and make it possible for aid organizations to distribute food to starving civilians. (Some 300,000 Somalis had died because factional fighting had made it impossible for aid groups to succor them.)

What was supposed to be a brief and relatively painless mission of mercy grew into an engagement that lasted well into the first year in office of Bush's successor, Bill Clinton. And it ended only after the American forces suffered an embarrassing and harrowing defeat at the hands of militia members in the streets of Mogadishu, the Somali capital.

The Somali episode no doubt was at the front of Clinton's mind when, in April of the following year, ethnic Hutus began slaughtering ethnic Tutsis in the small East African nation of Rwanda. In an action for which he later publicly expressed regret, Clinton declined to send American troops to help stop the slaughter, which ultimately claimed an estimated 800,000 lives—the largest genocide since the Nazi Holocaust of World War II.

Clinton also was reluctant to intervene in the Balkan civil wars that attended the breakup of Yugoslavia in the early nineties. Ultimately, however, he and America's NATO allies were spurred to action by the 1995 Srebrenica massacre, in which Serb militia members slaughtered more than eight thousand Muslim men and boys and raped countless Muslim women while an undermanned force of international peacekeepers from the Netherlands stood by.

Clinton, who had won election in 1992 in an unusual three-way contest with Republican incumbent Bush and independent H. Ross Perot, without question was the public personality of the decade. He made his mark as president in domestic policy. One of his most notable acts—to the distress of many liberals—was to sign a bill that, for the first time, made work a requirement for receiving federal welfare payments.

But the most consequential legislation of Clinton's presidency came in the first year of his first term. With the support of only Democrats, he won passage of tax increases, mainly on wealthier taxpayers, aimed at reducing the federal budget deficit. Despite predictions of fiscal calamity by his opponents, the economy took off with a roar. Inflation declined, unemployment fell, and Clinton's last four federal budgets featured something that hadn't been seen since the days of Lyndon Johnson: surpluses instead of deficits, black ink instead of red.

Clinton indelibly stained his record—and gave his legion of enemies a cudgel with which to pummel him—by engaging in a sexual liaison in the White House with a young intern, Monica Lewinsky. When the affair became public, Clinton initially denied it, but later confessed. Led by Newt Gingrich, the Republican speaker, the House of Representatives impeached Clinton. He was tried in 1999 by the Senate, but was acquitted and remained in office, completing his term in 2001.

Clinton had been in office just over a month when an event occurred that prefigured many more like it in the years ahead. Islamic terrorists detonated a car bomb in the basement of the north tower of New York's World Trade Center. It failed to bring the building down, as the bombers had hoped, but it killed six people and injured hundreds. Later in the decade, terrorists would bomb the US embassies in Kenya and Tanzania, killing hundreds.

But terrorism wasn't just a foreign or an Islamic franchise. In April 1995, Timothy McVeigh, a twenty-seven-year-old Army veteran and militia member, set off a truck bomb at the Alfred P. Murrah Federal Building in Oklahoma City. It destroyed the building, killed 168 people, and injured hundreds more.

When the nation was not fixated on political events, there was much else to occupy it. And most of it came right into America's living rooms, courtesy of CNN and its cable TV rivals.

Two events in particular riveted the country and revealed a deep chasm in perceptions among the races. There was, first, the videotaped beating of black motorist Rodney King by Los Angeles police in 1991, the subsequent trials of the police officers, and the massive riot that followed their initial acquittal. And in 1994, there was the bizarre, slow-motion police chase of former football star O. J. Simpson, followed by his arrest and trials for the murder of his former wife, Nicole Brown, and her boyfriend, Ron Goldman.

Racial divisions became manifest at Notre Dame in the early nineties also, even as the new president, Father Monk Malloy, vigorously pursued policies aimed at fostering racial and cultural diversity. Over the course of the decade, Malloy's inner circle included two African-Americans in key positions: Roland Smith, executive assistant to the president, and Chandra Johnson, special assistant to the president.

But in 1991 that mattered little to the students who created SUFR—Students United for Respect—and mounted a campaign to transform Notre Dame into an environment more hospitable to blacks. They wrote and published reports; they staged a sit-in at the registrar's office; they published a list of demands; and, crucially, they attracted media attention.

Malloy met with the leaders of SUFR, who also presented their case to the university's board of trustees. Some of their demands were met and some were not. But at a minimum, SUFR served notice to the Notre Dame community that there was serious work to be done to make the university a truly diverse, welcoming place for minorities.

To his credit, Malloy recognized that doing that work was necessary to the achievement of Notre Dame's ambitious overall goal: to become a national Catholic research university. Thanks to the robust economic growth during the decade, the university made enormous strides toward that goal. New buildings sprouted like mushrooms, endowed professorships multiplied, the student population grew, and student academic achievement flourished.

The football team also flourished during the first part of the decade under Coach Lou Holtz, falling just short of a national championship in 1993. Holtz retired after the 1996 season and was replaced by an assistant, Bob Davie. Davie compiled a middling record—thirty-five wins and twenty-five losses over five seasons. As important as his record, however, was the fact that, on his watch, Notre Dame suffered two major embarrassments.

One was a lawsuit filed by former assistant coach Joe Moore; he charged that Davie had defamed him and engaged in age discrimination in firing him. The latter charge was upheld at trial and the university paid a settlement. The other embarrassment stemmed from the actions of a South Bend woman, Kim Dunbar, who embezzled more than $1 million from her employer and used the proceeds to win the attentions and the company of Notre Dame football players. Davie was not responsible for the Dunbar-related infractions, but the university was found liable for a major infraction by NCAA for the first time in its history, and suffered penalties.

In 1997 Notre Dame Stadium was modernized and expanded to seat more than 80,000 people. And in 1999, Michael Brown became the first black student chosen to serve as Notre Dame's official mascot, the leprechaun.

Earlier in the decade, Jubba Seyyid—then known as Jubba Beshin—became one of only eleven male fencers in Notre Dame's history to hold an NCAA individual title when he won the 1990 championship in epee.

The same year, David Duerson (Class of 1983) became the first African-American to win the Moose Krause Award, the Monogram Club's highest honor.

IRIS OUTLAW

(Class of 1990 MSA)

---

*Iris Outlaw came to Notre Dame as a graduate business stu-
dent in autumn 1987. A graduate of New Prairie High School
in New Carlisle, Indiana, she earned her undergraduate degree
at Indiana University Bloomington. After earning her master's
degree at the Mendoza College of Business, she became head of
the Office of Minority Affairs at Notre Dame.*

AS AN AFRICAN-AMERICAN FEMALE AND FIRST-GENERATION
collegian living twenty-seven miles from South Bend in 1969, Notre
Dame was not an option for my post-secondary education. It was a
male-only institution then. I ended up going to Indiana University to
earn my bachelor of arts degree.

That I would later earn a graduate degree with honors from the
University of Notre Dame was beyond my comprehension. This part
of my journey in my higher education happened completely by
chance.

In the spring of 1987 I was a wife, a mother, and a full-time worker
out one day with my girlfriends. One of them, Jessie Whitaker, was
enrolled in the master of science administration program in the Mendoza College of Business. As she discussed her courses and how the
program was enhancing her professional development, she encouraged the rest of us to consider pursuing a master's. My husband was
employed at the university, so I was eligible for the spousal discount.
Funding was a non-issue; fear and nervousness were my obstacles.

However, I thought that if my friend and sorority sister, Felice Dudley-Collins, would join me, we could establish our own study group cohort. Never had I thought of attending Notre Dame, yet there I was shortly after, calling the MSA program office to discuss the admissions process. A few weeks later I began completing my application and gathering letters of recommendation from my Indiana University mentor, Dr. James Holland, and from employers. Outside of my immediate family and Felice, I told no one of my plan.

Even though I graduated from high school among the top ten in my class, was a member of the National Honor Society, and did well at Indiana University outside of my chemistry courses, I thought my acceptance into the Notre Dame program was questionable. I was naïve about the academic rigor of Notre Dame's curriculum. That was to my advantage, because if I had known, I might not have applied.

During the summer of 1987 Felice and I received our letters of acceptance. Denise Steen, one of Felice's co-workers whom she had told about the program, also had applied and was accepted as well.

Denise, Felice, and I enrolled in our first class, strategic management. Little did we know that this was actually the capstone class for the program, so most of our classmates were in their last or next-to-last semester. Although Notre Dame's undergraduate student body was predominantly white, our MSA cohort was generationally, socio-economically, and ethnically mixed.

After strategic management, our group of three was fortunate to be together in most classes throughout our time in the program. Often we were the only persons of color in group projects. In most instances, the group was welcoming to our input. This was not the case in one class. In that instance I informed the group as we were preparing our case study that we needed to note the current status of the corporation. I presented several rationales, including that I had had the professor before and knew she would expect it. The others argued and decided to eliminate the company update based on the stance that she did not request it in the assignment.

We gave our final presentation and waited anxiously for our grade. As we watched the following groups, each incorporated a company update in its presentation. We received an A- for our group project. The professor commented that, if we had included the current status of our company, we would have obtained an A. It was difficult for me to maintain my composure. I questioned whether I should have fought harder or if this occurrence was necessary for my team members to learn that each person is valuable and can offer worthy contributions.

Throughout the three years of the program, I discovered that the professors were supportive and wanted to see the students succeed. Most of the professors were adjuncts and professionals in their areas of expertise. For that reason they were able to demonstrate the practicalities of the theories. As a graduate student, I tended to sit in the front of the classroom to ensure the instructor knew me. I would either stay after class or come early to engage them in conversation. There was only one who was not receptive. She team-taught the class with a male. She was knowledgeable but had horrendous interpersonal relationship skills. I assumed she lacked relationship skills, but the other persons of color in the room felt the same. We were apprehensive when we submitted our assignments. It was interesting with the dual grading system that her male counterpart would provide higher grades and constructive criticism, while her grades were lower with negative comments. In spite of her, I graduated with honors.

My success in the program was due to my exceptional support network. Family members, Notre Dame administrators, and classmates kept me grounded. They allowed me to vent; they challenged me and kept me focused. Those more advanced in the program taught me how to navigate the system. They shared advice on what courses and professors to take. My core group did not hesitate to seek help in areas where we struggled. My brother-in-law tutored us in statistics in return for a promised dinner. Glenda Graham, a sorority sister who was also in the program, spent several Saturdays explaining accounting practices where a credit is noted as a negative and debit a positive. Logic for us was completely thrown out the window and we had to go with it.

We were astute in opening our group to others who appeared to be surviving as opposed to thriving. David, a hairstylist, and Mary, a single mother with two young boys, were two who eagerly joined us. David had taken a three-course load for several semesters and warned us not to attempt this. Working full-time and handling the course work, he said, often had him struggling to stay focused and function at his maximum potential. Heeding his wisdom, the members of this diverse team made sure we took no more than two classes per semester.

Our initial goal was to complete the program in three years, even though it was marketed as a part-time program that would take seven years to complete. Our advisor assured us our diverse cohort could graduate in three years. That meant we would make sacrifices in our personal lives to achieve both goals. We allowed times of weakness, but we also knew that we began this journey together and were going to end it the same way.

At times we studied at someone's home or apartment, while our families celebrated holidays without us. Individually, I studied at home with my children joining me at the dining room table. My daughter did her homework, and my son colored. Role-modeling and bonding were two benefits of being in the program. The anticipation of seeing their pride when I graduated and realizing the role they played in helping me achieve that goal was inspirational. My husband provided access to his computer for writing papers. He served as a sounding board when I became overwhelmed and quizzed me when I was preparing for exams. My family was truly the wind beneath my wings.

Because of their support, I was empowered to pursue employment where I could use my newfound skills. This led me to apply for the position of director of minority student affairs in the summer of 1990. It was ironic that my commencement speaker, Patricia O'Hara, was the person who hired me. She and Roland Smith, executive assistant to Father Edward Malloy, then the university president, were instrumental in my formation as a student affairs professional. They ensured that I obtained professional development and joined the appropriate organizations to flourish in higher education. Through the American Association for Higher Education's Black Caucus and the American Association of Blacks in Higher Education (AABHE), I worked on numerous conference committees and held board leadership roles ranging from secretary to vice president for administration. I used my position to expose African-American doctoral candidates to AABHE, where five Notre Dame applicants won awards for their research impacting African-American communities. My Notre Dame degree opened a variety of doors that permitted opportunities to conduct diversity training for parochial and public school systems and present at national and international conferences.

Reflecting on the past twenty-six years, the pursuit of my master's degree has brought interactions with thousands of young people from every walk of life. This life choice placed me on a trajectory that I never envisioned when I graduated from New Prairie High School. As a student affairs administrator in an institution where I can freely express my faith, I easily assist current Notre Dame students on their life journeys. We laugh, cry, and pray as they face the challenges before them. Perhaps knowing all too well that the path is never easy but you can only find out by going down it. I have learned that you never stop learning.

The future will bring more challenges and reasons to enlist hard-fought experiences. My vocation is ever-changing, spiritually fulfilling, and always engaging. Student enrichment comes every day; so does my pride. "Love Thee, Notre Dame" is not just a song lyric.

ROD WEST

(Class of 1990)

---

*Rod West came to Notre Dame in autumn 1986 from New Or-
leans. He majored in American Studies and was a member of
the football team. After graduation he earned JD and MBA
degrees at Tulane. He currently is executive vice president and
chief administrative officer at Entergy Corporation. He also is
a member of the Notre Dame board of trustees. He and his
wife, Madeline, live in New Orleans.*

MY PATH TO NOTRE DAME WAS, LIKE THOSE OF SO MANY
African-Americans growing up in the South, far from preordained. I
was raised in the Catholic tradition in New Orleans, despite the fact
that my family was predominantly Baptist. My parents' divorce pre-
cipitated my move to New Orleans in 1974, when I was six years old.
It was also at that age that I began to discern religious and cultural differences among my childhood friends and classmates. We didn't realize it then, but we were among the first generation of children who
never experienced a legally segregated school environment.

I attended public schools through the eighth grade. We lived in a
working-class neighborhood. We were never poor, never did without
the basics, although I recall often feeling like I was always "broke"
relative to the kids I went to school with. We lived close enough to the
neighborhoods we considered "rich" or well-off to daydream about
how the "other side" lived. But we lived in an apartment complex,
and there was no shortage of reminders about what we didn't have.

Interestingly, New Orleans is as poignant a narrative about class as it is about race. But that's a story for another day.

My neighborhood parish church, St. Maria Goretti, was my first portal into the Catholic Church and what would be my ever-evolving identity as an American black Catholic. I attended Brother Martin High School, an all-boys Catholic school founded in 1869 by the Brothers of the Sacred Heart. Brother Martin was the first school I attended that was predominantly white and Catholic. The irony is that New Orleans has historically had the largest concentration of black Catholics in the United States, so there was no shortage of black Catholic schools, like St. Augustine High School. Brother Martin had a strong tradition of athletic success to balance its stellar academic reputation, and it was my success as a student-athlete in that environment that set the stage for my tenure as a Notre Dame student-athlete.

I walked onto the Notre Dame campus in the fall of 1986 feeling like I was one of the luckiest people on the planet. It wasn't because of some lifelong dream of attending Notre Dame, a la Rudy. It was far simpler than that: I had made it to college, to a very well-respected university, and my parents would not have to worry and stress about how we would pay for it as they did when I was in high school.

My Notre Dame experience as an African-American student was so influenced by my responsibilities as a football player that I barely had time to reflect. But when I did reflect—my God!—the stark contrast to my upbringing was startling. Notre Dame looked like the whitest place I'd ever seen. Everyone, it seemed, was white, from a well-to-do family, Catholic, and, with few exceptions, of Irish descent. I remember early in my first semester my father called to ask how things were going. I remember telling him that football was rough because Lou Holtz was trying to rebuild the program. I also recall telling him that classes were extremely tough because everyone at Notre Dame, including the athletes, was off-the-charts smart. But the conversation came to a pensive pause when I said, "And Dad . . . if you take away the football and basketball players, there aren't a whole lot of brothers on campus at all." We laughed out loud together. This was a stark cultural contrast to my father's experience playing for the legendary coach Eddie Robinson at historically black Grambling State University.

The black athletes at Notre Dame were really easy to identify on campus. What was harder to pick out was the black student who was *not* an athlete, many of whom had to suffer the indignity of being asked what sport they played every time they were introduced to someone on campus, or worse, the indifference they sometimes felt from others when it was clear they were not athletes. My life as a football player isolated me from so much of what my fellow black students had to endure trying to "fit in." The athlete at Notre Dame is embraced by the Notre Dame community from day one. You're a campus celebrity; students and alumni alike want to get to know you, to introduce you to their friends, their parents, their bosses. If you're black and not an athlete, you might as well be invisible. I recall feeling a tremendous sense of guilt when one of my classmates was proudly introducing me to his parents. He'd obviously told them that he'd become friends with this "really cool" football player. I happened to be walking toward the North Dining Hall with another black male student who was not a football player. I introduced him to the couple and, of course, they asked him, "What position do you play on the team?" When he told them he was not a football player, they, too, were a bit embarrassed and tried to feign interest in continuing the conversation.

I never got the sense that there was ill will or neglect on the part of the campus leadership. In fact, the university tried mightily to address the cultural divide and improve the campus experience for minority students. I recall the Office of Multicultural Affairs as the main conduit for most of the programs designed to break down the cultural barriers on campus. Most were well-intentioned and a few were really successful. Some, like soul food week during Black History Month, were downright disastrous. The Office of Student Affairs struggled mightily in the 1980s and early 1990s to get its hands around what role it could or should play in fostering an environment on campus that was welcoming, and not just tolerant, of the growing number of minorities. It was evident that the university was aware of its problem, but wasn't quite sure how to respond.

The black students on campus, athletes and non-athletes alike, tended to lean on each other for support. The overwhelming majority of us came from similar backgrounds. No one forced us to attend Notre Dame, and we each certainly had other options. As a result, I always felt that the onus was on me to figure out how to "fit in." To me, that pressure was more debilitating than any academic challenge I ever faced at Notre Dame. Thankfully, many of us had black (and sometimes white) "families" off campus. These were blessed souls who provided a place of refuge when we needed the familiar comfort of a Sunday meal, or an understanding shoulder to cry on. They affirmed who we were as young black men and women working hard to make our way in an often unforgiving white academic and social environment. I will always be grateful for Delores Smith and her husband (we called him "Smitty"), and for Mr. Charlie Watkins. They and the many black families in South Bend like them were the difference between young black kids thriving at Notre Dame or just surviving, as so many of us did.

I believed as a student just as I believe now that Notre Dame was not always the place to be, but if I could gut it out and finish, Notre Dame would always be the place to be from. I graduated from the College of Arts and Letters in 1990 and went on to receive both a Juris Doctor and an MBA from Tulane University. The value of the Notre Dame brand and the alumni network means far more to me today than it did when I was a student. As an undergraduate I was constantly sold on Notre Dame's aspirations as a university. It was those same aspirations that I have, in turn, sold to my daughter, who is a current Notre Dame student.

I made a conscious decision to give back to Notre Dame with my time, talent, and treasure the moment I graduated. I chose to engage the university through the alumni association, National Alumni Board, advisory councils and, now, as a university trustee. I made a decision to be a part of the change I wanted to see in the university when I was a student. I do believe that Notre Dame's aspirations are worthy of my and our best efforts. The university is grappling with its identity as a Catholic institution and what that means in an ever-changing Catholic diaspora. The face of Catholicism is changing as the church seeks to hold on to both its historical roots and its relevance across the world. The Irish Catholic ethos still speaks louder at Notre Dame to black students than does her Catholic ethos. Nevertheless, what Notre Dame stands for and what the Fighting Irish fight for is worth protecting.

God. Family. Country. Notre Dame. We Are ND!

LISA ROBINSON HONORÉ
(Class of 1992)

Lisa Robinson came to Notre Dame in autumn 1988 from Bra-
zoria, Texas. She majored in government. After graduation, she
earned a master's at Northwestern University and a PhD at
LSU. She worked as a TV reporter in Louisiana, and taught
briefly at Southern University in Baton Rouge. She now is com-
munications director for Louisiana's teacher retirement system.
She and her husband, Tyrone, have three daughters.

A CONVERSATION WITH MY UNCLE, BRIAN WYCLIFF (CLASS OF
1985), set me on my path to Notre Dame. During my junior year in
high school, he asked me where I planned to go to college. Today, as I
think back on our conversation, I am amazed that, at the time, I hadn't
thought much about it. Apart from reading a brochure I'd received in
the mail from Mount Holyoke College, I hadn't done much research
on where I was headed after high school.

There was the University of Houston—my mother's alma mater,
located about forty-five minutes north of where I grew up. And my
father sometimes spoke of another Houston institution—Rice University, the "Harvard of the South," as he always called it. Those
schools didn't interest me, though. They were too close to home.

It was Brian who posed the question, "Have you ever thought
about going to Notre Dame?" I knew he had graduated from Notre
Dame, as had his two older brothers, Francois Wycliff (Class of 1971)
and Don Wycliff (Class of 1969). My uncle Chris Wycliff also attended

Notre Dame, but didn't complete his degree there. Even with this family legacy, Notre Dame had never been on my radar.

But during my senior year in high school, I applied, got accepted, and was invited to visit the campus during the annual Minority Student Weekend trip in the spring. When I received my acceptance letter, I knew I wanted to go. The weekend trip sealed the deal. Coming from a small, rural high school in southeast Texas, where athletics were the priority, I had never been among such a large group of black students of my age who were academically minded and driven. I was meeting people who were applying to Georgetown and Stanford, Cornell and Harvard. "What am I doing here?" I thought.

In retrospect, my decision to attend Notre Dame had little to do with my own assessment of how its academic programs meshed with my career goals and interests, and more to do with my desire to experience another part of the country and to interact with the types of people I'd met that spring weekend in 1988. Importantly, I had the luxury of knowing that Notre Dame wasn't completely unfamiliar territory. My family had history there. The university had been tested by my uncles. They had survived and appeared to be doing well in their lives and careers. I reasoned that I could, too.

At Notre Dame, I settled on government as my major. I was an average student, doing just enough to maintain a decent grade point average. Academically, I was more concerned with satisfying degree requirements than availing myself of the opportunity to become a serious scholar or discovering a passion for a particular field of study.

Yet some classes and what I learned in them still stick with me, like Dr. Marcia Sawyer's African-American survey class, where I first heard about the Middle Passage and became familiar with details of slave life. Notre Dame was where I took social dance, and absolutely loved it. My art appreciation class opened my eyes to the cultural, political, and moral symbolism artists seek to convey in their work. And as a Domer, I was required either to pass a swim test or take swimming my freshman year. Unfortunately for me, passing the swim test was not to be. I wasn't at all happy about having to walk across campus after swim class with wet hair my first winter in South Bend. Three hurdles for me: swimming, getting my hair wet, and going outside with wet hair in the dead of winter.

Spiritually, Notre Dame wasn't a place where I felt I grew or, probably more accurately, allowed myself to grow. Although I attended mass every Sunday with my family before going to Notre Dame, I can count on one hand how many times I attended mass on campus (or visited the Grotto) while I was a student. I did join the gospel choir, and fell in love with a style of faith music that was so different from what I was used to singing in my small, Catholic church in Texas. Despite the many opportunities to volunteer on campus or in the South Bend community, my efforts there were lackluster as well. I did feel pangs of guilt for not attending the evening 10 p.m. mass in my dorm, where pajamas were the clothing of choice. I still feel guilty for not embracing the spirit of volunteerism that Notre Dame fervently champions.

It has been more than twenty years since I graduated from the university. Much of my four years there are a blur these days, but I'd have to say the social experiences I had were its greatest impact on me. At Notre Dame, the dorm you lived in played a significant part in your social life. I lived in Lewis Hall all four years. It didn't have the amenities of the newer dorms like Siegfried and Knott, or the charm of older dorms like Walsh and Badin. It looked and felt institutional, but it was the center of my social world. The people who lived there became my closest friends.

I still keep in touch with Sheri Barker Hawkins (Class of 1992) and Chelsea Latimer Smith (Class of 1992). They are two of my oldest and dearest friends. My best memories of Notre Dame revolve around my time with them and the experiences we had. Sheri and I were in the same freshman English class and became friends then. She lived in Breen-Phillips but became my roommate in Lewis Hall our sophomore year. Chelsea, a triplet whose two sisters considered Notre Dame but chose Stanford and Cornell instead, also lived in Lewis all four years. During school breaks, I'd go home with Sheri to Chicago or to Detroit with Chelsea. On campus we'd go to mixers; watch Bookstore Basketball and participate in An Tostal events in the spring; treat ourselves to the occasional Tippecanoe Sunday brunch; and attend the Black Cultural Arts Council's annual fashion show. Since school, we've been there for each other through our weddings, children's births, and our fathers' deaths. Our continued friendship is a blessing.

Although my social experiences are my strongest memories of Notre Dame, I don't mean to minimize the university's impact on my professional life. Through the years, I've seen the look of surprise when I tell people that I graduated from Notre Dame. More than a few people have asked me how I came to attend that school. And I recognize that it's Notre Dame's reputation as an elite, academically competitive institution that has gotten me job interviews and offers. The weight that a Notre Dame diploma carries has influenced my life for the better, and it is a source of pride that I was fortunate enough to be accepted into and graduate from Notre Dame.

I haven't been back to campus since I graduated in 1992. But as my teenage daughters, Hannah and Holly, get closer to graduating from high school, I'd like, at least, to show them where I spent my undergraduate years. Should they wind up at Notre Dame, maybe they'll have an even better experience than I had.

JUBBA SEYYID

(Class of 1992)

---

*Jubba Seyyid came to Notre Dame in autumn 1988 from New-
ark, New Jersey. He majored in film and television and was a
national champion on the Notre Dame fencing team. After
graduation he worked as a producer for NBC in New York
City. He currently is senior director of programming and production for TV One. He lives in Los Angeles.*

WHEN I GOT THE CALL FROM MIKE DECICCO, HEAD COACH
of the Notre Dame fencing team, I was already committed to Penn
State. As a matter of fact, I even had a dorm room, a roommate, and
mailings with maps of the university grounds and other orientation
information. I told Coach DeCicco that I was excited about Penn State
and that I had a scholarship and new equipment and friends and lots
of cute girls waiting for me in central Pennsylvania. (I met a few coeds
on my campus visit who claimed they couldn't wait for my return.)
But Coach was undeterred by my alleged commitment to Penn State.

The following minutes are fuzzy in my memory, but Coach
DeCicco talked about the significance of the University of Notre
Dame and how the education was unparalleled, which I already knew
from my limited research. That's where my knowledge of the school
ended—if you don't count my father's proclamation that it was the
"whitest university on the planet."

Notre Dame wasn't even on my radar. I had never visited the
campus and I knew only one student who was attending. But DeCicco's
promises of a scholarship after freshman year were alluring, and his

silver tongue painted a picture of unparalleled mystique and tradition. Apparently that was enough to seal the deal for a gullible seventeen-year-old from Newark who was sitting on two full scholarships: one from Penn State and the other from Rutgers. Suddenly, my eyes were seeing green—clovers *and* dollar bills—so one year of student loans didn't seem like a mountain of debt, but rather chump change I could shake off with a Notre Dame education. Where do I sign?

Although my father wasn't particularly fond of Notre Dame, he was extremely proud I was attending. He was particularly delighted to tell anyone white he met that I was going to be a Notre Dame student. He was certain it would frustrate them, since Notre Dame is the one school every white parent wanted their kid to attend. That being said, I'm sure my dad was just a little frustrated that I had to pick one of the most expensive schools in the country. It shouldn't have been a surprise though, as my decision was in line with everything I had done in life to that date.

I had expensive tastes for a kid. I liked skiing and had dreams of racing cars. And fencing was my sport of choice, for crying out loud. The only more costly sport I could have chosen would have been polo. (But where would I have boarded my horse in Newark?) So, apparently we had beer money and I had champagne taste, and Notre Dame was about to be my first bottle of Perrier-Jouët.

I remember the afternoon my father and I arrived on campus. We unpacked the car and filed into Dillon Hall for the first time. Two things stood out. One was a student moving an entire rack of Polo shirts into his dorm—I mean, like, thirty shirts. I had one, and this guy had a Ralph Lauren store full! The second thing was that my roommate was obviously going to be a slob because his dirty underwear, books, and other junk were on the floor. He also had heavy metal cassette tapes on the dresser, so I knew I was in for a culture clash. White metalhead meets black hip-hopper from Newark. It was unfortunate to think I needed a new roommate already.

The Polo shirts were significant because for the first time I realized my socioeconomic standing in the community. Anyone who could afford that many shirts of one kind was clearly operating on a different financial tier than I. It didn't make me feel subjugated or small, but for the first time I was peeking behind the doors of people whose concerns were far different from mine. As a fencer I had certainly rubbed elbows with the elite, but never had I shared a living space. It was thrilling! I was open to the grand experiment. This is what dorm life was all about. The slob, on the other hand, I was not looking forward to meeting.

As I put my clothes in the closet and hung my Vanity 6 and Lisa Lisa posters, I blasted the stereo with "Strictly Business" by EPMD. And that's when the metalhead stranger walked through the door: a six-foot, soccer-playing black kid from Houston. "Hey man. I'm Bobby," he said. "What's this you're playing? Sounds incredible." We've been best friends ever since.

I reluctantly got a lesson in Black Sabbath and Iron Maiden, and with it a new appreciation for variety—and not just in music. It was a lesson that carried through all aspects of education and life and that I still proudly claim as a personality trait. Variety truly is the spice of life, and an ability to open yourself up to it is a characteristic to be cherished, as the best experiences in life happen when you're open to the possibilities of the unknown. That's the first lesson I ever learned at Notre Dame.

The four years I spent on campus were filled with life-changing moments—some good and some bad. I remember my first football game. I remember people crying when the Notre Dame Fight Song and the Alma Mater were played. Crying? Really? At first I thought it cultish, but it didn't take long for me to realize that students, alumni, and fans alike had a spiritual connection to the university. I was reluctant to buy in, since I never loved anything like I loved my family. But it became clear over a short time that these people saw the university as a member of their family, albeit a structure and a symbol of faith and endurance. It also became clear that I was part of a club, maybe even an enormous secret society. Secret because it's nearly impossible to articulate. It has to be experienced.

I never got that full scholarship after freshman year as promised, even though I won the national championship as a sophomore and the silver medal as a junior. The smooth-talking coach was apparently good at his job, God rest his soul. Not having a full scholarship meant I had to get a student job to make ends meet. I suffered through battles with the office of financial aid, not knowing if I was going to be allowed to attend class. Grueling work hours, study hours, and practice hours make for a challenging time as a student-athlete. I was bitter for a while, especially since a few of my white teammates had full scholarships but no championships under their belts. If I am honest, I must admit it is something that I have never truly come to terms with. If sports, in particular, are supposed to be a meritocracy, then I got the proverbial shaft. Clearly, inequality was afoot and the race card was played. But youth and inexperience were my Achilles heel, and now my experience is a life lesson.

I can say without hesitation or doubt that I would not have achieved the professional successes that I have had in life were it not for my experiences and relationship with Notre Dame. For the first few years after graduation, during job interviews there were two things people wanted to discuss from my resume: my David Letterman internship and my experience at Notre Dame. Interviewers either loved or hated the Irish; there was no middle ground! But even the haters respected the Dome. I've been interviewed by several Trojans—USC grads—over the years and always got the stink eye. But I always got the job, too. I think that speaks volumes about Notre Dame culture, education, and the indelible impression the university has left on the American and international landscapes.

When I think of Frazier L. Thompson and what his experience must have been like as Notre Dame's first black student, my tribulations feel trivial. He was a pioneer, and we were able to reap the benefits of his existence on the planet and at the university. I am honored to share my story in tribute to him and those who followed, and I am humbled to know that someone will one day read this and smile, get a laugh, or relate to my experience. That makes me proud to be a member of this secret society we call the University of Notre Dame.

MICHELE D. STEELE

(Class of 1992)

Michele Steele came to Notre Dame in autumn 1988 from Indianapolis. She majored in government and was involved in the Black Cultural Arts Council and Students United For Respect. After graduation she earned a law degree at Indiana University Bloomington, and then a master of law degree at Capital University. She lives in Indianapolis.

I WAS ALL SET TO GO TO BROWN UNIVERSITY UNTIL I VISITED Notre Dame in April 1988. That day changed my life. When I walked onto the campus, I knew that Notre Dame was where I wanted to be. I met students who looked like me, sounded like me, and made me feel part of a family. I felt that I was going to be embraced for who I was, get a great education, have a fun college experience, yet still be close enough to my parents that I could go home if I ever got homesick.

I had reason to second-guess myself many times over the next four years, and to think my father, Walter Steele, a 1973 graduate of the Notre Dame Law School, had been right when he urged me to go to the East Coast and an Ivy League school, where diversity was more eagerly embraced. But now, twenty years later, I look back and realize that I would pick Notre Dame all over again.

I grew up in the suburbs of Indianapolis, in a majority white environment. So I thought Notre Dame would be just like my high school: I'd have my white friends and I'd have my black friends. I was used to being the "lonely only" black in many situations, so I thought

I would feel relatively comfortable at a school that was more than 70 percent white males.

Was I surprised! My sophomore year in my philosophy of law class, we debated affirmative action and I was deemed the "spokesperson" because I was the *only* black person in my class. As an example of the beneficial diversity that comes through affirmative action, I told of the Council on Legal Education Opportunity (CLEO) program that my father went through and, upon successful completion, was accepted to Notre Dame Law School. Because of the opportunity he received, he had the financial ability to send his children to Notre Dame.

During the follow-up discussion after the affirmative action debate, I was told by one of my classmates that I didn't belong at Notre Dame. I was told that I didn't deserve to be there because the only reason I was there was the color of my skin. Not because I was twenty-third in my high school class of 323 students. Not because I was an A student throughout high school and graduated with all academic honors. Not because I brought something different to the school that people could learn. Not even, for that matter, because my father was a Notre Dame alumnus and I was a legacy as much as any other child of a graduate. To that classmate—and maybe to all the others, since nobody spoke up in opposition to him—I was the black girl who had taken the spot of someone else who was more deserving.

His words—and their silence—hurt me and cut deep. They angered me. I felt like I had to defend myself. I began to tell them my credentials, how I deserved to be there, and basically told them all they could kiss my butt and walked out of class.

After I had missed two classes in a row, the professor called me to apologize for the other students' behavior and for allowing the debate to go as far as it did. I accepted his apology and returned to class.

I felt I wasn't embraced as being part of the Notre Dame family, which was why I had wanted to attend Notre Dame in the first place. What troubled me was how could a school with such deep religious roots make minorities feel that they didn't belong? How could you love the Lord and believe that Jesus died for all of our sins and loved everyone, and still treat someone who doesn't look like you so differently? The attitude seemed to be that if a black person didn't play a sport, why were they there?

I cried many nights because that was the first time that I had experienced to such a degree a sense of isolation and rejection due to the color of my skin. I questioned myself. I even tried to transfer to the University of Michigan! My mother told me that she would not let me quit. I would stay there and graduate, she said. I would succeed. And if I got through Notre Dame, then I could get through anything. She told me to get used to such rejection, because a lot of people in this world would not embrace me, so I needed to embrace myself, pray, and seek guidance from God.

So I went to the Grotto, and there got the guidance that I needed.

Instead of trying to fit in, I embraced my black self. I made a niche for myself. I joined the Black Cultural Arts Council and became an active member. I participated in Students United For Respect (SUFR), when we protested to the administration about the treatment of minority students on campus and the firing of Ken Durgans, who headed the Office of Minority Affairs. I wrote research papers on black issues, about parallels between Malcolm X and his journey to Islam and Catholic leaders and their spiritual journeys to Catholicism. I wrote about the hypocrisy of Catholicism and slavery in my theology class. Whenever I had to write a paper for any of my classes, I always chose a topic in which I could discuss issues that were important to African-Americans. All those negative comments from that affirmative action debate pushed me to want to learn and embrace my blackness even more. I took every class that I could that dealt with black people, different cultures, or diversity. I went from being a person who had little self-confidence to a person who was strong and confident and knew that I could succeed anywhere.

I pushed the envelope at Notre Dame. Some professors embraced the fact that I challenged the white mainstream of thought and some did not. But at the end of the day, I was growing as a proud black woman.

Being at Notre Dame helped me grow spiritually as well. There is something about being at a place as spiritual as Notre Dame that makes you get in touch with God. Even though I was not Catholic, I was fascinated by all of the rituals and philosophies behind Catholicism. I admired the deep faith that the school promoted and that so many students embraced.

So I stayed. I met people from all over the world. I met people from all different backgrounds. No, they were not the majority, but they were there and going through the same struggles that I was going through. We became our own family within the Notre Dame family.

And eventually, Notre Dame was home. It was a place where all of my friends were, a place where I was growing and developing into a strong, independent woman. It was a place where, even though there were not a lot of people who looked like me, I made it my own. I found my footing and began to truly embrace all that Notre Dame had to offer. Four years after my arrival, when I received my diploma, I thought: Thank God! I'm done! I made it! And when I drove away from campus, I felt somewhat nostalgic, but was glad that I wasn't going back. I could now go to law school at a big state school and be embraced and be in a more diverse environment.

It took me ten years to go back to campus. And when I did, I came with a different set of eyes. I had been out in the world and started seeing how influential Notre Dame really was, how I got more interviews, how people wanted to ask me what it was like going to Notre Dame and to tell me how they had always wanted to go there. That is when I realized how special a place it really was.

Notre Dame prepared me for the real world in the sense that, most times in my professional career, I have been the only black person in my department. Many times people did not embrace me. And once I went back to campus, I did feel a bit more embraced. I did feel I was a part of something special. I can look back and see how far Notre Dame has come since my father attended. I realized that Notre Dame was becoming more sensitive to diversity students and was trying to change the atmosphere on campus to be more inclusive.

So in 2006, when I was approached to be a board member of the Black Alumni of Notre Dame, I said yes. And now I recruit students to come to Notre Dame. How ironic! I tell them of my dad's struggle and explain to them how I survived. But my vision for them, I tell these future students, is to see them shine. And I tell them lastly that, when I really thought about it, even though Notre Dame was a hard place to be, it's a great place to be from.

AZIKIWE T. CHANDLER

(Class of 1994)

Azikiwe T. Chandler came to Notre Dame in autumn 1989 from Charleston, South Carolina. He majored in architecture and studied abroad in Italy. Since graduation he has worked in a number of community service and educational endeavors. He currently is earning a master's degree in teaching and hopes eventually to lead a public charter school for African-American males.

I HATED MY FRESHMAN YEAR AT NOTRE DAME.

For some reason, when it was time for me to apply to college, I was under the impression that all universities were incredibly diverse centers of debate and cultural exchange like Cal Berkeley, where Andrew Martinez made national headlines for expressing his First Amendment rights by attending classes in the nude in 1992. I was in for a shocking surprise.

Overwhelmingly Catholic, conservative, upper middle-class, and white, Notre Dame was the most alien, most homogeneous environment I had ever experienced. There was very little cultural diversity on campus. No Kwanzaa celebrations. No reggae music. No student activism. And as the lone African-American kid with dreadlocks, sporting a Bob Marley–emblazoned coat everywhere I went, I stuck out like a fly in a bowl of milk. Of course, being a six-foot tall, 145-pound weakling who couldn't attract a girlfriend amid a sea of 200-plus pound NFL pros-in-training didn't help matters, either.

How had I let Dr. Lannie talk me into this? Dr. Vince Lannie had taught at Notre Dame for a few years prior to becoming my high school's assistant vice principal. He was determined to send someone from Charleston's all-black Burke High School to Notre Dame. After earning the highest SAT score in the school, I had become his candidate.

By my sophomore year at Notre Dame, things were turning around. The director of the Office of Minority Affairs, Ken Durgans, and his colleague, Brother Sage, became mentors who organized support groups and Afrocentric symposiums, which helped keep my head above water.

Fred Tombar (Class of 1991), who was like a big brother to me, also began his term as Student Government Association (SGA) vice president during my sophomore year. Deputizing me his minority concerns commissioner, Fred said, in essence, "Stop whining and start creating the environment you want."

Employing the principle of Kuumba—"To always do as much as we can, in the way that we can, to leave our communities more beautiful and beneficial than when we inherited them"—I started a reggae music show on WVFI, the campus radio station, and helped organize a "Black Man's Think Tank," which brought to campus intellectuals like Naim Akbar, Wade Nobles, and Jawanza Kunjufu. I was a part of various teams that set up debates and brought the plight of minority students to the attention of the university administration. And I started hitting the gym. Thanks to Fred and Ken, I was applying one of the most valuable lessons I learned at Notre Dame: it's better to light candles than to curse the darkness.

Of all the organizations with which I was involved during my sophomore year, my work with Students United For Respect (SUFR, pronounced "suffer") was the most rewarding. It wasn't a preexisting, administration-sanctioned student organization playing by the rules. SUFR was a movement, a coalition of disgruntled, disenfranchised students who had come together to take the university by its shoulders and shake it until it snapped out of its lethargy and took action to improve our predicament.

At a Black Cultural Arts Council meeting at the beginning of my sophomore year, we found out that, after an extensive interview process, Brother Sage would not be hired as the assistant director of the Office of Minority Affairs. Having served as a *de facto* counselor whose encouragement helped keep many of us afloat in the hostile waters of Notre Dame, Brother Sage had the unwavering support of most students of color, and we felt dissed by the university's decision to disregard our recommendations and let the assistant directorship go vacant instead of hiring him.

Needing to vent, we started listing other ways in which the university was disrespecting us. One brother endured unpunished racial harassment at a dorm party where the n-word was written in large black letters on a bathroom wall and residents wore blackface to a "soul food dinner" of fried chicken and watermelon. Another student reported a professor saying black people were better off as slaves. Tuition was rising every year, yet our financial aid packages stayed the same. We were being unfairly targeted and scrutinized by campus security, rectors, and resident assistants. Out of eight hundred faculty, only eight were minorities from the United States, and the few classes on non-Western cultures were all cross-referenced in such a way that taking the classes was nearly impossible for most students. Why was the Office of Minority Affairs tucked away in a tiny closet of an office off a hidden staircase in the student center? At a school that had professed its commitment to diversity, why was there no multicultural center or a racial discrimination policy?

We decided something had to be done to help the university take these problems seriously, but we didn't want to have to seek administrative approval for the steps we planned to take. Furthermore, we didn't want any of the existing minority clubs to be targeted, ostracized, or disbanded because of our actions. So we set about creating a new group.

Brainstorming names for the new group, I started thinking about the double entendre of an acronym that came to mind (SUFR). The idea was that if life were a little less comfortable for everyone on campus, perhaps the administration would take steps to assuage our pain. Thus, Students United for Respect (SUFR) was born in the fall of 1990.

Among the ten demands we presented to the administration were calls for a comprehensive racial harassment policy; hiring minority professors until they made up ten percent of the faculty (like the percentage of minorities in the student population); student approval of the two people who were to be hired as assistants to the director of the Office of Minority Affairs (so they would be *our* advocates, as well as administrators); tenure for minority professors already teaching on campus; a multicultural center with a library; and financial aid packages that increased as tuition increased.

Subsequently, the SGA Minority Concerns Commission convened to review and update a 1980 diversity report whose recommendations had been disregarded.

It was a three-pronged offensive designed to spur the university into action. On the faculty level, Ken Durgans lobbied for us through the Office of Minority Affairs. We were also producing a university-sanctioned document through the proper, administration-approved student channels in the form of the SGA diversity report. And SUFR's student activism would show the administration that Ken's suggestions and the report's recommendations weren't idle talk, but heartfelt issues that needed to be addressed as soon as possible.

On Dr. Martin Luther King Jr. Day in 1991, we held our first non-violent protest on the steps of the Main Building, just before filing into Patty O'Hara's Office of Student Affairs, demanding a meeting. A month later, while Fred Tombar and I presented the 1980 and 1991 SGA diversity reports to the Notre Dame Board of Trustees, the rest of the group picketed the meeting with signs expressing our grievances.

"As you can see from the students picketing outside," I said, "the recommendations from these reports should be implemented as soon as possible to demonstrate that the university is not just paying lip service to the cause of diversity, but is actually taking concrete measures to make the university more hospitable, and less hostile for its minority students."

In addition to open letters published in campus and off-campus periodicals, we chalked the sidewalks to educate the student body on the grievances, and we held other demonstrations, including a 150-student sit-in, which shut down the registrar's office for a day during minority recruitment weekend.

In the end, most of the demands were not met, but over the course of the semester there were some concessions, including the administration's designation of a large space in LaFortune for meetings and multicultural events, and the faculty senate's approval of the racial harassment policy we had drawn up. Before the policy was approved, there had been no recourse for a student complaining of racial harassment. The new policy, which is still in place today, makes racial harass-ment punishable in the same way as sexual harassment.

Using his vice president's office well, Fred set up a meeting with university president Father Edward Malloy on the night of the sit-in. Those of us spearheading the coalition met with him shortly after midnight in his room in Sorin Hall to hash out next steps.

In the spirit of compromise, we allowed ourselves to be assimi-lated. Father Malloy gave us his word that no one would be punished for the sit-in and committed to fast-tracking SUFR's official approval so that it could be part of the committee he would be forming to look into meeting the demands and implementing the diversity report rec-ommendations.

Ten days later, after Father Malloy had run a two-page ad on cul-tural diversity in the *Observer*, SUFR was recognized. Shortly there-after, the task force on cultural diversity began meeting.

It wasn't the grand victory we had hoped for, but I was proud that we had stood up, united, for what we believed in. The trials, tribula-tions, and successes of SUFR were blessings for which I give thanks.

I am also grateful to Notre Dame for making my first trip abroad a reality. I had always dreamed of traveling the world, but if spending junior year in Italy hadn't been an integral part of Notre Dame's ar-chitecture program, I don't know if I ever would have made it happen on my own. While I spent the two years after Italy working thirty-six hours a week at three jobs (while still taking eighteen credit hours!) in order to cover the gap between financial aid and school fees, including bills acquired in Rome, and never did pursue a career in architecture, I'm proud of the bachelor of architecture degree I earned.

I'm grateful not only for the wanderlust my year abroad stimu-lated, but also for the mettle I realized I possessed at the completion of that five-year degree.

Notre Dame also nurtured the spirit of community service my parents instilled in me through the Nguzo Saba, the Seven Principles of Kwanzaa. My first "job" after graduation was serving as a team leader for AmeriCorps–National Civilian Community Corps, after being interviewed and hired by campus director Jeff Biel, a fellow Domer. So now, after living in, traveling through, and leading experi-ential learning and community service trips to forty-one countries, in a way, I also have Notre Dame to thank for contributing to the where-withal to pursue the three greatest passions in my life: travel, youth development, and community service.

While no leprechauns or "Fighting Irish" slogans grace any of my apparel, there is a blue and gold Notre Dame vanity plate on the front of my car, and on game days I do proudly wear my Notre Dame shirts and proclaim with the rest of the faithful, "We are ND!"

FRANK MCGEHEE

(Class of 1994)

Frank McGehee came to Notre Dame in autumn 1990 from Chicago. He majored in accountancy. After graduation he went first into banking and later into loyalty marketing. He and his wife have a daughter and live in Maplewood, New Jersey.

NOTRE DAME WAS MY FIRST CHOICE. ALTHOUGH I ATTENDED Mount Carmel, a prominent Catholic high school that was a football powerhouse on the South Side of Chicago, I knew little about Notre Dame's football lore.

For me the allure was academics. As the product of parents who were both educated to the postgraduate level, the importance of education was perpetually stressed in my home. Notre Dame's academic reputation was well known to my family.

We did not know any alumni, nor did we have any connections to the university. Our Catholic heritage also did not factor into Notre Dame's being my first choice. It was the moment that I stepped foot on campus that the love affair began.

My first visit to Notre Dame occurred in October 1989, the fall of my senior year of high school. A graduate student from China who had tutored me in chemistry the year before had accepted a teaching assistant position and invited me to visit.

That weekend I soaked in all Notre Dame could offer a first-time visitor. I walked the campus landscape from end to end. I visited dorms, popped my head into major academic buildings, the Hesburgh

Library, and public facilities like the LaFortune Student Center and the Grotto, and attended the Notre Dame–USC football game. I was hooked. This was the place for me.

April 4, 1990, was one of the happiest days of my life. It was the date that I received my acceptance letter. Now I was assured of my dream.

I loved Notre Dame and I still look fondly upon my years there as a cornerstone in the development of my character and my maturation into manhood. It was during these years that I learned about adversity, friendship, love, victory, responsibility, leadership, and camaraderie.

The idea that being an African-American made my experience different is true, but not in the way that most people would generally conceptualize it. The way I saw it was that every person at Notre Dame was different. Students came from varying backgrounds. So I carried myself as a person who was not only black but also a Chicagoan, a baseball fan, a lover of all things breakfast, and a runner. I refused to give off the vibe of "the black guy."

The root of this mindset could be traced back to my youth. I grew up in Hyde Park, Chicago, one of the most diverse communities in the Midwest. Although my grade school was 80 percent black, my high school was predominantly Caucasian. I guess you could say that I was educated on the "real world" before I stepped foot on the Notre Dame campus. So because of my childhood, I had no issues transitioning to life at Notre Dame.

It was natural and comfortable for me to, in a single day, hang out with my close black friends in the student center between classes, eat lunch with my white friends at the dining hall, and bring both groups together in my dorm room to play SEGA. Dorm and black parties were all fun.

But the rigorous demands of the academic landscape resulted in some initial struggles. I was always a hard worker in the classroom and had self-confidence, but by the end of spring semester of my freshman year, I was in trouble. My struggles continued into the fall semester of sophomore year and adversity stared into my face. But it was at that moment, when it appeared that my dream would become a nightmare, that the Notre Dame family wrapped their arms around me and would not let me fail.

I was given a second chance. I was provided the right tutor in a subject I had struggled to pass, and then a proper class selection that presented the material in a better format than other class offerings. With that, I was able to achieve academic success.

Fast forward to today and people still marvel and want to talk with me about Notre Dame. I wear my class ring every day and many times I have been approached on the elevator, in the subway or at the airport with "Wow! You went to Notre Dame?" or, "What year did you graduate?"

Having Notre Dame on my resume has only been a plus professionally. It has afforded me numerous career and networking opportunities. It is a brand in corporate America that inspires tremendous respect.

I have maintained ties to the university both financially and in service to the alumni association. I feel that it is important to give back when a place or experience has helped you.

Notre Dame is intertwined in my family life. My daughter visited the campus when she was six, and she thinks of Notre Dame as "a place where smart people go to college." She now thinks about going there, which would make her a second-generation African-American Domer. Of course she already knows the fight song.

Because of my love for Notre Dame I am often asked by friends, especially African-American friends who did not go there: Is there something in the water? How did you survive that place? Would you really choose Notre Dame again?

My answer time and time again is, "Yes, it was a great experience."

My Notre Dame experience can be summarized in two words: the people. Amazing people of all races, backgrounds, financial statuses, sexual orientations, and religious affiliations.

Dedicated people who worked for the university and went the extra mile to make sure that I did not become a statistic, but a Domer.

Kind people who gave me rides to the train station instead of letting me spend my last couple of dollars on a taxi.

Great people who became my best friends, shared deep personal moments, read at my wedding, assisted in coaching youth baseball, and attended football games with me all over the country.

Remarkable people who wrote recommendations for me to get into graduate school.

Passionate people who showed me how I could serve people and the community.

Caring people who said, "I love you brother. I love you man."

Hilarious people who made me laugh.

For me it was the people. They made my Notre Dame experience great. Good people. Family.

The Notre Dame family.

My family.

LeShane Saddler

(Class of 1994)

LeShane Saddler came to Notre Dame in autumn 1990 from Waterloo, Iowa. He majored in sociology and was a member of the football team. After graduation, he spent thirteen years as a high school social studies teacher and coach in Iowa. Today he, his wife, and two children live in South Bend, where he works for the University of Notre Dame as an assistant director of undergraduate admissions.

AS A RECRUITED STUDENT-ATHLETE, I HAD THE OPPORTUNITY to visit universities across the country during my junior and senior years of high school. Northwestern, Missouri, Illinois, and Iowa were among my final five to consider attending, along with a small Catholic school in northern Indiana.

When I made my official visit to Notre Dame, I knew that this place was different from all the others in two ways: the students were genuinely kind and the school was Catholic.

Football recruitment trips are better than your wildest dreams, as schools go to the extreme to showcase their programs, giving you stadium tours with your high school highlights playing and other such attentions. Amazing.

But my visit to Notre Dame consisted of nothing extreme but the cold temperature. I met the coaches, had dinner, and hung out in a dorm with my future teammates and classmates. I remember simply chatting about what Notre Dame meant to them and how I could live out my passion for sport and life as an undergraduate in this unique campus community.

Being from Waterloo, Iowa, the cold winters did not cause me concern. What did cause concern was that Notre Dame was a Catholic university. As a Baptist I was not so sure what this place was all about. I knew that it would be a great fit academically and athletically. But I wondered: would I fit in as a non-Catholic?

I soon learned that I not only would fit, but I also would come to love the opportunity to continue to grow in my faith life at Notre Dame. The theology course requirement was perfect; I found that the ability to study the Bible and keep God first was what I really needed in my life, as I struggled at times to find my place academically and athletically at Notre Dame. The one constant I always had during my five years at Notre Dame was my faith life and the understanding that, regardless of your religious beliefs, at Notre Dame you could pray and not worry. (Thanks, Mom.)

I thank my mother most sincerely for gifting me with the understanding and the knowledge that prayer changes things. She, a single parent, raised five college graduates with one simple rule, the Golden Rule: "Do unto others as you would have them do unto you." The power of prayer is real, and at Notre Dame I needed every bit of her teachings.

Playing football at Notre Dame was not all fun and games; there was a constant expectation to compete. I played strong safety for the most part, and really found my niche as a nickel back, the fifth defensive back inserted into the game to help prevent teams from passing. I had some ups and downs while playing, but injury was the biggest down.

We were in preparation for our January 1, 1992, Sugar Bowl game against Florida when it happened. Practice was going well; I had worked really hard that sophomore year and had earned some valuable playing time. The bowl game was where I would be able to showcase my talent. It was later in the practice session, and we were in our seven-on-seven period when another player, attempting to catch a pass, dove into my leg, causing my left knee to hyperextend. There was no pain, but I could not walk. The trainer ran out to check on me, and with a pull and a tug and a little twist it was determined that damage had been done to the knee. In the training room, after a few more tugs, came the news: torn anterior cruciate ligament (ACL).

When playing football, one has to expect that an injury is always just one play away, but an ACL tear is one of the worst injuries. The recovery, the sitting out and watching, the wondering if I would ever regain my speed and agility, was enough to make me go insane. I was blessed time and time again during my recovery. Having a supportive family and special teammates like Marvin Robinson, Bryant Young, Anthony Peterson, Aaron Taylor, and Jerome Bettis, and our team trainer, Jim Russ, made the journey back possible.

Jim encouraged me, coached me, and put me in position to be able to contribute to the success of the Notre Dame football team after many doubted that I would ever return to form.

I will always remember Coach Holtz as not just a superior coach, but a masterful motivator and human being. (You'll have to read my book to hear my stories and all of my reflections on him and on being a member of the Notre Dame football team.) What I can and will share here is a poem that he would recite every night before a football game.

"What Will Today Bring"
This is the beginning of a new day.
God has given me this day to use as I will.
I can waste it or use it for good.
What I do today is important because I am exchanging a day of
    my life for it.
When tomorrow comes this day will be gone forever,
Leaving in its place something I have traded for it.
I want it to be gain, not loss;
Good, not evil;
Success, not failure;
In order that I shall not regret the price I paid for it
Because the future is just
A whole string of nows.

My older brother, Obie Saddler Jr., two years my senior, attended the University of Iowa, and I thought my dorm experience would be much like his. I soon found that to be totally untrue.

The dorm life here at Notre Dame is more of a community than I would have thought. Many students choose to stay in the same dorm for all four years, and since Notre Dame does not have fraternities or sororities, being part of your dorm community becomes a special part of your experience. There is no need to fight to try to find your fit or your place of acceptance. Meeting young men and women in the dorms from all over the world was interesting and as educational as attending any lecture or class.

Sensitivity and appreciation for culture is what I learned quickly at Notre Dame. I'm not sure if my freshman roommate, a Caucasian brother, was kidding or not when he asked me why I used lotion, but I immediately realized that my history was a mystery to him. It was early in our first semester when he popped the question: "LeShane, why are you putting that cream all over your body?"

I had been well educated prior to entering college on race relations and that my being black could cause some discomfort for some people, but this was not one of those moments. He *really* did not know what lotion was. We had some interesting conversations, starting with the lotion and moving on to my *JET* Beauty of the Week collage, Black History Month, and my grandmother's recipe for banana bread. That entire year was an education not just about race, but about how little unknowns could be big moments of discovery that could lead to understanding and appreciation.

I grew a lot at Notre Dame. Sure, there were times when I thought, "Wow this situation would be a lot easier if I was a white kid." But I was not brought up to have self-doubt; I actually found strength when faced with adversity. (Thanks, Mom.)

If I had to do it over again, I would choose Notre Dame without question.

The friends, or, should I say, the relationships, are what I value greatly from my student days at Notre Dame. Making friends was easy. What I have learned since undergrad is that the gatherings of friends tend to happen less and less, but the memories last forever.

But on occasion I get the opportunity to see some of those friends again—old football buddies Reggie Fleurima, Emmit Mosely, Cliff Stroudt, and Oscar McBride; one of my freshman year roommates, Glen Cassidy—and what seeing them instantly reminds me of is their honesty, conviction, and joy in being at and attending Notre Dame. Their sincere passion for service, their dedication to family and to their communities is something I think a lot of as an adult. Every day of my life I can only hope to live the way I believe a Notre Dame person should live.

After reading this one might think: "Wow, what Kool-Aid did he drink?" I am a firm believer that Notre Dame does not create good people or faith-filled people or people who value service; I do believe, however, that Notre Dame simply allows people to be their best without shame or fear. To be brave in the face of the many of the ills of our society is what one gains from attending and experiencing Notre Dame.

CHRISTINE ASHFORD SWANSON

(Class of 1994)

Christine Ashford came to Notre Dame in autumn 1990 from Detroit. She majored in film, television, and theatre. After graduating she earned an advanced degree in filmmaking at NYU and, along with her husband, Michael Swanson (Class of 1993), has worked as a filmmaker ever since. She and her family live in Pasadena, California.

I WISH I COULD SAY THAT MY PARENTS, GRANDPARENTS, EVEN great-grandparents graduated from the University of Notre Dame. I wish I could say that I knew early on that this highly lauded institution would be my destiny because attending Notre Dame was in my DNA. Many of my classmates at Notre Dame claimed this as their legacy, and I saw how important and meaningful it was to their families.

I am a testament to the fact that there are many paths to Notre Dame. My path, while atypical, is still imbued with a sense of destiny that rivals all the folklore of generations past. My story, however, just happens to start out as a love story.

The year was 1989, the summer before my senior year of high school. I was a school representative attending Presidential Classroom, a weeklong seminar in Washington, D.C., designed to inspire civic responsibility and activism in government. Little did I know that I would meet my future husband, Michael Swanson, at Presidential Classroom that week. I was so smitten by this brilliant young man that I would follow him all the way to his and my future alma mater, Notre Dame.

When I met Michael he had already been admitted to Notre Dame in the freshman class of 1989. He courted me long-distance my whole senior year of high school—he at Notre Dame and I in Detroit. Eventually he convinced me that Notre Dame was a great choice for me. After many visits to the campus, I felt that the university was a good fit. Its academic reputation was high, yet it maintained an appealing small-campus feel. So, twenty years of marriage and four children later, I'm still very pleased with my decision to attend Notre Dame.

My educational experiences at Notre Dame ranged from challenging (required math and science courses) to mind-blowing (all the film theory, art, and literature courses). I remember distinctly the very day I decided what I wanted to do with the rest of my life. In my freshman year, filmmaker Spike Lee visited campus. During his lecture, I had the realization that I, too, wanted to make films. Until I heard Spike speak, I had no idea that I could earn a living making movies. I'd never met a filmmaker before.

That encounter changed the trajectory of my life. I immediately changed my major from finance to film studies, and I never looked back. In fact, I went on to graduate school at New York University Film School and earned an MFA in filmmaking. In serendipitous fashion, Spike, also an NYU Film School graduate, was my directing teacher.

Many years later, Notre Dame contacted Michael and me to create and produce commercials for the NBC broadcasts of Notre Dame football games. Although we are African-American, neither of us (like a whole lot of others) played sports at Notre Dame. We proudly created three dynamic ads, including one titled "Not Just Football," that highlighted all the wonderful aspects of Notre Dame outside of athletics.

Three professors at Notre Dame made indelible impressions on me as a student, and I know their tutelage opened my mind in ways that still inspire and serve me today. I never studied African-American culture formally until I took Dr. Marcia Sawyer's freshman seminar course. I've been a student of African-American studies and culture ever since. The late Dr. Erskine Peters taught two of the best classes I took at Notre Dame. Professor Peters was prolific, eloquent, and passionate about African-American literature. He opened up a world of language and art as told through the African-American experience that still informs my own work as a writer and filmmaker. Feminist theory in film and literature was something new to me. Professor Hilary Radner instilled in me a hunger to disseminate images and cultural cues in media and pop culture. Film studies was a relatively new major when I was at Notre Dame. Today it is a large program with resources and facilities that rival some of the best film schools in the country.

Some of my fondest memories stem from my time spent studying abroad. Twice. I studied in Japan my entire sophomore year and participated in the Saint Mary's College Semester Around the World program during my senior year, traveling throughout Southeast Asia, Europe, and India. Some of my most enduring friendships were made abroad. While in Japan, I became fluent in a foreign language and conversant with an energetic and historically rich culture that still intrigues me. Studying abroad pushed me outside of my comfort zone and forced me to navigate uncharted waters where I either had to sink or swim. Culture shock was the least of my concerns; I had to figure out how to ride a bike to a bus station, take a bus to a train station, then take a train to my exit, and finally, walk two miles to school.

I lived a year with a host family in which my eleven-year-old host sister had more homework than I did. Every night her parents sat with her at the table and helped her until she finished. I learned to appreciate, at a young age, the level of sacrifice and commitment Japanese families make to their children's education. Those lessons still stick with me as I raise my own four children.

Part of what made Notre Dame special to me is the commitment of the university and its students to a deep sense of service. Everywhere I turned, students were active in service-oriented events. You couldn't escape it. It was just a part of what it meant to be a student at Notre Dame. I was fortunate to participate in Big Brothers Big Sisters. I was placed with a nine-year-old little sister from South Bend. I had the opportunity to mentor her and spend time with her over many years. Today that little girl has a master's degree and teaches science.

As I approach my twenty-year reunion, I reflect upon all that Notre Dame has meant to me. The university's name has always garnered a certain level of respect wherever I went. Some of the connections I made with friends at Notre Dame became catalysts for various breaks in my career in the entertainment industry.

On a more personal note, when our family moved to Pasadena, California, we were referred to highly recommended pediatricians for our children. When I called the pediatricians' office, I was disappointed to learn that the practice was no longer accepting new patients. I learned the doctors were Notre Dame graduates, and I e-mailed them about our desire to have them as our children's pediatricians. When they heard my husband and I were also Notre Dame alumni, they immediately reached out and welcomed us into their practice. I'm happy to say, as a member of the Notre Dame family, we love our own and we take care of our own.

As our oldest child considers high schools, my mind has already wandered to potential college choices for him. My husband and I have considered all the possibilities. Maybe he could go Ivy, perhaps Stanford or even Northwestern? Our desire for all of our children is that they do better than we did. The older our children get and the longer we live, we keep coming back to our alma mater.

We know that our son would be challenged intellectually, while keeping faith at the forefront of all of his endeavors. To us, that means everything. There are many institutions where our children can receive a world-class education, but very few put at the forefront of their mission a commitment to faith and service.

If our children decide to attend our alma mater, they will officially be considered "legacy." That is no small feat for us, first-generation college graduates. For the next generation to receive an education at Notre Dame by following in the footsteps of their parents would be a great accomplishment for our family. We are creating a legacy, one that will live on for generations after us. Perhaps one day our great-grandchildren will say, "My great-grandparents attended this storied institution, and I, too, am a student here."

OWEN HAROLD MICHAEL SMITH
(Class of 1995)

Owen Smith came to Notre Dame in 1991 from Prince George's County, Maryland. He majored in finance and was 1995 Bookstore Basketball champion. After graduation, he became a stand-up comedian, writer, actor, and producer. Currently, he is a writer, producer, and performer on The Arsenio Hall Show. *He lives with his wife, Ralinda, in Santa Monica, California.*

The black population at Notre Dame is 2 percent. That's like skim milk. You couldn't skip class cuz they knew. I'd be walking across campus and white people would pop out the bushes like, "Missed you in class today, Owen."

—from Owen Smith's comedy special, *Anonymous*

IN AMERICA, BEING BLACK USUALLY QUALIFIES YOU AS A minority. And although I've been black all my life, I never truly knew what being a minority felt like until I attended the University of Notre Dame. Let me explain.

I was born in Nassau, Bahamas—a place where we have black people on our money. What's blacker than that? I was raised in Prince George's County, Maryland, a suburb right outside of Washington, D.C. In the nineties, *Ebony* magazine called PG County, as it's more affectionately known, "the blackest county in America."

Growing up I saw black doctors, black lawyers, black dentists, black business owners, black bus drivers, black teachers—PG County was like Smurf Village, except all the Smurfs were black.

Being teased as a kid is nothing new. Everybody gets it. Some kids were tormented for wearing glasses or being overweight. I got slammed for being smart, always doing my homework, and getting good grades. My grades were so good I got put in the "not black enough" category. Michael Jackson got whiter from vitiligo; I got whiter by making the honor roll.

Then at seventeen, I finally had an opportunity for a reprieve from my childhood angst. Going to college gave me the chance to pick my own world. Fortunately, because I kept my grades up and had decent SAT scores, I had lots of options. Maybe I'd attend a historically black college like Howard, or an Ivy League school like Princeton, or I might explore new territory out west like UCLA.

Then one day, seemingly out of the blue, I received a letter from the University of Notre Dame in South Bend, Indiana, asking me to apply. Initially it didn't seem like the right fit. I mean, South Bend, Indiana? What black person looks in the mirror and goes, "South Bend, Indiana—now that's where I need to be"? Definitely not seventeen-year-old me.

But then the strangest thing happened. When I would tell people the colleges I was considering, Notre Dame always got the biggest reaction. From my guidance counselor to the lunch lady, all of them may not have known where Notre Dame was—hell, I didn't know where it was until I got that letter in the mail—but they all agreed it was a great school and would be a tremendous opportunity. And my mom made no secret that Notre Dame was *her* first choice. So when the time came for my decision, in the words of the great LeBron James, "I decided to take my talents to South Bend."

And in the summer of 1991, I left the blackest county in America for quite possibly one of the whitest places on earth, or what a friend of mine would later call it after a visit, "Disneyland for white people."

Yes, I experienced a lot of the classic fish-out-of-water scenarios at Notre Dame. I had a white girl from Idaho tell me she never saw a black person before, and good luck finding any black magazines or hair-care products on campus.

I remember spending hours in the Basilica of the Sacred Heart looking for one black angel. When it came to food, I learned that everybody doesn't necessarily use seasoning. And I got so used to being mistaken for a football or basketball player that I started having fun with it. My favorite was the time a little white kid saw me, raced across the quad, and begged me to sign his football. I didn't want to be rude so I wrote, "Stay in School," and signed it "Daffy Duck."

I'm still waiting for that football to pop up on Ebay.

However, something unexpected happened over on the Ebony Side of the Dome. You know how in the X-men movies Professor Xavier has a school for gifted mutants? And at this school, mutants come from all over the world to develop their skills? To me, the greater gift this school provides is that it's where these outcasts discover they are not alone. For a lot of them it's the first time they encounter others out there who are just like them.

This is how I felt as I got to know the other 1.999 percent of the black community at Notre Dame. Being black at Notre Dame was the first time in my life I was in a room with so many other black people with white names. At times it felt like I was at a "Black People with White Names" convention.

If you were black at Notre Dame it meant that growing up you were probably teased for being smart and getting good grades, and you knew what it felt like to be put in the "not black enough" penalty box by your own people.

If you were black at Notre Dame that meant you came from a support system that stressed the importance of education and made the necessary sacrifices to ensure you had access to the best opportunities.

If you were black at Notre Dame, it meant you didn't accept "no" for an answer.

If you were black at Notre Dame it meant you were raised to say "please," "excuse me," and "thank you"—just like me!

If you were black at Notre Dame it meant you had finally found your tribe. And I can't speak for anyone else, but for me it felt great!

It was at Notre Dame where I felt safe enough to dream. I remember taking long walks across that beautiful campus and envisioning myself being a huge star in the world of comedy. I was going to sit on that couch with Arsenio; I was going to have several successful comedy specials, star in movies and television shows, and the world was going to know and love me for making them laugh.

Being black at Notre Dame was where I got the courage to dream big and, if I had it all to do over again, I wouldn't change a thing.

ROCHELLE VALSAINT

(Class of 1995)

Rochelle Valsaint came to Notre Dame in autumn 1991 from New Orleans. She majored in communications. Since graduation she has bridged her vocation as an entrepreneur and branding professional and her avocation as a servant leader on the university's alumni board and in civic organizations. She and her children live in Doraville, Georgia.

MY JOURNEY TO AND THROUGH NOTRE DAME IS FULL OF FATED details. As a senior at New Orleans's John F. Kennedy Sr. High School, I was summoned to the counselor's office one day to have that conversation about where I would apply to college. As I awaited my turn, I noticed a picture of the Golden Dome on a folder in the office. When my turn came and the counselor asked what schools I was interested in, I answered his question with a question: "What's that folder with the golden building on it?"

Mr. Counselor's eyes lit up and his face brightened with a smile. I left the office with information about Notre Dame and an application for admission. At that moment, I just felt good that I had completed the task of finding a college to apply to, as I had been instructed to do at my college-prep program.

Notre Dame was the only university I *applied* to. I was guaranteed admission and a scholarship to the University of New Orleans, where I attended a college-prep program for high achieving, low-income, minority students. And at that time, I was the first in my family to consider entering college. So I had no idea that you were supposed to apply to multiple schools.

My counselor's enthusiasm was the momentum that started me skipping down the road of admission requirements. But it was the response of my English teacher, to whom I had gone to have my essays reviewed, that turned my skip into determination. Mr. Applebee—his name is clear in my memory—discouraged me from applying to Notre Dame. He wanted to save me from disappointment, since he was convinced that I would not get in. He was sure of it because he had been rejected when he applied. And since he was everything I was not—white, male, privileged, and surely more prepared to go to and succeed at Notre Dame than a little black girl from this inner-city public school—he wanted to save me the sting of rejection. But I was encouraged by his discouragement and, ultimately, I was all too happy to prove Mr. Applebee wrong with, first, my acceptance letter, and eventually, my degree.

I still smile, reminiscing on my serendipitous Notre Dame story. However, what I find most arresting is the ever-evolving tale of Notre Dame and me.

"How many black alumni of Notre Dame are there?" I asked this question of the group of peers I sat among in the conference room on the second floor of the LaFortune Student Center. It was 2007 and I was asking in reference to a marketing strategy for our organization, Black Alumni of Notre Dame. I was already several years into my eventual fifteen-year tenure on the organization's board of directors. As marketing director, I wanted to reach as many black alumni as possible. And the best way to do that was to think about the details of who, where, and how they were to be reached. My question was a spontaneous one, as many things are for me. But the answer came as a surprise. Someone responded, "About 2,300."

"What?!" I was dumbstruck.

I had always known that I was one of the few black students in my classes. I knew every black person in my class by face, and most by name. I'd guess there were, at most, 115 black students on campus any given year during my time at Notre Dame. But, even with that knowledge, I was not prepared to know that I had such a small number of alumni peers.

Part of my shocked disbelief was rooted in the fact that, for me, the black alumni presence was and is so prevalent in my life. Two of my closest friendships were developed the summer before our freshman year with two black classmates who now are alumni, Letitia "Tish" Bowen McGuff (Class of 1995) and Tonya Callahan Perry (Class of 1995). A program developed for diverse students brought a handful of us to campus to acclimate us to all the changes we would be exposed to on a campus barely sprinkled with people who looked like us.

(I would be so grateful for that summer in subsequent times, when the campus seemed so white, figuratively and literally. Times when I felt on display, being the only black person in a class of thirty. Or when for the first time I put a relaxer in my hair in my room as my white roommate looked on. I had to explain what I was doing and why I was doing it to Heather, who had never seen the process. Later I became the campus go-to for many who could not do their own re-laxers, or get to or afford a hairdresser in South Bend. Or the times when those cold, long, dark South Bend winters reminded me of my sun-filled, steamy roots in Louisiana, a place where snow was foreign.)

Those relationships are what got me through. Tish and I ate most meals together in the North or South Dining Hall. We hung out to-gether in Breen-Phillips, my dorm, or Farley, Tish's, every chance we got. We had different majors, so we had no classes together after fresh-man year. But we made up for it in LaFortune and at social gatherings on and off campus. There was lots of dancing, laughing, and talking involved. And the best weekends were going to Tish's family house in nearby Buchanan, Michigan. We'd go there to share in family, food, and fun, and sports were always involved, since she was from a basket-ball family and a student-athlete. Those weekends were the closest thing to being back home with my own family in New Orleans. Those experiences made my everyday life culturally and colorfully familiar in what seemed at times a different world.

I graduated in 1995. And after a short stint in Chicago, I settled in Atlanta. I didn't know anyone there outside of my family. So I decided the best way to meet people would be to connect to the local Black Alumni of Notre Dame. A notice of an opening to represent the southeast region led to a position on the BA of ND board. That led to constant involvement with black alumni in Atlanta. From 1997 to 2012, I flew to Notre Dame two or more times a year to develop local, regional, and national efforts to connect and engage black alumni.

With such a small number of black graduates, our matriculation into black alumni status comes with the special distinction of being among the few to make it to these distinguished ranks. The ranks are distinguished, in my opinion, because we made it from whatever our fated backgrounds were to the hallowed halls of historic buildings, sitting in classes despite whatever our perceived weaknesses and labels, whether given to us by others or ourselves. Those ranks are distinguished because some of us, like me, were the first in our families to go to college, and because others, like Tonya and Letitia, continued a legacy of education started not long ago by a determined lineage, overcoming what seemed like insurmountable odds. Those ranks are distinguished because we can say we made it through many "worst of times" and some of the most important "best of times."

And even though the stories of our past are important, we are also distinguished by what is being accomplished now, both big and small. I have helped shape the organization that gave foundation to my post-college life, Black Alumni of Notre Dame. Over fifteen years, this organization taught me lessons in collaboration, negotiation, service, compromise, and leadership. And in return, I have become a woman of leadership. Those are the big, public lessons.

The small, private lessons have been of love, family, loss, uncertainty, persistence, and reinvention. The greatest gift of the public and private life lessons has been in balancing it all. And even as I walk my path and continue on my journey, I get to watch the depth, breadth, and beauty of others' stories. Stories of films written, performed in, or produced by Jeremy Rall, Jeremy Sample, Michael and Christine Swanson, or Stephen Pope. Stories of big business deals made by Manny Grace. Stories of legal victories by Qiana Lillard. Stories of fundraisers by Richard Ryans. Stories of babies born to Annie Denson and parents getting care from Eleanor Walker. It's the sum of these stories that make us distinguished.

Some years have passed since I first posed the question about the number of black alumni. Our ranks have swelled and, with the popularity of social media, I get to hear and see many stories unfold.

As for the story of me, individually, I turn forty-one this year. And this particular chapter is one of growth, rebuilding, and reinvention. I am no longer the young, married, black mom creating a place for myself as an educated woman with aspirations of being both an at-home mom and an entrepreneur. I am embarking on middle-age, divorced and starting a new chapter, with dreams of a second career that's bigger and better than my first. As for what I'll do, I'm not completely sure just yet, maybe something in education, maybe something nonprofit, contributing to the world my talents and gifts through work that bridges my vocation with my avocation. My contributions have been and will be big, beautiful, colorful, multidimensional, marvelous, awe-inspiring, and breathtaking, all at once. And I stand boldly in the present to take a breath before stepping confidently toward a future of greatness. I can do this all because I know the grandness of those that stand behind me, in front of me, and beside me.

So stay tuned. Where we'll take you is not certain. But I assure you, it will be worth the ride.

ROWAN RICHARDS

(Class of 1996)

Rowan Richards came to Notre Dame in autumn 1992 from Bloomfield, New Jersey. He majored in marketing and played on the baseball team. After graduation he was drafted by the Texas Rangers and played professional baseball for several years. He now heads The Stewards Market, developing micro-enterprises in underresourced communities in Chicago. He and his wife, Stacia (Class of 1997), live in Oak Park, Illinois.

PRIOR TO 1991, NOTRE DAME WAS LITTLE MORE THAN A PLACE of legend to me. It was a name used by many of the people in the northeast New Jersey neighborhood where I lived—Irish and non-Irish, Catholic and non-Catholic—to describe a sacred place. It was the school that my tenth-grade biology teacher, Juanita Moss, mentioned while detailing the many accomplishments of her dear friend Aubrey Lewis (Class of 1958). Notre Dame was the university that a previous alumnus of Bloomfield High School, Kelly Tripucka, attended and played basketball for.

Based on the sentiment of others, the University of Notre Dame always seemed to represent a place of hope and opportunity. It was never a place that I seriously considered for *my* future. But that all changed during the summer of 1991.

A baseball coach encouraged me to try out for the Garden State Games, which is a statewide all-star tournament. I made the team and performed well enough to earn the attention of Notre Dame's assistant baseball coach, Mike Gibbons, although not right away.

Coach Gibbons came to the games to recruit New Jersey's top baseball players. He came initially not to see me play, but rather to recruit my closest childhood friend and teammate, Brian Lindner. Brian had been named an All-American, but his academic record was not strong enough to meet the standards of Notre Dame.

Gibbons sat in the stands with John Kroger, a former minor league teammate of his who also had been my high school freshman basketball coach. As the two men discussed the selection of players, Kroger steered Gibbons's attention towards me. This timely reunion of two friends set my life on a new course.

By Monday of the following week, the recruiting and admission process had begun. By October 1991 I was accepted and chose the University of Notre Dame for my college education and experience.

My four years at Notre Dame were a period during which I experienced several high and low points of my life. My earliest experience at Notre Dame was one of complete culture shock. I am sure many incoming freshmen have a similar experience. But when you are going through it, you sense that you are the only one who does not quite fit in.

The three areas that created the greatest challenges for me were economics, race, and culture. Financially my family and I most likely fell into the lower tenth of the income distribution of families represented at Notre Dame. Thanks to my baseball scholarship, much of my schooling was paid for, but there was the additional financial strain of covering the remaining costs. My parents definitely carried the burden, as they wanted me to focus my energy on my studies and athletic endeavors.

The economic disparity was closely linked to the cultural differences. I grew up in an era when culture was defined not only by race and ethnicity, but also by experience. Many of my Notre Dame classmates came from backgrounds that, unlike my own, included private school, frequent travel, and at least one parent having attended Notre Dame. I never begrudged anyone these opportunities, but I certainly could never fully understand that lifestyle. And even to my youthful eyes, it seemed obvious that there was a link between race and the possession or lack of these opportunities.

Nevertheless, I had the great fortune of meeting incredible individuals. My first connection to these wonderful people was the dormitory I lived in for four years: Morrissey Manor. I developed several lasting relationships with other residents of that dormitory. The first person I met in Morrissey was a young man named Richard Rolle. Today he is Dr. Richard Rolle, DDS. Back then he was just Richie, the skinny kid from Minnesota, living in the dorm's basement and hoping to make the football team.

Unfortunately, Richie's football experience was short-lived after he was diagnosed with cancer during his sophomore year at Notre Dame. I won't attempt to understand how Richie felt during that period. I can say, however, that I witnessed a brave young man handle that experience with grace and joy.

The next person I met was Dan McConnell, a young man from Alton, Illinois. Dan was the first of three roommates I would meet that day. We had written to each other during the summer months as a way of learning a bit about one another. Although we are not of the same race, we realized that our upbringings had been very similar. Although I remain friends with my other freshman-year roommates, Dan was the only one that I lived with for all four years. To this day we remain great friends, and, in fact, Dan was the best man in my wedding.

During the years I attended Notre Dame, 1992 to 1996, "Morrissey Manor" was considered one of the worst dorms on campus because of the small section of rooms in the basement. Conditions there *were* quite spartan, but that almost added to the appeal. I complained as much as anyone and had many opportunities to move to other dormitories. But for some reason, I could never pull myself away. Good people have a way of making everything around them better.

Over the years I met many other great people. Among these people none is more important than my best friend and wife, Stacia. Stacia Masters and I became friends the first day of math class during the spring of 1993. Our relationship continued to grow over the next three years, first as friends and eventually as a couple. During that time, we shared in the ups and downs of each other's lives. I believe these experiences allowed us to withstand the challenges of being apart for five years while Stacia was in Chicago and I was playing minor league baseball in various small cities.

Outside of the dorm, I spent my waking hours in two places: the classroom and the baseball field. Both would prove extremely challenging during my first semester. By the time that semester was over, I was barely keeping my head above water. With the help of tutors and professors, I was able to turn things around in the classroom. As for my time on the field, just one month into the fall season of my freshman year, I was sidelined with an injury that required surgery. As in the classroom, I recovered and finished strong during my remaining years at Notre Dame, even earning the role of captain on the 1996 baseball team.

During the four years of baseball, I experienced two different head coaches, many teammates, two home stadiums, numerous road trips, multiple injuries, amazing victories, crushing defeats, championships, and individual honors. Yet the one constant throughout was the camaraderie between my teammates and myself. It wasn't always rosy. There were plenty of arguments and the occasional physical altercation. Even so, I knew my teammates would be around whenever I needed them.

After graduating in 1996 with a bachelor's degree in marketing, I went on to be selected by the Texas Rangers in the amateur draft. It was not an easy road to professional baseball, but truly a dream come true. After four years of moving up through the organization, a severe knee injury brought my baseball career to a halt. Injury in sports is a very common occurrence. For many of the young men I played with or against, the challenge of finding other opportunities with equal potential was an uphill battle. I was fortunate to have opportunities come to me right away. I attribute these opportunities to being part of the Notre Dame family.

I worked in the front office for the Rangers for eighteen months doing a variety of tasks. At the time, Doug Melvin was general manager, and he put me on track to be a general manager of a major league team someday. I quickly realized that I really didn't have the passion for that side of the game. Around the time I made that realization, a former Notre Dame teammate reached out to me and asked if I would be interested in joining the futures trading firm he worked for. I didn't really know anything about the industry, but figured I could learn. I flew to Chicago and interviewed with the two principal owners of the firm. They were not concerned about my lack of experience or knowledge of the industry. They were, however, very interested in my Notre Dame experience. I was offered the position on the spot.

It has been seventeen years since I graduated from the University of Notre Dame. I travel back to campus at least once a year and am proud of the advancements the school is making in areas such as student diversity and its focus on global justice issues. As I look back on my experience at Notre Dame, I thank God for how He challenged me during those years and how He developed my character. Both good and bad, my four years at Notre Dame were like no other.

TANYA WALKER

(Class of 1997)

Tanya Walker came to Notre Dame in autumn 1993 from New Orleans. She majored in marketing, sociology, and African-American studies, and participated in the African-American Student Alliance, the Student Alumni Relations Group, and the Voices of Faith Gospel Choir. Since graduation she has worked in marketing professional services for architecture, engineering, environmental, and construction firms. She lives in Atlanta.

I ONCE WOULD HAVE SAID THAT I CAME TO THE UNIVERSITY of Notre Dame almost by accident. However, in retrospect, it seems a series of fortuitous events brought me to Notre Dame, and to the Catholic faith—as if Mother Mary herself looked out for me.

I grew up a Methodist girl in New Orleans, a largely Catholic city, in a family that held on to certain Catholic traditions despite its Protestant religious affiliation. I grew up at the knee of a great aunt who would cook and clean for priests of the Notre Dame seminary in New Orleans. Although there was no formal affiliation between the seminary and the university, I developed an affection for the name "Notre Dame" and Our Lady.

With the same great aunt, I would participate in the local New Orleans Catholic tradition of visiting St. Joseph Church for prosperity beans (fava beans) on the feast of St. Joseph. Together with my mom and my sister, I would visit the historic St. Ann Grotto during my childhood. I wouldn't become Catholic until many years after leaving

Notre Dame. But the beauty of my early childhood Catholic experiences and people who held dear the name "Notre Dame" would plant the seeds of openness to attending the University of Notre Dame. Ultimately, the university's Catholic character, the ability to be openly spiritual there and to have a personal relationship with Jesus, and the feeling of closeness with Our Lady would all play a large part in my choosing Notre Dame.

A black engineer and mentor at Shell Oil, where I interned while attending McDonogh 35 Senior High School, would challenge me to apply to Notre Dame. His sister, Marcia Sawyer, whom he admired, was a professor at Notre Dame, and he felt I should aspire to her level of achievement. Almost as one would take on a dare, I took on the challenge of applying to Notre Dame.

As smart as I thought I was, I wasn't wise enough then to understand the significance of a place like Notre Dame. I pursued Notre Dame with blind faith. My senior year in high school, I would have a series of prophetic dreams that showed me walking among snowy landscapes and gave me glimpses of vistas that I could experience only as a student at Notre Dame. I didn't quite understand what I was seeing in my dreams, as I had never visited the campus; but these dreams would lead me in search of those experiences in real life, and Notre Dame seemed to be the key.

Visiting during spring diversity recruitment weekend would also be instrumental in my attending Notre Dame. That weekend I would make friendships that I would retain during my four years on campus. Most importantly, I would walk the campus and feel a mystical sense of connection with the place—as if I belonged. It was an indescribable connection that I cannot explain but I am certain others have felt. And it's that feeling I first felt at Notre Dame—the connectedness, a joy that feels like being home—that I would use in the future as a gauge on whether a community, a place, or an environment was where I was supposed to be. If I could feel the same love in a place that I first felt at Notre Dame, that place is where I want to be.

It seems impossible for me to talk about Notre Dame and not think of it in magical terms. The journey to Notre Dame was magical for me. It was also one of the most challenging times of my life. My time at Notre Dame was also a polarizing experience. I would grow into the new energy of being a young woman far away from everything that had been familiar, on a campus where being a racial minority became the most salient part of my identity, and with the academic challenges of a marketing/sociology/African-American studies major in the Mendoza College of Business. Diversity dynamics would cast me into the role of outsider, along with two hundred or so other students who would make up the 2 percent African-American student population during my time on campus.

Like many others, I would react by overly identifying with my blackness. I would cling to definitive black student events and community. I would also take on limiting views of what was possible for my life and not dare to take advantage of the global opportunities that Notre Dame offered as part of the educational experience, like studying abroad or for a semester at a partner college in another part of the US.

I can recall being so angry while attending Notre Dame. I recall being among friends who shared my fondness for phrases like "Notre Dame is a microcosm of the world at large and whatever happens in the world happens here," to explain why things were so racially tense and divided. I think this was the way we—the young, brilliant adults we were becoming—learned to deal with the pain of feeling alienated, by intellectualizing it and creating bonds through our alienation.

I can also recall being very loving, finding love and camaraderie among other souls having similar experiences, and finding the impetus to be the woman that I am now. At Notre Dame, I would study marketing, sociology, and African-American studies, and become the only student my graduating year with an African-American studies double major. This would lend itself to a career in business development for architectural and engineering firms, following graduate studies in sociology. I would work in a computer lab on campus. This would translate into skills utilized on my first job post-college, with a software firm. I would become co-owner in Siegfried Hall Food Sales and that same entrepreneurial spirit would drive me as a staffing manager and operations leader with CH2M HILL, a company ranked among Fortune's "Most Admired Companies" and Ethisphere's "World's Most Ethical Companies."

While in school I would become co-president of the African-American Student Alliance. This student leadership connection would foster my seven-year commitment to serve on the board of the Black

Alumni of Notre Dame. On campus, I would be among the student leaders who, against enormous odds, funded bringing a major rap group, Outkast, to campus. While on the BA of ND board, that same grassroots organizing and teamwork would help deliver the first-ever, simultaneously held, five-city fundraising event for the BA of ND's Frazier Thompson Scholarship Fund, and celebrations of the contributions of blacks at Notre Dame and the black alumni legacy.

College shapes your life experiences in ways you never quite understand when you are in the middle of it. At age thirty-eight and more than sixteen years post-graduation, I can truly appreciate Notre Dame for what it was and would become—a safe space to explore your interests and come into your own, and a place that anchors you in its tradition as it connects you with future generations in a shared experience. It is safe to say that the person I discovered myself to be during those formative years is the person that I am still becoming today. As I continue my life, I hold both Notre Dame and Our Lady sacred within my heart.

REGGIE BROOKS

(Class of 1999)

Reggie Brooks came to Notre Dame in autumn 1989 from Tulsa, Oklahoma. He majored in management information systems and was a standout running back on the Notre Dame football team. After graduation he played four years in the NFL and two years in Europe. He returned to the university in 2004 and now serves as manager for monogram relations. He and his wife, Christina Arnold Brooks (Class of 2014), and their five children live in Granger, Indiana.

"DID YOU SIGN THAT LETTER OF INTENT?" MY FATHER ASKED.

"Yes sir," I replied.

My answer prompted my father to hang up, leaving me alone on the phone with only the dial tone and my word. I had called him hoping to gain a sympathetic ear concerning my desire to transfer from Notre Dame.

My freshman year had been tough. Everything about Notre Dame was foreign to me—from the nuns doling out discipline in the office of student affairs; to DuLac, the student handbook; to parietals; to priests in residence checking you at the door of your dorm after dark; to white kids drinking with their parents and leaving cases of beer at my door as gifts. I was constantly surrounded by people I didn't understand and who, I felt, didn't understand me. But my dad let me know that night that I had to own what had been my first adult decision: to follow my big brother Tony (Class of 1992) to Notre Dame.

I had been recruited heavily by "the U" (the University of Miami), Oklahoma State, UCLA, Arizona State, and Princeton, and in the end made the choice to attend Notre Dame. Now I had to make the best of it. And eventually I did.

Most people have no idea what it's like to be a student-athlete for a Division I football program, especially one that has the kind of storied history that Notre Dame does. Under Coach Lou Holtz, Notre Dame had amassed a bevy of blue-chip players at every position. In my case, I was an underclassman at running back behind my brother Tony, Ricky Watters, Rodney Culver, Raghib Ismail, and Anthony Johnson—each an all-American who would later be drafted into the NFL, making an indelible mark.

Essentially I had to operate at a high level at the busy intersection of academics and football, while navigating the cultural and religious divide my own life experiences brought to the table. It came to a head for the first time the summer after my freshman year. My schedule was grueling by any standard. Every day during summer school I ate an early breakfast, had a full morning of classes side by side with some of the brightest young people in the country, and then went straight to the kind of workouts that would leave you vomiting until the dry heaves took over—all before the unofficial afternoon practice without coaches, a kind of voluntary seven-on-seven.

On one particular day, instead of eating I used my break between workouts and afternoon practice to head back to Grace Hall for a quick nap. But I forgot my key. I was hungry and exhausted and beginning to question the worth of the "ND" experience. The rector let me into the dorm and I walked toward the elevators, explaining my predicament and being only halfway conscious of his disapproving glare. He followed, lecturing me on responsibility and how I had disturbed him. The disgust in his voice seemed to escalate with my silence.

The elevator doors opened and I stepped in, but he was not finished telling me about my entitled football player mentality and so he grabbed my arm. "Don't walk away from me when I'm talking to you!" he hissed.

With one clean jerk, I broke free of his grasp and the elevator doors closed. My tired muscles—the same muscles I had worked incessantly to earn a spot on the field to represent Notre Dame, to represent him—had responded by reflex. When I got to my room, I fell into my bed and immediately fell asleep.

A week later, I received a notification in my mailbox concerning a meeting with Sister Jean Lenz of student affairs. When I arrived she told me I had been "charged" with assaulting a rector. The student affairs version of the story said I had pushed the rector to the ground. I told her that version was false. I told her that I did not like white people grabbing me in an aggressive manner and, if I had hit him, there would have been a mark. I had been taught to defend myself, but I did not hit, shove, or push him. I had simply jerked away from him. With no witnesses, it was my word against his and his word carried more weight. I was put on disciplinary probation with the university and sent to Coach Holtz for athletic discipline.

At the time, I don't think Sr. Jean understood the depth and breadth of the racial experience I had walked onto campus with. I had grown up in a very segregated city—Tulsa, Oklahoma, in the late 1970s and 1980s. Tulsa was a city known for a few things—big oil, Oral Roberts University, singer Charlie Wilson and the GAP Band, and, infamously, the 1921 Race Riots, a two-day orgy of violence by the white community during which untold numbers of black citizens were massacred and "Black Wall Street," at the time the wealthiest black community in the country, was destroyed.

That episode had been fueled by a false story. The contrived tale of a black man attacking a white woman on a downtown elevator still haunted the people and the dilapidated structures on the north side of Tulsa where I grew up. Their story was never told in the history books, and survived only through the whispered stories around the dinner tables of black families that had survived or knew people who had. It wasn't until a few years ago, when a documentary film and several books about the riots were published, that the world recognized and recounted the tragedy.

Although roughly seventy years had passed since the riots in my hometown when I came to Notre Dame, that day—the day I was placed on disciplinary probation without evidence—I felt I was again experiencing the painful residuum of racism. My voice, my word, *my being* lacked the credibility to garner a fair review of the situation before I was sentenced. And where could I go from there?

My Dad knew what I had already been through in my short time at Notre Dame when I called him. He had been born in Texas and moved to Tulsa a few years after the race riots. He had experienced the harsh realities of racism growing up in segregated Tulsa as the first four-sport letterman student-athlete at Booker T. Washington High School. He hadn't just heard the stories; he had survived them. He raised me to persevere in the beautiful face of challenge. I could not quit, but I had to ask and answer some serious questions. I had to be willing to work harder than the average Notre Dame student to succeed.

I questioned how the Notre Dame community could know and understand the historical baggage I carried without taking the time to talk to me and find out what experiences culminated in what I considered a normal, reflexive reaction. I wondered if my new Notre Dame family was willing to know me beyond a one-dimensional image of a black student-athlete. And I pondered whether I was willing to stick around long enough to get to know Notre Dame and help the university discover the necessity of valuing the voice of every student—athlete or not.

Almost twenty years after leaving Notre Dame as an undergraduate, I came back to work for the university as an administrator in the athletic department. I was still trying to answer those questions I asked as a kid, but was determined not to quit.

After all, my signature will always be on that letter of intent.

DANIELLE GREEN

(Class of 1999)

Danielle Green came to Notre Dame in autumn 1995 from Chicago, Illinois. She majored in psychology and was a member of the women's basketball team. After graduation she remained at Notre Dame to play a fifth year. Two years later she joined the United States Army, and in 2004 she deployed to Iraq. Today she resides with her son and her father in South Bend, where she works for the Department of Veterans Affairs.

AS A SEVEN-YEAR-OLD, I VIEWED NOTRE DAME AS A MYTHICAL place. The football team was on television every Saturday when there was little else on. I saw Touchdown Jesus and the Golden Dome, and I thought: "This place must be special." So I decided that I wanted to attend someday.

My other dream was to serve my country. As a child raised in poverty in the inner city of Chicago by a single parent who battled with substance abuse, it was imperative for me to dream big so I would not fall victim to my environment. I wanted to be somebody; I wanted to matter in life.

Shortly after I decided that I wanted to attend Notre Dame, I told my mother. She replied that she didn't have the money to send me there. I recall telling her that I would make good grades and play a sport so I could earn my way. As a preteen and then a teenager, I would share my Notre Dame dream with others. But they would simply look at me bewildered or say, "Do you understand the prestige of Notre Dame?" This lit a fire in me, and I devised a plan: I was going to earn a basketball scholarship.

In the summer of 1994, as I was about to enter my senior year of high school, Coach Muffet McGraw came to watch me play one day in a summer league. I performed well enough that some of the high school coaches who were present said she was interested. I realized that my dream was about to become a reality.

A couple of months later, I was on the Notre Dame campus for an official visit. Fear and doubt had entered my mind. The thought that I might not be smart enough and other people saying I would not be successful almost propelled me to consider another school. However, I never wanted to look back later in life and regret not attending Notre Dame. So at the end of my recruiting trip, I verbally committed to Coach McGraw during Sunday breakfast. I dared not leave campus without committing.

Coming from a melting-pot high school—Roosevelt High School on Chicago's North Side, where at one point there were students of no fewer than twenty-six nationalities—Notre Dame proved a complete culture shock to me. I had a difficult time connecting. Everything about the university was grueling: my class schedule, basketball practice, and socializing. I felt awkward and out of place, and a part of me thought about returning home. But I knew returning would be a bad decision, and I knew my Granny—my mom's mother, who was an enormous influence in my life—would not allow it.

As the weeks passed during freshman year, I connected with Dr. Miguel Franco, a sports psychologist on the Notre Dame staff, with whom I worked weekly for five years on a plethora of psycho-social-emotional issues. I looked forward to our meetings. When I was in his office, I had a voice, and over the years he helped me work through issues stemming from my childhood, build my confidence and self-esteem, and maximize my performance on the basketball court.

By sophomore year I was starting to feel that I belonged at Notre Dame. Besides Dr. Franco, I was getting vital support from several teammates: Julie Henderson, Niele Ivey, Katryna Gaither, Diana Braendly, and Imani Dunbar. And then, on the first day of practice, I tore my Achilles tendon. That sidelined me for the entire year. But this injury proved to be a blessing. Not only did I have the opportunity to focus exclusively on my academics, but I also watched in astonishment as a depleted, senior-led Notre Dame team reached the Final Four with only seven healthy bodies.

This was the fuel that I needed to change my mentality about Notre Dame, to learn how to work hard at the collegiate level, to become a team player, and to let the past rest. I came back to the team as a starter, and went from averaging 1.1 point per game as a freshman to a pace that allowed me to finish as Notre Dame's seventeenth all-time leading scorer.

I graduated in 1999 but completed my tenure as a scholar-athlete at Notre Dame in 2000. Leaving Notre Dame was very difficult and scary, and I felt a certain bitterness and a sense of abandonment. The university had been my home for five years. Now, at age twenty-three, I was going into the unknown with no job and no direction or plan.

After a couple of years of teaching in Chicago, I felt hollow inside. I thought I should be doing more in life, so I decided to enlist in the United States Army, even though I knew that war was looming.

In January 2004, my military police unit deployed to Iraq. I admit that I was terrified at first, because at Fort Lewis, Washington, where I had been stationed, I had observed soldiers who had returned from deployments and appeared a little "off," apparently suffering from mental health problems. But as the weeks in Iraq passed, my fear diminished and I started to feel invincible. After all I was the company commander gunner, the chief protector of our unit commander.

Two months into my tour, I returned home and married Willie Byrd, whom I had known as a coach, a colleague, and a friend for several years. Then I returned to Iraq. Several weeks later, on May 25, 2004, I was working security on a rooftop in Baghdad when a couple of rockets whizzed past me. Immediately, I reached down to grab my weapon to return fire. As I did so, a rocket-propelled grenade hit me.

My comrades came to my aid, carrying me to safety. When I awoke in the hospital, my entire chain of command was waiting by my bed. My master sergeant gently told me that my dominant left arm was gone. Against the company commander's orders, two of my sergeants had returned to the rooftop to find it under seven inches of sand. Now, standing at my bedside, my master sergeant slipped my recovered wedding rings onto my right hand. And then the brigade commander stepped up and pinned a Purple Heart on me.

A couple of days later, I arrived in Landstuhl, Germany, for additional surgeries in preparation for my return to the United States.

Little did I know that a Notre Dame graduate, Captain Tim Woods, would be performing my surgery. A further coincidence: Captain Woods's mom and dad, David and Eileen Woods, were friends of the Notre Dame women's basketball team and a couple I knew very well.

They were visiting their son at Landstuhl at that time and, after learning I was there and what had happened to me, they came to visit me at the hospital. They entered the room with tears and smiles; they immediately pulled out their phone to call Coach McGraw. I said, "Coach, all those years you wanted me to use my right hand, now I have no other choice."

I learned then that Notre Dame is not only a local entity: we are global. From that day forward, I started to rekindle my relationship with Notre Dame and feel love.

Obviously, lots of therapy and rehabilitation followed my injury and my return to the United States. After that, I earned a master's degree in counseling at St. Xavier University and became a licensed clinical professional counselor. I went to work for the VA in the Chicago area and, in January 2013, returned to South Bend as a supervisor in the Vet Center. There was progress—and also tragedy: in February 2011, my husband died unexpectedly of cardiac arrest.

After twelve years of being an amputee, I often am asked whether or not I regret joining the military. Although my tenure in the Army was cut short, I am proud to say that I am one of the fewer than 7 percent of Americans who have served their country in the armed forces and the fewer than 1 percent who have ever fought in a war. I have said numerous times that I have no regret or self-pity for my decision to serve my country. I refuse to accept a role as victim; I want to be known for courage, hope, and resiliency and victory in the face of danger. Yes, I was angry and disappointed because I did not want to lose a limb, but the greater picture is that *I am still here*. Still here to serve others and to leave behind a legacy with deeds and action.

CHAPTER 6

The 2000s

More than any other decade since the 1960s, the 2000s were a decade of convulsions. We were convulsed by wars, terrorism, political change, and natural disasters; by acts of mass, murderous violence and, at the end, by economic collapse.

Two events at opposite ends of the decade vie for the status of most consequential. In 2001, in a development whose ramifications are still unfolding, the United States experienced its worst-ever attack on "the homeland." Nineteen hijackers, commissioned by terrorist mastermind Osama bin Laden, seized control of four domestic airliners and piloted them into the twin towers of New York's World Trade Center, the Pentagon in Washington, D.C., and into a field near Somerset, Pennsylvania.

The "9/11 attacks"—so named for the date on which they occurred, September 11, 2001—collapsed the twin towers at the southern tip of Manhattan, took the lives of almost three thousand people, and ushered in a new era of indefinite war against terror, of concern about national security, and of curtailment of the personal liberty Americans were accustomed to enjoying.

In 2009, with the nation's economy approaching cardiac arrest as a result of years of excesses in the financial world, America inaugurated a new president, its first black president, Barack Obama. African-Americans in particular rejoiced, seeing Obama's victory in the 2008 election as evidence that America really was becoming what it had long professed to be: "one nation, under God, indivisible, with liberty and justice for all."

But some Americans, it appeared, were having none of it. Even before Obama's inauguration, the drumbeats of birtherism, accusations of socialism, and undisguised racism began—and continue.

Between these two poles of the decade, we saw a major American city, New Orleans, almost obliterated in 2005 by Hurricane Katrina. We saw the United States invade two countries, one (Afghanistan) in justifiable (if not indisputably wise) retaliation for the 9/11 attacks, the other (Iraq) on what turned out to be a pretext, a false assertion of a threat to our national security from so-called "weapons of mass destruction." We saw a series of sinister attacks against public officials and unwitting bystanders through the use of weaponized anthrax molecules. We saw madmen exercise their Second Amendment rights to commit one mass slaughter after another, including, in one instance, thirty-two people shot at random on the campus of Virginia Tech University. We saw in hurricanes and tornadoes and droughts and forest fires the result of centuries of climate change. We saw the Catholic Church in America brought to shame and disrepute by a clerical sex abuse scandal that extended over many decades and dioceses. We saw a pope, John Paul II, die after many years during which he made the church a major force in geopolitics, and we saw his chief deputy elected to replace him. We saw high-flying American companies—WorldCom, Enron—brought down by the excesses of their corporate leaders who, like Icarus in the ancient myth, became so carried away with their ability to fly that they lost sight of their limitations. We saw an American president, George W. Bush, brought low by a similar failure to appreciate limitations: of American military power, of "The Market," and the magic of deregulation.

Even before the 9/11 attacks, the 2000s had produced two major items for the history books. One was the 2000 presidential election, which required the equivalent of an overtime period and a still-disputed decision by the Supreme Court of the United States before Republican George W. Bush was declared the winner over Democrat Al Gore.

The other was Bush's appointment of two African-Americans, one of them with Notre Dame in her resume, to the top two foreign policy positions in his administration. Colin Powell, former chairman of the Joint Chiefs of Staff and one of the nation's most admired public figures, became America's first black secretary of state, fourth in the line of succession to the presidency. Condoleezza Rice, like Powell a veteran of George Bush the elder's presidency and recipient of a master's degree from Notre Dame in 1975, was Bush the younger's national security adviser.

Later in the decade another major "first" occurred when Representative Nancy Pelosi, a California Democrat, was elected speaker of the House of Representatives. In Liberia, meanwhile, Ellen Johnson Sirleaf became the first woman elected a head of state in Africa.

Among other prominent names of the decade: Fidel Castro, longtime, longwinded dictator of Cuba, finally stepped down in 2008, yielding power to his brother Raul; Martha Stewart, domestic maven, was convicted of a securities violation and served several months in federal prison; Michael Jackson, so-called "King of Pop" whose life had looked for years like a slow-motion train wreck, died of a drug overdose in 2008; Saddam Hussein, the bone in the throat of President Bush who led him into the ruinous invasion of Iraq, was captured and hanged; Harry Potter, the boy wizard created by British author J. K. Rowling, saw his last chronicle published in 2007; Pluto, for years considered the most distant of the planets in our solar system, was downgraded in 2006 to a "dwarf planet"; Apple Computer, at one point almost given up for dead, began a comeback under CEO Steve Jobs that eventually made it the world's most highly valued company and gave us such revolutionary products as the iPod, the iPhone, and the iPad.

Less easily discerned than the events of the decade were some of the trends and developments that built up and occurred over time. Among them: the replacement of the Clinton surpluses with more national debt after President Bush's 2001 tax cuts (the national debt doubled from $5 trillion at the start of Bush's presidency to almost $10 trillion at the end); the climate change that made the ten years starting in 2001 the warmest since modern measurement of such things began in 1850; the growth of the "national security state" as Americans got used to stripping down in airport security lines and their government got used to collecting more and more data on the activities of terror suspects and ordinary citizens; the continued growth of the nation's prison population as the so-called war on drugs proceeded.

One of the worst of these developments was the so-called housing bubble, the run-up of housing prices created by easy money and lax oversight in the mortgage and other financial industries. That bubble popped in 2007, leading to dramatic drops in home values, rampant foreclosures, a recession, and, ultimately, a full-blown financial crisis that brought the nation and the world in 2008 to the verge of another Great Depression.

President Bush, in probably the greatest indignity of his administration, found himself forced to sign a bill providing $700 billion to bail out the financial industry—the government bailing out the marketplace.

It was this financial collapse, as much as anything else, that opened the door for Barack Obama's historic victory over veteran Arizona Senator John McCain in the 2008 election. Obama's first year in office was largely devoted to pulling the US economy, and the world's, back from the brink of disaster.

Obama became a focal point of protest and political contention in the nation, including at Notre Dame, where he was invited to give the 2009 commencement address and receive an honorary degree. Opponents of the invitation argued that honoring a president who supported a constitutional right to abortion betrayed the university's pro-life Catholic principles, and Mary Ann Glendon, the Harvard law professor who had been awarded the Laetare Medal, declined the honor in protest of Obama.

Despite the protests, Father John I. Jenkins, who had succeeded Father Monk Malloy as Notre Dame's president in 2005, refused to withdraw the invitation.

The Obama controversy marked an end to a decade at Notre Dame that was characterized by a convulsion over an issue of tenure—not in the usual academic sense, but in the sense of time in office.

Monk Malloy, after a presidency of eighteen years, during which the university grew prodigiously, yielded the office on July 1, 2005, to Father Jenkins. The board of trustees had elected Jenkins to succeed Malloy more than a year earlier, and the two men reportedly had worked out an agreement allowing Jenkins to take the lead on any issues that would extend into his tenure. Jenkins used that authority to initiate the firing Tyrone Willingham, Notre Dame's first black head football coach and, indeed, its first black head coach in any sport. Willingham had been hired in 2001, after the brief, abortive hiring of George O'Leary, who had to withdraw after it was revealed his resume included falsifications.

Black Domers were as distressed and outraged by Willingham's firing—he had completed only the third year of a five-year contract—as they had been elated by his hiring in 2001. Maybe more so. Willingham was replaced by Charlie Weis, who lasted through the 2009 season, when he was replaced by Brian Kelly.

CAROL D. ANDERSON

(Class of 2000 MBA)

Carol D. Anderson came to Notre Dame in autumn 1998 from Los Angeles. She was a graduate student in the Mendoza College of Business. After graduation she returned to Los Angeles to a career in corporate finance and strategic management, and continues in her coaching and entrepreneurial consulting practice. She lives in Los Angeles.

OCCASIONALLY, WHEN I NEED WORDS OF INSPIRATION, I REFER to the commencement speech delivered by President Barack H. Obama to the University of Notre Dame class of 2009, one of his first after becoming president of the United States. In it he cited President Emeritus Father Theodore Hesburgh's description of Notre Dame as both a "lighthouse" and a "crossroads." The lighthouse stands apart, shining with the wisdom of the Catholic tradition, while the crossroads is where, in Father Hesburgh's words, "differences of culture and religion and conviction can coexist with friendship, civility, hospitality, and especially love."

The University of Notre Dame has been both a lighthouse and a crossroads for me! As a proud undergraduate alumna of the University of Southern California, living in Los Angeles and preparing for a career in medicine, no one, including myself, expected my ultimate choice for graduate school to be the University of Notre Dame in the Mendoza College of Business. But when I met her, Notre Dame became my lighthouse. Looking back, I chuckle at the contrast between what I thought I wanted and all I ultimately became!

There I was, frantically in the midst of the MCAT exam and medical school applications, then the anxiety of rolling off waitlists, and deciding to spend time in corporate America while I waited. This transitional period became the opportunity for me to experience the business world. It had always fascinated me, yet I never expected I'd be able to experience it in a career in medicine. During this introduction to the corporate experience, my supervising vice president asked, "Are you sure you're on the right path? I think you'd do well in business school." His observation gave me pause. Not because I did not believe in my abilities, but because I thought I had expressed passionately enough my commitment to becoming a cardio-thoracic surgeon. That day changed my life, as I began to entertain the possibilities. It was the first time I consciously chose to stay open to life and step out on faith.

Here again, President Obama's words rang true: "But remember, too, that the ultimate irony of faith is that it necessarily admits doubt. It is the belief in things not seen. It is beyond our capacity as human beings to know with certainty what God has planned for us or what He asks of us, and those of us who believe must trust that His wisdom is greater than our own."

And as the universe would have it, Notre Dame chose me. My beautiful gold-embossed "Preview Weekend" invitation arrived unsolicited. I thought, "Notre Dame? Hmm, Notre Dame!" I hadn't given it a thought, since in my preliminary review it did not meet my "desired location" criterion on the short list of schools I was considering. I mean, me, a single Caribbean-American LA girl and diehard Trojan, in small-town northern Indiana, cheering on the Irish? Was a meaningful existence there possible for me? After all, this was my professional future being considered, so the appropriate due diligence was necessary. I stayed open, continued stepping in faith, accepted the invitation, and the lighthouse met the crossroads.

Notre Dame's reputation as a premier academic institution certainly preceded it. But experiencing the university firsthand—its standards for quality and rigor; its rich athletic tradition, Christian values, and commitment to social justice; its loyal alumni and devoted fan base; its serene and picturesque campus; its dedicated faculty and staff; and its global reach—was transforming. Like my beloved USC, Notre Dame held the qualities and traditions that made it a perfect fit. With new dreams to fulfill, and by Notre Dame and I choosing each other, the journey had just begun. I immersed myself in everything business, from theoretical and structural perspectives to practical applications. My goals were: earn an MBA in finance, expand my travel and international business experience, contribute actively to the university and community, develop a sound professional network, create lifetime memories at Irish sporting events, and, most importantly, shift the trajectory of my professional career to management.

In my first week as a Domer, I introduced myself to Dean Carolyn Woo, to learn what her aspirations were for the business school, particularly as a relatively new hire. Dean Woo took my meeting as a walk-in despite her schedule. Not only did she share her plans to grow the program and raise its visibility, which she successfully accomplished within a few short years, but she demonstrated sincere interest in my academic and professional aspirations and my desire to become fully integrated in the Notre Dame community. I left our conversation inspired, determined to fulfill every goal I set, make as big an impact as I could, embrace all that the "Becoming Irish" class welcome banner intended, and, per Dean Woo, use my "business education to *bring about the greater good.*"

Then came the rigor, accompanied unceremoniously by the merciless trappings of competitive environments: conflicts, egos, and even questionable integrity among some peers. Everything Father Hesburgh had defined as the crossroads, where "differences of culture and religion and conviction can coexist with friendship, civility, hospitality, and especially love" was challenged in ways I could never have imagined. My naiveté in believing this lighthouse attracted only those pure in integrity, compassion, and acceptance caused me considerable growing pains. I had been sheltered by my life as an immigrant, raised in a relatively conservative middle-class family in Belize (Central America) as a cradle Episcopalian who was educated in Catholic schools, and in my subsequent life in Los Angeles, a culturally and ethnically diverse city where self-expression was the norm. Not even my world travels had prepared me for this. The realization began a shift in my idealistic expectations of Notre Dame, and ultimately the world and life itself.

I learned that navigating politics and personalities in competitive environments such as this required an emotional intelligence that I needed to cultivate, since my formative years were influenced by a different set of cultural sensibilities. In addition, being the first in my family to attend college and graduate school meant I had to navigate this maze on my own, perfect this skill, or risk losing myself. I was in for the long haul, so I stayed the course and gifts began to reveal themselves, the most treasured of which was the opportunity to expand my travels via this world-class education.

Notre Dame's global reach and my dream to visit every country in the world continued to drive me. And, along with my early exposure to travel and my voracious appetite for reading, which had developed my perpetual curiosity to experience the world in person, when travel opportunities presented themselves, without hesitation I said, "Yes!" While at Notre Dame, I experienced one of my best travel years yet: seventeen countries, some multiple times within that year, as I studied, interned, and consulted abroad (outdone only by my most recent trip around the world, twelve years later). While studying and doing research in Santiago de Chile, a visiting Notre Dame professor asked what I thought of my experience there. Overwhelmed at all it was, I could only summarize, "I am living my dream!" And when I consulted with non-governmental organizations (NGOs) in the townships outside of Cape Town, South Africa, or drove through the Swiss countryside, hiked the trails of Machu Picchu, Peru, or visited manufacturing facilities in Monterrey, Mexico, I was Notre Dame, the lighthouse and the crossroads. God's wisdom had surpassed my every expectation!

Today, fourteen years after graduation, I have achieved the goals I set when I said "yes" to Notre Dame. My unconventional, sometimes unpredictable, yet fulfilling journey has reaped an exceptional return on investment, the greatest of which include the community that Father Hesburgh described, and the courage, growth, and rewards that faith can bring, which President Obama spoke of in his commencement speech. These returns inspired me to commit twelve years of service on the alumni board, recruiting, fostering connections, mentoring, and fundraising for the university. My spiritual life as a practicing Christian has flourished and remains my centering force. My travels ramped up exponentially, and I've now visited six of the seven continents, with plans to get to Antarctica, my seventh, soon. I continue to expand my life's purpose with courage and conviction and a commitment to inspire all whom I encounter to live their dreams. Best of all, my professional life experienced the trajectory I desired. It took me as a corporate finance and strategic management professional from leadership in multinational corporations and NGOs to an independent consultancy for entrepreneurs. I provide comprehensive strategic solutions to developing entrepreneurial ventures that capitalize on their operational potential to maximize profits. In addition, I am creating a fully integrated business that incorporates acculturation training, business English, and business etiquette across cultures for foreign enterprises. When I take stock of my life, as I do in daily meditations of gratitude, and on that Saturday each fall when my two beloved schools meet on the field, I know I am one lucky girl.

AVA R. WILLIAMS

(Class of 2003)

Ava Williams came to Notre Dame in autumn 1999 from Detroit. She majored in political science and German. Since graduation she has pursued a variety of activities related to languages, leadership, and cultural programs for children. She is executive director of a foundation she created that promotes excellence in those same areas worldwide. She lives in Royal Oak, Michigan.

NEWS OF MY ACCEPTANCE TO THE UNIVERSITY OF NOTRE DAME in the spring of 1998 spread quickly. Everyone from close relatives to the postman who delivered the mail to our home on the east side of Detroit was *uber* excited. The congratulatory calls were endless. The problem, however, was that the excitement seemed to extend to everyone but me.

Thanks to a reading habit that developed early and exposed me to people, ideas, and cultures far beyond my small backyard in Detroit, and to supportive parents who emphasized that with hard work and creativity any obstacle could be overcome, I had developed a global perspective. I had spent the summer after my junior year of high school studying in Brazil. Immediately following my senior year I would spend a year abroad as a foreign exchange student in Germany. My perspective was global. I was excited about Notre Dame, but I was *ecstatic* about Germany. The world was waiting!

Eventually I did begin to develop the unwavering appreciation of and dedication to the University of Notre Dame that is so notable in most Domers. It began, ironically, during the year that I spent in Germany as a recipient of the Congress-Bundestag Scholarship, a study-abroad opportunity offered jointly by the US Department of State and Germany's national legislature in order to strengthen diplomatic relations between the two countries. I had deferred my enrollment at Notre Dame.

Prior to my departure for Germany, a refund check arrived one day from the university. I called the university to alert them of the error: No refund was in order because I had not made any payment yet. Months earlier I had been informed it was not necessary to pay any fees since I would not officially be starting that fall. After conversations with several employees and officials in various departments, the matter was resolved.

A little later that same day the phone rang once more. On the other end was Daniel Saracino, the assistant provost for enrollment. Mr. Saracino had heard about the accidental refund check and called to congratulate me on my acceptance to Notre Dame and my receipt of the Congress-Bundestag scholarship, as well as to commend my honesty. It was a lengthy and inspiring conversation. A few days later, a care package from Mr. Saracino arrived; it was filled with Notre Dame apparel. During my stay in Germany I received additional letters and packages filled with advice and goodies. Although I had not yet stepped foot on campus, I already had a lifelong mentor and friend.

Finally it was the big day! In the fall of 1999 I arrived on campus. To describe what greeted me as beautiful would be an understatement. There is a reason Notre Dame's campus has been so highly lauded.

One of my earliest memories at Notre Dame is of the epic argument between my mom and the mother of one of my three roommates. Our basement quad in Lyons Hall was the setting for the showdown. The catalyst was the bottom bunk bed and the fact that both of our moms insisted on our right to it. I had arrived first so the answer seemed obvious. Not so. The argument lasted hours! At one point all of my new roommates and I left and shared our first meal together in South Dining Hall. We also shared a chuckle over the antics of the Southern Belle (my roommate's mom) and the Detroit Diva. The silly argument eventually ended and, although it did not prevent my roommate and me from becoming friends, the exchange did contain undertones. Undertones that could be neither concretely defined nor completely dismissed.

There were other moments during which such "undertones" were present. They were present at the one large table where most of the students of color sat in the dining hall. They were present in the constant inquiries, and even insistence, that I must play or must have played a sport. They were present in the fact that in many of my classes I automatically became an expert on subjects ranging from apartheid to welfare, since it was assumed by many of my peers, and even some professors, that these were topics with which I was intimately familiar. They were even present during the dorm-wide cultural diversity presentations that, while well-intentioned, somehow never quite hit their mark. Such undertones did not necessarily negatively impact my experience at Notre Dame. In truth, they were a small part of my experience that served only to make the place seem a little less than perfect.

In contrast, there were experiences, moments, and people that were absolutely incredible. Within the first few weeks of arriving on campus I was able to fulfill a lifelong dream. As a child I had always wanted to learn to ride horses. As dedicated as my parents had been to providing my siblings and me with as many opportunities as possible, riding was cost-prohibitive and simply not an option.

I attended a freshman leadership seminar offered by Dr. Kathleen Sullivan, the senior director of service and spiritual programs. At the end of the seminar, which had been phenomenal, Dr. Sullivan, an avid equestrian, offered the participants the opportunity to join her at the stables in Granger, Indiana, where she rode. I did, and for the rest of my time at Notre Dame, either Dr. Sullivan drove me or I rode my bike there. Dr. Sullivan continues to follow my progress as both a mentor and a friend.

Such instances of professors taking an interest in my personal, academic, and professional development were not rare. Mario Borrelli, for example, professor of mathematics, served not only as a mentor helping to guide me through the rigors of college life and better understand and prepare for graduate studies, but he also became a surrogate grandpa. In the years since I graduated, Professor Borrelli has remained a fixture in my life, championing and encouraging every endeavor.

Some of my classes surpassed anything I had ever been able to imagine. Guest professors such as former Ambassador Curtis Kammen stepped off the pages of history to prepare my classmates and me for the future. He had been intimately involved in some of the historic events—such as the ending of the Cold War—that had influenced my decision to become a political science/international relations major.

Courses such as Dr. Vera Profit's Self-Definition and the Quest for Happiness haunted me with their profundity and implications for my life. At the ripe old age of twenty-two, I found myself questioning my purpose and mortality, and genuinely concerned about the contribution that I would make to humanity. I recall Dean Ava Preacher joking that, at age twenty-two, I was experiencing a quarter-life crisis.

Joking aside, a few years later when I was called to be a full-time caregiver for my mother at various times during her nearly seven-year battle with lymphoma, lessons from that course helped me understand what was being required of me and provide the level of care, dedication, and, at times, sacrifice that was necessary. Faith, having accompanied my mother's courageous battle and a myriad of positive Notre Dame experiences, would also influence my decision to take the road less traveled and start the PREMBEL Foundation, a philanthropy dedicated to promoting excellence in language, leadership, and culture worldwide.

Often prospective Notre Dame students stand before me at college recruitment fairs and express shock that I spent three semesters and two summers studying overseas in Brazil, Estonia, and France. They are incredulous that I would have spent so much time away from the mystical place with the Golden Dome. I redeem myself by quickly adding that I was the first student to ever successfully participate in the university's year-long study-abroad program at Sciences-PO in Paris. I also mention that I pioneered the international studies office's study-abroad program in Brazil. To dispel any remaining skepticism, I regale them with tales of my incredible meeting with Father Ted Hesburgh. That encounter, in itself, provides the basis for an essay!

When I speak to prospective students I explain that Notre Dame was not a place that defined me. Rather, it was a place that allowed me to define who I wanted to become and then gave me the resources, encouragement, and continued support to travel along my chosen path. In that sense, for me, the University of Notre Dame truly was magical. Looking back, I often find myself agreeing with the hopeful high school students that I meet at college recruitment fairs. I understand their awe and wonder.

JAMIE L. AUSTIN
(Class of 2004)

Jamie L. Austin came to Notre Dame in autumn 2000 from Youngstown, Ohio. She majored in chemical engineering and theology and was a Notre Dame cheerleader. After graduation, she earned master's degrees at Johns Hopkins University and the University of Michigan, where she is a PhD candidate. She is a regulatory affairs professional in the pharmaceutical industry. She and her husband have four children and live in Illinois.

THERE'S SOMETHING ABOUT THE FALL THAT MAKES ME THINK of Notre Dame. Year after year the colorful trees and the brisk and sunny mornings make me smile and remember what it felt like to walk across South Quad. I think about those beautiful old trees that shaded the path between the quad and the basilica—so rich and full of history. I can recall, as if it happened just last week, stopping under the canopy of neighboring trees on my way to Crowley Music Hall.

Occasionally I just take a break from my busy days, close my eyes, and silently wish that I were walking up Notre Dame Avenue, catching a glimpse of a sparkling dome between the trees. For just a moment it feels so real that I can almost smell the familiar scent of ethanol in the air. Without fail, I begin to reminisce about the excitement of football weekends on campus, and, before I know it, my heart lets out a great big "Go Irish!"

Yes, indeed, it seems that every fall, I take a moment to think of Notre Dame and proudly acknowledge that I am a Domer.

Although I now have such pleasant memories of my alma mater, the truth is that I have not always felt so well connected to Notre Dame. In fact, there were many times when I wished to be almost anywhere other than South Bend. When I enrolled in the fall of 2000, there was not much to connect me to Notre Dame other than my hopes for a great academic future.

Determined to overcome the challenges of my circumstances, I was by all means a fighter, but I certainly wasn't Irish. My black Baptist heritage stood in stark contrast to that of most Irish Catholics. I was a product of an inner-city school system in a blue-collar town. So, as you can imagine, my life experiences were quite different from those of my Notre Dame peers.

Unlike most of my classmates, no one in my family had attended Notre Dame before me, and there was no legacy for me to follow. In fact, while most parents would be thrilled to have a child attend Notre Dame, my mom resisted right up until the first day of frosh orientation. It was *my* choice to attend Notre Dame, and I chose the university because I wanted the opportunity to be considered among the world's brightest scholars. Yet, in such an environment, I faced the enormous challenge of discovering my individuality within the confines of unfamiliar and overwhelmingly homogeneous surroundings. I wanted to be known as more than just "the black girl" in class, but I felt the need to hold onto my "blackness" so that I didn't lose my identity.

Although most students were making a lot of social adjustments to transition into young adulthood, it was difficult for me to engage in social activities that aligned with my interests when I first came to Notre Dame. I bought football tickets in the fall, but I ultimately spent every weekend of my freshman year visiting with my high school sweetheart in Ohio. And when I was on campus, I found myself intentionally gravitating to students of color in hopes that there would be some familiarity and welcoming acknowledgment of how our differences unified us among the majority. As a Balfour-Hesburgh Scholar, I was fortunate to enter the university with a handful of minority friends. Once the fall semester began, however, we became overwhelmingly concerned with our individual pursuits, and the extent of our socializing was soon diluted to occasional Friday night mafia games in Zahm Hall and chance meetings at the "black table" in South Dining Hall.

Being one of only a handful of black engineering students made my transition to Notre Dame even more challenging. With few exceptions, my instructors never gave the impression that they genuinely cared about my progress as a student, and I experienced more than one case of unfair or unkind treatment in my department. I wanted to quit several times, and I have a vivid recollection of breaking down in tears of frustration in front of South Dining Hall. I'll never forget how my advisor all but laughed in my face when she explained that—simply put—I wasn't smart enough to go to graduate school. (I am really looking forward to mailing her a copy of my PhD thesis.) Academically, there were numerous gloomy days on campus. Sometimes it seemed that even those big, leafy trees were mocking me and waiting for me to fail.

Gratefully, I soon encountered brighter days and reached a turning point in my career at Notre Dame when, having access to a vehicle, I discovered a local church during the fall of my sophomore year. The familiarity and support of the church helped me cope with student life just a few blocks away on campus. My faith sustained me, and I found a sense of balance—becoming more confident of my identity. The church members saw me as part of Notre Dame, and, without realizing it, I began to embody that role.

As I adapted to life at Notre Dame, I began to notice how other black students were acclimating as well. All around me, Notre Dame's black students were treading down new paths and setting new precedents. Naturally I saw great athletes, but I was also privileged to know the first black leprechaun, the first black female drum major, and a black member of the Irish Guard. With the inspiration of these trailblazers in mind, I found the courage to pursue my interest in cheerleading and try out for the squad. I barely made the cut, but I was delighted nonetheless. Even though I cheered before only a few fans at the soccer games in the fall, I presented to them a part of Notre Dame that was often overlooked.

As a Notre Dame cheerleader, I sensed a definite connection to the university. When in uniform, *I* became the university's ambassador and formed a bridge of familiarity to the community at large. And as I became more comfortable with my own identity and my deserved place within the university, I slowly embraced the notion of the Notre Dame family—a concept I had heard so much about.

Now, I have tried to explain the Notre Dame "family" to those without ties to the university, but they struggle to understand it, much as I did at first. Ironically, however, my experience shows that it's the outsider's perspective of the privileges and challenges of experiencing life at Notre Dame that somehow unites us into one of the world's most notable alumni networks. Truly, no matter how different our circumstances, we are Notre Dame to the outside world. By default, we're expected to stick together and look out for one another. Hence, we begin to operate as a family, held together by our love for Notre Dame.

Because the latter half of my student career was so unusual, I experienced and grew to appreciate the strength of my Notre Dame family shortly thereafter. My dormmates in McGlinn Hall rejoiced with me when my high school sweetheart proposed on a bright fall day at the start of junior year. Fellow members of the Voices of Faith Gospel Choir celebrated our union by traveling to sing at our wedding. And although it was very challenging to finish my senior year while carrying our first child, my engineering peers were overwhelmingly supportive and accommodating.

When I think of my years at Notre Dame, there is no denying that they were challenging. Yet I somehow manage to think about them fondly. The sights and sounds of campus are bright memories and I remember them with warmth. Now, my family makes it a point to visit campus nearly every fall. As we stroll beneath those tall trees on the quads, I can only hope that our four children will experience the privilege and challenge of attending Notre Dame. While there are many things I would love to change about the university to make it more inviting for future generations of black students, I am grateful for my own experiences there. These experiences helped me become the woman I am today. I can honestly say that, if given the choice to reconsider, I would still choose to do it all over again . . . beginning in the fall, of course.

ARIENNE THOMPSON

(Class of 2004)

Arienne Thompson came to Notre Dame in autumn 2000 from Memphis, Tennessee. She majored in history and Japanese and was co-founder of Shades of Ebony. After graduating she earned a master's in journalism from American University and has worked since 2006 at USA Today. She is an entertainment reporter and on-air personality. She lives in the Washington, D.C., suburbs.

WHAT'S THE OLD ADAGE? WHEN YOU STOP LOOKING FOR love, it will find you? Well, that certainly tells part of the tale between me and Notre Dame.

I was a stressed-out, overwhelmed high school senior who had applied to more than a dozen schools when my parents insisted that I try one more.

"Fine," I told them, the cockiness of youth mixed with type-A burnout seeping into my tone, "but you have to fill out the application yourselves. I'll give you my essay and sign the application, but beyond that, you're on your own."

(Still not sure how I got away with that one.)

To put it plainly, Notre Dame was not on my radar. At all. However, for my born-and-bred Catholic father and convert mom, Notre Dame was the holy grail, and they prayed that their dream school would become mine.

Fast forward a few months and I was accepted, and with a good deal of money to boot. "Wow, Notre Dame is a great school," I thought. "I'll give it a shot."

And just like that, the decision was made. No wrangling, no tears, no bargaining, no long discussions. It was done. (Hey, not all love stories start with a bang.)

It was clear even before I enrolled that I had made the right decision. My parents and I made the first of many ten-hour treks from Memphis to South Bend that spring of my senior year, and when I stepped on campus for the first time, I knew that my instinct had led me to the right place.

It was finals week, and Notre Dame looked literally like a living, breathing brochure. Students were lazing about on the lawn and reading inside the library and throwing frisbees and chatting on benches and enjoying the short-lived warmth of the season. And, some—a small sum, obviously—of those kids happened to be black, so I just knew this was the place for me!

A few months later, when it was time to move into the dorm, I gave myself over to the place body and soul, never doubting my blasé decision to say yes to this lily-white, freezing, middle-of-nowhere place.

My four years went by in a glorious blur. And how did I spend my time-of-your-life moments? I fell in love with Japanese, studied abroad in Tokyo, founded the first student group for black women, recruited hundreds of diversity students, met some of the best people I had encountered in my life, discovered my deep disdain for snow, and succumbed to the mania that is "Love thee, Notre Dame."

When I left I was head-over-heels, warts-and-all in love with Notre Dame. And that's when the love affair truly blossomed.

I went directly to graduate school the fall after graduating from Notre Dame and soon discovered that most of my fellow students were not as enamored of their undergraduate institutions as I was. I had naively assumed they'd want to gush about their schools as I did about Notre Dame. I heard a lot of, "Wow, you really love that place!" and "You go back to campus how often?!"

And they were right—I went back a lot. In fact, I made a promise to my younger sister, who started at Notre Dame the semester after I graduated, that I would visit at least once a semester all four years that she was there.

Not only did I make good on that promise, but I also discovered a new way to love and give back to the place that had given me so much.

Just a few years after graduating, I was appointed to the board of directors of the Black Alumni of Notre Dame as a young alumni representative. When that term was up, I stayed on as the board's historian and, halfway through that term, I was elected to the Notre Dame Alumni Association's board of directors as a young alumni director, a position that I will hold through summer 2014.

During my alumni association board term, another opportunity presented itself when Father John Jenkins appointed me to the Undergraduate Experience Advisory Council as a young alumni representative, on the advice of former University Vice President and Associate Provost Dr. Don Pope-Davis.

I offer up these accomplishments not as an opportunity to brag, but rather as more proof of how much I love "that place." Whenever non-Domers question why I'm on another plane to South Bend or why I take the time to respond to any Notre Dame student who e-mails me for coffee or why I'm always dialing in for a conference call about this or that, I just think, "They don't get it. They don't love like this."

I think it's true that Cupid's arrow hits straighter and truer when you least expect it. All those years ago, I never knew a love like this was possible, and, all these years later, I know how special a place it takes to engender such emotion.

I will always love Notre Dame, and, when I daydream, my fantasy involves my future children being Domers and loving Our Lady, too. And, when their time comes, I hope Cupid is ready to aim and hit his mark one more time.

Jetaun Davis

(Class of 2005)

Jetaun Davis came to Notre Dame in autumn 2001 from At-
lanta. She majored in sociology and gender studies. After gradu-
ation she spent eight years as an internet marketing professional
with AT&T. She recently returned to Notre Dame as assistant
director of new media communications for the undergraduate
enrollment division. She lives in Granger, Indiana.

AS I RECALL MY INTRODUCTION TO THE UNIVERSITY OF NOTRE
Dame, it is ever so clear to me that destiny was at hand. Though my
mother hadn't attended college, I always knew that I would. However,
I hadn't heard of Notre Dame.

In my junior year of high school, I accompanied a classmate and
her mom on a road trip from our hometown, Atlanta, to visit a few
colleges, one being the University of North Carolina at Chapel Hill
(UNC-CH). That is where I had my sights set on going. I bled Carolina Blue through and through.

As my senior year started, my basketball coach from a couple of
years past suggested that I consider Notre Dame. I remember saying,
"Notre Dame? Where is that? I don't want to go anywhere that it
snows."

She encouraged me to look beyond the snow and apply anyway.
She was such a proponent of Notre Dame because her nephew, Sky-
lard Owens (Class of 2000), had played basketball there and had
graduated the previous spring. She told me that Notre Dame was a
really special place and that they were looking for talented minority

students and even flew them to the campus for a visit. Though I wasn't convinced, I agreed that I would at least apply.

Winter came and, sure enough, I received an invitation from Notre Dame to attend its all-expenses-paid spring visitation program. I thought, "Sure, I'll go on the trip, but I'm going to UNC-CH." In the weeks before visiting the campus, I got at least two phone calls from Notre Dame: the first from a student, the second from a member of the black alumni board, a board on which I eventually came to serve with that same alum, Rochelle Valsaint. After getting those calls and looking forward to my free trip, I started to question whether UNC-CH would see me as an individual as Notre Dame obviously did, or just lose me in the shuffle of its larger class sizes. Still, I remained pretty sure that I would ultimately attend North Carolina.

Then the time for "spring vis" came around. My host was a black woman, also from the Atlanta area, so I felt I could get a candid view of the university from her. She gave me a heads-up that the weekend was filled with multicultural activities, but that campus life was nothing like that the rest of the year. I appreciated her frankness and enjoyed the weekend with that wisdom in mind. Of course, the BCAC Fashion Show excited me the most. I knew that if I did decide to attend Notre Dame, I would be in the fashion show as a student.

After returning home, I thought Notre Dame was a pretty good choice. Its being predominantly white was a good attribute in my opinion. Although I attended a public high school with a rather diverse student body, I had still been raised in Atlanta, where there was a large black population. Therefore, I wanted a college experience that would prepare me for the world outside of Atlanta, where I would need to know how to interact and thrive among people with different perspectives and backgrounds. Stepping outside of my comfort zone, I thought, would give me the best reward in the end.

Still, I wasn't sure about signing up for the snow. After all, although Chapel Hill had a larger population of minority students than Notre Dame, it was still predominantly white. I could get the benefit of stepping outside of my comfort zone there as well.

However, by mid-April I still had no financial aid decision from UNC-CH. So there it was: the sign that I would not be seen as an individual. Meanwhile, Emory had offered me a financial aid package very similar to Notre Dame's. I called Notre Dame's admissions office to see if they could offer me a little more gift money to reduce my loans. And after the admissions counselor, Cindy Santana, went to speak with the financial aid office, they made it work and reduced my loans! That last show of support sealed the deal, and Notre Dame became the place I called home for the next four years.

When reflecting on my experience at Notre Dame, the relationships that I had with administrators and staff stand out the most. Christy Fleming Greene (Class of 1996), an advisor in the first year of studies, was a great support for the multicultural community, often in matters that went beyond the academic. For example, in my junior year, she learned that I had bought a car at the dealership sale that used to take place in the Joyce Center parking lot. Long story short, the interest rate was astronomical, and she thought that there was no way that I should have been sold the car. So after she had notified another administrator, Bob Mundy of the admissions office, we all went over to discuss the situation with the dealership. After going back and forth about the sense of integrity at hand, they encouraged the dealership to buy the car back from me! It did, and while I had enjoyed having a nice ride with leather seats, I was very relieved to no longer have a car note.

Another administrator who comes to mind is Dr. Cecilia Lucero, who directed the Balfour-Hesburgh Scholars Program. She has always been a great example of quiet strength and intelligence without arrogance. We worked together throughout my Notre Dame years, and, besides giving me the only gift that I received for graduation (she didn't and still doesn't know this fact), she shared some words of wisdom that stayed with me throughout my time working in the corporate world. She made me aware that, in business, women often try to emulate men in order to succeed. She encouraged me to maintain my sense of self in my journey. I must say that I witnessed the dynamic that she described as I progressed in my career, and I knew that I had to make an exit from corporate soon before I adopted the "survival of the fittest" mentality essential to rising through the ranks.

Lisa Mushett, a staff member in the sports information office, helped me secure a dream internship with ESPN just because she knew that I had a personal interest. How awesome it was to have an opportunity like that without being a film, theater, and television major or going through a massive interview process!

In addition to those three, staff members Elizabeth Hilson in the admissions office and Jannifer Crittendon in student welfare and development in the athletic department, also served as confidants in a community that could be much too small at times. To all of these people, I am eternally grateful. They manifested the family that Notre Dame prides itself on being.

From a social perspective, I kept a very intimate social circle that included and expanded beyond the black community. I had done this since grade and high schools, so college was no different. Still, I was fairly active in the black campus community and participated in the BCAC Fashion Shows and Black Images talent show.

Additionally, I served as a multicultural student recruitment coordinator in the admissions office, was a facilitator for the Balfour-Hesburgh Scholars program (having been a scholar myself), was the interview segment producer for NDTV, was a freelance writer for the *Observer*, and attended the "Interrace Dialogue Forum" of the office of multicultural programs and services—all the while keeping a few campus jobs to have spending money in my pocket. I was happy to have so many outlets to pursue a variety of interests.

Being a Notre Dame graduate has influenced both my personal and professional life greatly. On a professional level, the cliché that "having the Notre Dame name on your resume will mean something" has been true for me. It has convinced my more experienced superiors to give me special projects as an entry-level employee. As I exceeded their expectations on small tasks, my responsibility increased. On a personal level, as I have moved around the country I have had an established network of contacts through the alumni clubs. Additionally, being an alum enabled me to participate in professional development opportunities, such as serving for four years on the board of the Black Alumni of Notre Dame and the Diversity Council. It was during this time, through my student recruitment posts, that I identified my passion to work in higher education, which prompted my recent change from corporate work to higher education.

Notre Dame has given me opportunities for growth and promise through both challenges and rewards—tangible and intangible. And because the university wasn't even on my radar when I started considering colleges, I am even more appreciative of the experience.

Shawtina Ferguson

(Classes of 2005, 2008 Law)

Shawtina Ferguson came to Notre Dame in autumn 2001 from Inglewood, California. She majored in American studies and African-American studies and was co-founder and first president of Shades of Ebony. After graduation, she stayed at Notre Dame to earn a law degree. She currently practices law in Los Angeles.

FEWER THAN THIRTY DAYS INTO MY FRESHMAN YEAR AT NOTRE Dame, two hijacked commercial airliners slammed into the World Trade Center's Twin Towers, a third into the Pentagon, and a fourth crashed before it could reach its intended target. Before the sun set that day, the Notre Dame student body, clergy, and members of the faculty and staff gathered on South Quad for a prayer service. While memorials and events took place around the country to allow people to grieve and draw comfort from others' presence, the speed and grace with which members of the Notre Dame community drew together was singular to Our Lady's university. It was clear to me very early on that this was a special place.

A year earlier, I did not know Notre Dame. Ben Finley, who graduated from Notre Dame in 1960 with a degree in electrical engineering, came to my small, Catholic high school in Inglewood, California, to introduce Notre Dame to me and other high-achieving students of color. Before Ben's comments, Notre Dame was nothing more to me than some elusive college with a rich football tradition located somewhere out there with attendance reserved for others, not me. What business did I have at Notre Dame?

I'll put all of my cards on the table. Fifteen minutes into freshman year, I, like many, loved the place. Cheering for friends in the marching band and on the team on football Saturdays was thrilling. Women with whom I lived in community at Welsh Family Hall became my closest friends. Daily access to professors who were eminent scholars in their fields seemed normal.

Still, it was quite strange to be surrounded by a sea of whiteness en route to DeBartolo Hall, in my dorm, at the dining hall, everywhere. Before then, I had been used to going home to people who looked like me. It was bizarre to observe that Abercrombie & Fitch seemed to outfit a significant percentage of the student body. I had never shopped there. When classmates asked whether I'd study abroad, my silent thought was, "I *am* abroad!" In many respects, Notre Dame was a different world. Over time, however, I would come to learn that, although I had not known about this university, Ben Finley was right: there was a place for me at Notre Dame.

Notre Dame was home for me and, as many of us do to make the places we live more comfortable, I did my part to make the campus a better place. My emergence as a student leader was born in part out of my desire to contribute to my community, but also out of necessity in an effort to enhance multicultural awareness. I enjoyed seven Februarys on campus, each one with a similar offering: freezing temperatures, Black Coffeehouse, a student-led celebration of African-American history, a student submission to the *Observer* discussing the merits of affirmative action, a question from a curious white student wondering why black students all sit at the same table in the dining hall. Co-founding and serving as the first president of Shades of Ebony, an official campus club and space where African-American women could see themselves and share their experiences without scrutiny, and vice-chairing Junior Parents Weekend were two of my proudest achievements at Notre Dame. They stand out in my memory even now, as faulty as it may be, because these experiences contributed to my lasting memory of this place.

On the road to becoming a Double Domer, I've known Our Lady to be an organic and evolving place with a steadfast commitment to its rich traditions. Any departure from tradition at Notre Dame did not go unnoticed. For most black students on campus, and I suspect for many blacks across the nation, it was a proud moment to see a black man at the helm of arguably the grandest stage in college football. It seemed that Coach Tyrone Willingham, too, embraced his place as "one of us," meeting with black student groups and faculty members to learn more about our Notre Dame experience. The unprecedented manner in which Coach Willingham, the first black head coach in any sport for the Irish, was fired was the first and only time that I felt disenchanted with Notre Dame. I vividly remember many black faculty and staff who stood on the front lines, as they had consistently done, to support black students who felt warring emotions about the university's decision and the decision-making process. At Notre Dame, football has always been more than a game.

My continued service to Our Lady, in my role as a board member of the national alumni association or as a volunteer in my hometown club, continues to broaden my perspective and deepen my understanding of what it truly means to be part of the Notre Dame family. I routinely meet people who, like me, have been made better, smarter, more generous citizens because of the professors who pushed us to excel or because of our interactions with students, classmates, and roommates from all walks of life who challenged our ideas or broadened our perspectives. Like them, my commitment to continued service to Our Lady stems from personal gratitude for the myriad ways in which the Notre Dame experience has become an integral part of my identity.

Memory fades. In the hectic day-to-day of our lives, joy can seem elusive and remote. But for me, the mere thought of Notre Dame, my connection to it, the memories of it, brings me joy. For me, Notre Dame is a phenomenal place to be from and was a blessing to be at.

JUSTIN TUCK

(Class of 2005)

Justin Tuck came to Notre Dame in autumn 2001 from Kelly-ton, Alabama. He majored in entrepreneurship and was a member of the football team. Since graduation he has played professional football for the New York Giants, winning two Super Bowl rings. He and his wife, Lauran (Class of 2006), have two sons and live in New Jersey.

IT'S A LITTLE IRONIC THAT MY JOURNEY TO SOUTH BEND STARTED with a wrong turn. On a Friday night in the fall of 1999, two members of the Notre Dame recruiting staff took a wrong turn and found themselves lost in Coosa County, Alabama. They were in Kellyton, a town so small it didn't even have a traffic light and about two hours away from their intended destination.

Figuring that the trip was a waste, they decided to stop at a gas station and ask for the nearest high school so they could at least watch a football game. Long story short, they ended up at Central Coosa High School, where a skinny linebacker had the game of his life. A few hours later I was surrounded by men in suits with briefcases, and being asked to answer all kinds of questions. Three weeks later I was offered a full scholarship to Notre Dame. I accepted!

My journey was very difficult at first. Going to Notre Dame was my first time being away from home and I hated it. All of my friends went to southern, i.e., *warm weather*, schools. I wasn't prepared for what seemed like days, weeks, months, of lake-effect snow. Plus, I broke my hand my freshman year and was red-shirted. I was ready to tuck my tail and head back south. But the thing that saved me was what makes Notre Dame so great: the people.

I was blessed to have some great people around me at this stage in my career. God knows I wouldn't have made it without my family, friends, professors, mentors, and teammates. This support system was a lifesaver. And at that point I hadn't even met yet the person who would have the biggest impact on my time at Notre Dame and beyond.

December 7, 2001. It was a Friday afternoon, class was letting out, and I was heading back to O'Neill Hall to get ready for my first football banquet as a member of the historic University of Notre Dame football team. A car flagged me down. The driver asked for directions to the Joyce Center. I gave him directions and went on my way. As the car proceeded I thought that the man must not be a good listener, because he made a wrong turn. I remember thinking he would probably be blaming me for wrong directions later, but I would most likely never see him again anyway.

Later, as I walked to the banquet, I was told that I would be sitting with a former Notre Dame football player and alumnus, Gregory Williamson (Class of 1982), his father, and his sister, who was an early admit to the university for the coming fall.

As I made my way to the table I saw a familiar face: the man to whom I had given directions earlier, Fred Williamson. And sitting next to him was a beautiful young woman. I'm sure you can imagine my thoughts: *Who* is the girl?

Lauran Elizabeth Patricia Williamson was her name, and little did I know that by the year 2014 she would be my wife of six years and mother to our two strapping baby boys.

Lauran and I both were extremely focused during our time at Notre Dame. I was focused on being the man around campus and she was engaged in trying to change the world. But after a few years of dating and getting to know each other, I realized that she was an angel sent from heaven. And now I truly know that she is my better half.

I received my Notre Dame degree in May 2005, shortly after being taken in the third round of the NFL draft by the New York Giants. A few years later, I found myself a starting defensive end on the team, playing for the Super Bowl.

Nothing can prepare you to play for a world championship—the Super Bowl is a stage second to none. That being said, at the collegiate level, you would be hard-pressed to find a better training ground for the big stage than Notre Dame. Being a captain at Notre Dame trained me to better serve in that role with the New York Giants. What to say and, more importantly, how to act while leading your peers is something I learned through trial and error. I learned how to have confidence when speaking in public, whether in front of a small group or in front of thousands.

As an athlete I rarely remember specific games or plays. I don't remember the sack that gave me the Notre Dame all-time record. But I do remember the jokes from teammates in the locker room and late-night studying sessions with friends. I remember road trips in the summer and barbecues at Lake Michigan.

My most vivid memories at Notre Dame are indeed, though, football related: The first was my first trip down the tunnel, hitting the "Play Like a Champion Today" sign, and running into Notre Dame Stadium to 85,000 screaming fans. I remember that like it was yesterday. The second was my sophomore year when we beat Michigan at home and the crowd rushed the field. That was unreal.

Off the field, my experiences were just as important and valuable. My parents always stressed that in the title student-athlete, "student" comes first! My education has opened so many doors for me, and I know how my education has been an equalizer. I believe that is the case regardless of where you're from, and that is why Lauran and I started Tuck's R.U.S.H. for Literacy in 2008. We wanted to promote the importance of reading to today's youth. We have been able to use our platform of a Notre Dame education and our success in New York City to promote change and make a difference in the lives of so many people. Thank you, Notre Dame.

So Notre Dame for me was four years of growth. And that word, growth, is very important. I went from a shy country boy to a poised, well-groomed man. From Kellyton, Alabama, to the brightest city in the world, New York City. From writing papers for Professor Richard Pierce's class to writing a children's book. From a shallow view of the world to traveling across the world and embracing how unique different cultures can be.

I've played in and won Super Bowls and Pro Bowls and I've conversed with both US and foreign presidents. I know a lot of powerful people, and I've done a lot of absolutely amazing things, but regardless of all that, there is still one staple topic that people want to hear about in my speeches or in casual conversations.

"Justin," they say, "tell us about Notre Dame."

And that's why Notre Dame is different. While I was at Notre Dame I didn't understand what alumni meant by that statement. I understand now.

Notre Dame, I have been and continue to be tremendously blessed to call you home. I will always "Love Thee, Notre Dame."

RHEA BOYD

(Class of 2006)

Rhea Boyd came to Notre Dame in autumn 2002 from Akron, Ohio. She majored in Africana Studies and Health, a program of her own design. After graduation she earned an MD at Vanderbilt University School of Medicine. She lives in San Francisco, where she is a practicing pediatrician and child health advocate.

ALTHOUGH OUR NUMBERS MAY BE FEW, IF YOU LOOK CLOSELY at Notre Dame's heritage, there are African-American families whose stories illuminate the breadth of the Notre Dame experience. As generations beget generations, these families define a Notre Dame tradition. Their legacy of scholarship and service bridges the divide between people of color and one of our nation's preeminent Catholic universities. To them, Notre Dame is home because it is where they formed the bonds that define their lives. We are one of those families.

It all began with my parents.

My father, Ralph Boyd, was raised in East St. Louis, Illinois, and was seventeen years old when Notre Dame recruited him as a track athlete. He was a quiet intellect who was both handsome and fit. To hear him speak of it now, it's clear he ventured to the university with little preconception. He was a student, and Notre Dame was a good school. The pairing seemed natural. And yet, upon arrival at Morrissey Hall in 1977, he was greeted as a stranger, an outcast.

While most students were grappling over loft and appliance purchases and the shared expenses of communal life, his roommates created a furniture barricade that barred him from entering the common space. Orientation had barely begun and, rather than being welcomed into the community where he would later meet his wife and send his children, he was ostracized to live alone, in a side room. So he did.

But he refused to be embittered and instantly befriended a freshman from New Orleans who lived down the hall. Their friendship, which has endured long beyond their time on campus, helped mitigate the sting of rejection and cultivated the space for my dad to experience Notre Dame beyond the limitations of his dorm room walls.

Early in his freshman year, the rector visited his suite. As my dad noted, he surveyed the room, obviously divided, and made no mention of it. Neither did my dad. And yet, without formal complaint or even direct acknowledgment of what occurred, my father returned to the university the next year to find he had been transferred to Carroll Hall, a dormitory of single-occupancy rooms. He continued as a civil engineering major and left the university as a senior, before receiving his degree.

To this day, however, he speaks highly of Notre Dame and says he cherished his time there—afternoons spent at the Rockne Memorial playing some of the best pick-up basketball games of his life, swimming in the pool on the weekends with friends, and all-out dance parties with the other black students who never required alcohol to get the festivities started. Most of all, he will tell you, he loves Notre Dame because that is where he met his wife.

If my father's introduction to the university showed the dark side of the Dome, unceremoniously indifferent and cold, my mother's showed its light. Avis Jones was an ROTC scholarship student from Jackson, Mississippi, and she loved Notre Dame. Hers was one of the millions of families across the country whose members fell in love with the university on Saturday mornings, through the eyes of their televisions, as the beloved football team took the field. Though they had never actually visited the university, her father regaled her with tales of the legends of Notre Dame football, and her mother, a devout Catholic, held a deep respect for the prestigious religious school. As the salutatorian of her Catholic high school and a loyal football fan, it seemed Avis was destined for Notre Dame. And she was, because it was there that she met my father and our family began.

As a spirited twenty-year-old, with strength and grit beyond her years, she and my father wed and she had her first child as a junior. When I think of the contentious debates my generation had over the complexities and wonder of female sexuality, it makes me proud to know that, little more than twenty-five years before, my mother had the brass and wit to thrive as a married, pregnant student on a Catholic college campus. I can only imagine how she must have felt. Notre Dame may be many things, but tolerance of difference has not always been its strong suit. Ask my father. And yet my mother not only did it, she excelled. And without missing a beat. She went into labor in her child psychology class, took a few days of maternity leave, and went back to graduate on time as a biology major.

Their baby, my older sister, Tona Boyd, was born in South Bend and spent her first year of life on Notre Dame's campus, in married student housing with our parents. Given the circumstances of her arrival, she was a quick study from birth, talking at eight months, reading by three years. Our parents say it was clear from very early on that she was a beautiful mix of my father's sharp intellect and my mother's strength. When the time came she had her pick of Ivy League institutions, yet she chose to return to the school of her birth. There she embraced all the university had to offer, both on campus and abroad. She spent a year studying in Spain, a summer doing service in Honduras, and was actively involved in the Kroc Institute for Peace Studies and campus ministry.

Although our father never received a degree, his first-born daughter would achieve that and more. As the first African-American student in the honors program, she triple-majored in government, Spanish, and philosophy, and minored in peace studies. In her senior year she was the first African-American to be awarded the Alumni Association's Distinguished Undergraduate Award, and she graduated from the university summa cum laude.

And then, of course, there was me.

Notre Dame, it seems, is one of those places where you either instantly feel a part of something or instantly realize you are on the outside. During my time there, I felt both. I chose the university, after all, for its familiarity. I found security in the halls where my mother and father had walked and the place of my sister's birth. And then, as a student, there were times at pep rallies and football games where the sway of the crowd and the metered rhythm of the band drowned out any feeling of isolation. I was with my roommates, and as I shouted "We are ND," I believed it.

And yet there were also times when I felt lost inside a vortex of sameness. For example, that moment in class when other students looked at me to represent "the black opinion" because, well, I was the only black person there. Or when California seemed like an exotic destination and North Face apparel was the only suitable solution to winter's bite. Or the times when uniformity seemed to extend from the architectural aesthetic to the points of view considered worthy of shared conversation and debate.

I remember the first time I publicly confronted what I considered the student body's homogeneous perspective on race in America. The memories of writing my first *Observer* article are still vivid in my head. I was in Lewis Hall, at my desk, on the phone with my mother, furious about an article written by a fellow student and published in my school paper. The article demeaned minority students, arguing they were "relying on pity in order to achieve" and "demanding that society lower the merit bar so that they can compete."

The ignorance was obvious, but I questioned the need to legitimize this blatant disregard for the scholastic ability of minority students by the largest vehicle for student expression on campus. So I submitted a letter to the editor and it was published. My article garnered so much attention that the author of the original article reached out to me and apologized. We mutually decided to host a town hall meeting encouraging Notre Dame students to start a dialogue about race on campus. Afterwards, we summarized the need for dialogue about these difficult topics in a joint piece in the *Observer*.

This public forum gave me the opportunity to be appointed the inaugural chair of the Student Senate's minority affairs committee, which led an initiative to create a cultural competency requirement for undergraduate students.

It seems I chose Notre Dame and Notre Dame chose me. During my time there, I met wonderful mentors, made lifelong friendships, and found the freedom to design my own major: Africana Studies and Health. I became the first graduate with a major in Africana studies (prior to that, only a minor was available) and used my degree to explore the dynamic relationship between health and society, particularly as it relates to marginalized and minority communities. As a senior, my efforts to promote diversity on campus and create a cultural competency requirement were honored as I was named the recipient of the Lou Holtz Leadership Award and the Frazier Thompson Scholarship.

In the end, my family's story is Notre Dame's story. Our legacy began with my father having the grace to look beyond the intolerance he met at the university. It continued with my parents' courage to raise a young, black family on a Catholic college campus. And it found meaning as my sister and I went on to unprecedented success at Notre Dame. What was started under the Dome finished under the Dome. And because our parents were willing to confront adversity with faith and love, the university benefitted from the scholarship and service of our family.

Today my parents have been married for thirty-three years. My father used his engineering background to work in civil engineering, professional construction management, and renewable energy development. My mother leveraged her biology degree to work in military space systems management, health care, communications, cable TV management, and nonprofit management. My sister took her interest in justice and peace to Harvard Law School and is now a trial attorney at the Department of Justice's civil rights division. And I am a pediatrician and child health advocate who continues to serve underserved communities.

We may not be the typical face of the university. But we certainly are ND.

LAURAN WILLIAMSON TUCK

(Class of 2006)

Lauran Williamson came to Notre Dame in autumn 2002 from Bensalem, Pennsylvania. She majored in marketing. After graduation she earned a master's degree at the University of Pennsylvania and co-founded a philanthropy, Tuck's R.U.S.H. for Literacy. She and her husband, Justin Tuck (Class of 2005), have two sons and live in New Jersey.

THE UNIVERSITY OF NOTRE DAME SERVED AS A PLACE FOR me to strengthen my values. As a biracial Catholic woman, I found that the desire to live a life focused on social justice was fostered at Notre Dame. Notre Dame also reinforced my family values, and, as a result, my wonderful family grew. Notre Dame, I loved you then and I love you now. This is my love letter to you.

A young man from Kellyton, Alabama (population 215), and a young woman from Bensalem, Pennsylvania, a suburb of Philadelphia, crossed paths in northern Indiana: both attended the University of Notre Dame.

We were so different. I grew up spending my summers in Europe and he grew up hunting and farming, but we met at a place that attracted a certain type of person, so we knew that deep down we had more in common than was apparent on the surface. Like many Notre Dame students, we grew up going to church every Sunday, singing in the choir. His parents have been married for over forty years and my parents for over thirty years.

Our strong faith in God allowed our relationship to survive many tests. In a society where being a virgin is often met with ridicule, my husband respected my desire to wait until marriage. I had many friends on campus with the same belief, so I was able to do it. Single-sex dorms and parietals helped to shape a culture that, in turn, helped to shape my future.

My husband graduated in 2005, and I graduated in 2006. We were married in 2008 and many of our Notre Dame classmates were in the wedding. In 2010 we welcomed our first son; in 2013 we welcomed our second, and our love continues to grow. Our children are blessed to have both our siblings and our college roommates serving as their godparents. Our Notre Dame family extends even beyond those we knew during our time on campus—I feel an instant connection with anyone who has attended Notre Dame.

So Notre Dame, thank you for the introduction to my husband, my bridesmaids, my children's godparents, and many of my mentors.

Who can describe their Notre Dame experience without mentioning Football Saturdays? I cannot. Waking up Saturday morning, putting on "The Shirt," tailgating, and then heading into Notre Dame Stadium to cheer on my boyfriend and the rest of the Fighting Irish football team—those are some of my favorite memories. Being thrown into the air to do pushups after the Irish scored a touchdown is such a euphoric feeling. And embracing your best friends while singing the alma mater was the icing on the cake!

Football Saturdays turned into Football Sundays when my husband was drafted by the New York Giants after graduation. Our time at Notre Dame helped set the stage for us to take on and take over New York City! Thank you, Notre Dame, for giving me an appreciation for the game of football.

I approached university just as I had approached high school. I joined a multitude of clubs and activities and aspired to be their leader. My favorite activities included flag football, Take Ten, Interrace Advisory Committee, and coed soccer. My dorm's flag football team was always good, and I had so much fun playing with my fellow women of Cavanaugh Hall. My coed soccer team was formed based on my existing group of friends, but we grew closer and had a great time. Take Ten was a wonderful program that worked in the South Bend community promoting techniques to prevent violence. As a team leader I enjoyed the challenges and rewards of that work.

The Interrace Advisory Committee served as a think tank for me, a place where I could come to terms with my unique place in our country and our world. Thank you, Notre Dame, for helping me to discover my gift as a "middle," the mediating position.

The company you keep says a lot about you and shapes many of your beliefs and actions. My fellow Notre Dame students were so motivated that it was and is inspiring! After graduating from the University of Notre Dame's Mendoza College of Business, I went on to earn a master's degree in nonprofit leadership from the University of Pennsylvania. I rose to the top among my peers in graduate school, and was honored with the Emerging Leader award. I truly believe this was because of my training at Notre Dame. Thank you, Notre Dame, for challenging me academically and igniting an insatiable passion for knowledge.

Two years after graduation, my husband and I founded Tuck's R.U.S.H. for Literacy, an organization that encourages children to Read, Understand, Succeed, and Hope. My own education has opened many doors for me, so I know firsthand how education is an equalizer. Research supports the notion that post-secondary education is still the surest way to economic mobility in the United States. Our organization focuses on literacy (preventing summer learning loss) and financial literacy (children's savings accounts), all in an effort to help children's dreams of a college education become a reality. Tuck's R.U.S.H. for Literacy has given more than 65,000 books to more than 11,000 students in Alabama, New York, and New Jersey. We have also awarded grants to youth-serving literacy and financial literacy organizations.

In 2013 we partnered with Citi Foundation, the 1:1 Fund, and the Children's Aid Society to support "CAS College Savers," a financial literacy initiative for low-income youth and their families. I also serve on the board of directors of New Yorkers for Children and the LINK School in Newark.

As an alumna, I have enjoyed working with Notre Dame on the Performing Arts Advisory Council, and my husband and I proudly support the ANDkids World Film Festival. Strategic planning, fundraising, program development and evaluation—Notre Dame prepared me to do all of these. But most importantly, Notre Dame strengthened my leadership abilities to enable me to change the world. With role models like the Reverend Theodore M. Hesburgh, CSC, I continue to strive to do more.

Thank you, Notre Dame, for strengthening my confidence and giving me the determination necessary to work in the nonprofit sector.

We are still learning, but I believe that our foundation, forged at the University of Notre Dame, is strong. My hope is that I can give to the world what Notre Dame has given me. I am so passionate about children and education, and I pledge to continue finding ways to provide opportunity and support, to answer the call when it is given.

Love thee, Notre Dame!

CHAPTER 7

The 2010s

On the morning of Sunday, May 16, 2010, the most significant event in the history of African-Americans at Notre Dame occurred: Katie O. Washington, of Gary, Indiana, mounted the podium at commencement and gave the valedictory address for the Class of 2010. After sixty-six years of black presence and accomplishment at Our Lady's university, one of our number had achieved the academic ultimate: graduating at the very top of her class.

"Over the last four years," she told her classmates, "I hope that all of us have taken the opportunity to step outside of our comfort zones, to build relationships with people from different places and backgrounds. Through service, time spent abroad, and our experiences with each other right here on campus, we've had the chance to find unity in the diversity of gifts with which God has blessed us."

Unity amid diversity. That goal, echoing our national ideal of *e pluribus unum*, proved to be the challenge of the decade for the United States. And as the decade's end came into view, it was not at all clear that the challenge would prove surmountable.

The fantasy of a post-racial America, entertained by some after President Obama's election in 2008, proved short-lived. By 2010, the Republican Party had served notice that it was not about loyal opposition, but about scorched-earth enmity. Nothing less than Obama's humiliation and defeat in 2012 would satisfy the GOP. In the end, however, it was Obama who had the last laugh, winning reelection by a comfortable margin.

Whatever may have been left of the post-racial fantasy was definitively interred in August 2014, when an unarmed black teenager,

Michael Brown, was shot to death by a police officer on a street in the St. Louis suburb of Ferguson, Missouri. Brown, like the biblical grain of wheat, fell to the ground and gave rise to Black Lives Matter, a new civil rights movement. Focusing on police killings of African-American men and boys, the movement spread across the American landscape like a prairie fire, finally reaching even the stuffy, conservative precincts of the National Football League, where in 2016 a young quarterback of biracial descent, Colin Kaepernick, ignited a protest by refusing to stand during pregame performances of the national anthem, in solidarity with Black Lives Matter.

But by far the most formidable challenge to American unity amid diversity sprang from New York and the fantastical world of "reality TV," in the form of billionaire real estate mogul Donald J. Trump. Trump decided in 2015 to take a plunge into politics at the highest level, announcing a run for the Republican nomination for president. Improbably, he won, beating out sixteen other contenders and becoming in the bargain the avatar of a movement of disaffected Americans, most of them white.

From the beginning of his campaign, Trump made clear that he was no respecter of established norms of politeness and civility, which he derided as "political correctness." By the time he accepted the GOP nomination in Cleveland in August 2016, he had publicly insulted and denigrated Mexicans, immigrants, Muslims, disabled people, women, African-Americans, Democrats, establishment Republicans, and many others.

And as the clock ticked down to election day and Trump stared at the possibility of defeat by Hillary Clinton, the first woman ever chosen as a major party presidential nominee, he redoubled his insults and fearmongering, declaring that the election was being "rigged" in favor of "Crooked Hillary" and hinting broadly that his followers might need to resort to means other than political ones to set things aright. And sure enough, some of those followers began to talk publicly about the need to "take out" a President Clinton.

As it turned out, however, Trump surprised everyone—including himself—by winning an electoral college majority and becoming the forty-fifth president of the United States. Clinton had to console herself with the knowledge that she carried the popular vote by a margin of almost 3 million.

Unified we were not.

Gun violence seemed to reach plague proportions in the 2010s. The Second Amendment was elevated by gun rights activists to the status of Holy Writ, and firearms—from the smallest and least powerful to the most potent and destructive—became so many graven images, worshipped and revered above all other gods—and God.

What many thought might break the spell of the gun occurred on December 14, 2012. A twenty-year-old gunman armed with a high-powered rifle and a pistol shot his way into the Sandy Hook Elementary School in Newtown, Connecticut, and in a matter of minutes killed six adults and twenty first-grade children. Surely, advocates of gun control thought, this slaughter of innocents would move Congress to pass at least some modest restrictions on firearms. Despite importuning by the president, however, Congress ended its 2013 session without taking any action.

By 2016, when a gunman in Orlando, Florida, invaded a gay nightclub and killed fifty people, no one expected—or even tried—to enact any gun controls. Indeed, in the superheated atmosphere of the Trump–Clinton presidential campaign, what attracted the attention of our political leaders was the gunman's religion, Islam, and his inspiration—the insane, homicidal ideology of ISIS, the so-called Islamic State.

ISIS seared itself into the national consciousness in August 2014, when it posted on the Internet a grisly video of American journalist James Foley being beheaded by one of its executioners. A number of similar videos followed over subsequent months. But by 2016, ISIS was on the defensive on the battlefields in Iraq and Syria, and it began to lash out with deadly terrorist attacks in Europe—including several major ones in France—and, when it could penetrate our defenses, in the United States.

At Notre Dame, the 2010s brought continued growth and progress. In spring 2016, the student body elected the second black student body president in the university's history, Corey Robinson, a member of the football team. Earlier in the decade, in 2013, with a black quarterback, Everett Golson, at the helm, Notre Dame played for the national football championship for the first time since 1988. The Irish fell to Alabama's Crimson Tide, 42–14.

On the basketball court, the Lady Irish basketball team, under coach Muffet McGraw and behind such standouts as Skylar Diggins, Jewell Loyd, and Kayla McBride, compiled a record of consistent success during the decade. Indeed, not since the Frank Leahy–coached football teams of the late 1940s and early 1950s had any Notre Dame team in any sport enjoyed such success.

By far the most notable event of the decade on campus was the death on February 26, 2015, of the Reverend Theodore M. Hesburgh. Ninety-seven years old at his passing, Father Hesburgh had served as president of Notre Dame for thirty-five years, from 1952 until 1987. More than any other individual, he was responsible for Notre Dame's growth from a small but respectable football school into one of America's top-ranked and most highly regarded universities.

Father Ted was of special importance to the university's African-American students and graduates. From the start of his presidency to its end, and even after, he pushed to increase and include blacks in the life of the university—as students, as faculty, as alumni. The results of his efforts are evident in the stories of many of the essayists in this book.

Father Hesburgh's passing was among the most significant in a decade that also claimed Steve Jobs, co-founder of Apple Computer and the genius who gave the world the iPhone, the iPad, and the Mac; Dick Clark, longtime host of *American Bandstand*, who was known as "America's oldest teenager"; Muhammad Ali, heavyweight boxing champion and civil rights and antiwar activist; Sally Ride, the first American woman to go into space; Dave Brubeck, jazz genius and a Notre Dame Laetare Medalist; Trayvon Martin, a black Florida teenager who was shot to death by a "neighborhood watch" captain in an incident that sparked national controversy; George McGovern, onetime Democratic nominee for president; Neil Armstrong, first man to walk on the moon; Joe Paterno, longtime Penn State football coach who came to ruin in the sordid Jerry Sandusky child sex abuse case; Arnold Palmer, golf champion; Elizabeth Taylor, actress; Charles "Bubba" Smith, a star of the 1966 Michigan State football team that played Notre Dame to a tie in an early "game of the century"; Elie Wiesel, Holocaust survivor and Nobel peace laureate; and Osama Bin Laden, Al Qaeda leader and mastermind of the 9/11 terror attacks.

Notre Dame remains the premier Catholic university in the world, and so had more than a passing interest in one of the biggest ecclesiastical developments of the decade. In February 2013 Pope Benedict XVI announced that he was resigning, the first pope to do so in six hundred years. Shortly after, the College of Cardinals elected to succeed him the first non-European pope since the eighth century: Cardinal Jorge Mario Bergoglio, the archbishop of Buenos Aires. Taking the name Francis I, the new pope immediately began advocating for a more humble, compassionate, merciful church.

Pax vobiscum, Pope Francis. And to all our spirits.

KATIE WASHINGTON COLE

(Class of 2010)

Katie Washington came to Notre Dame in autumn 2006 from Gary, Indiana. She majored in biological sciences with a minor in Catholic social tradition. She was director of the Voices of Faith Gospel Choir, student coordinator for Center for Social Concerns immersion courses, and a vocalist for the Notre Dame Jazz Band and New Orleans Brass Band. She and her husband, Charles, live in Baltimore, where she is completing an MD and a doctorate at Johns Hopkins.

IN THE DAYS AND WEEKS AFTER I GRADUATED FROM THE University of Notre Dame as the first African-American valedictorian, I found myself asking my parents how we got to this point. In the course of searching for answers, we found the words of Charles DuBois Hubert, my great grandmother's brother. In 1909, after graduating from Morehouse College in Atlanta, he found himself at the Rochester Theological Seminary. In this passage from a letter to his future wife, Mayme, my Uncle Charles writes about his experiences as the only African-American student at this predominantly white institution:

> They somehow feel here that [black men] cannot grapple with hard subjects, but I aim to show them, and I can do it here, that the black man can lead the white man in Ethics and Hebrew and Greek and Philosophy. It is up to me and I am going to do what they have felt that the black man cannot do.

I started my freshman year knowing very little about my family history and nothing about Notre Dame. I had never heard of C. D. Hubert or his tenure as a professor and acting president of Morehouse. I knew very little about the educators, healers, and innovators in the branches of my family tree. Similarly, during the first days of my freshman year, Notre Dame traditions felt foreign to me. I was not a legacy student, I had never watched a Notre Dame football game, and I had not set foot inside a Catholic Mass since I was a first-grader at Sister Thea Bowman Elementary School in Gary, Indiana. Yet during my time at Notre Dame and in the years since graduation, I've learned to see and understand family tradition—and my place in it—in a new light.

By the time I started college, I knew from my parents' example that excellence in education was my responsibility. None of my grandparents graduated from college, and my parents faced tremendous hardship in their pursuit of higher education. They both entered college and professional training with small children in tow and very little money. By the time I enrolled at Notre Dame, my mother, a registered nurse, and my father, a physician, had been practicing in their respective fields for many years. Every time I was too tired to go to class or too distracted to study, I remembered the sacrifices they made and the example they set for my siblings and me.

I spent my time at Notre Dame doing my best to live out the values that my parents instilled in me, but I certainly struggled to find my way. I often worried that I could not compete with students who had graduated from high schools with more resources than the public schools I attended in Gary, Indiana. I always had dedicated, loving teachers, but they worked under severe constraints. Even though I was a hard worker, I still internalized negative stereotypes about young, black women from cities like my hometown. I felt isolated in my classes as one of ninety-nine black freshmen in a class of two thousand students, and I found myself struggling to figure out where I fit in.

However, amidst these struggles, I found a community of friends, advocates, and mentors. Some aspects of this community, like the Voices of Faith Gospel Choir and the Black Cultural Arts Council, had been handed down as a safe space for students—especially black students—for decades. Other aspects of community surprised me. I found friends, with a range of backgrounds and experiences, in the

Center for Social Concerns—people who shared my vision for faith-driven service as vocation. My mentors and advocates in the College of Science and throughout campus were a diverse group of women and men who nurtured me and challenged me to reach my full potential.

Becoming a member of the Notre Dame family was transformative. While moments of isolation were often in conflict with my feelings of being part of a special community, this tension was essential to my growth. My experiences led me to constant questioning and examination of my life and the world around me. They challenged me and informed my walk of faith and transition into adulthood. Over the course of four years, I learned to embrace my identity as a member of the Notre Dame family and all the ways that my experiences on campus affirmed the lessons my parents instilled in me.

On May 16, 2010, Father Theodore Hesburgh found and embraced my mother in the audience just as I took the podium to begin my valedictory address. Father Hesburgh's leadership at our university and on the United States Civil Rights Commission paved the way for me to be valedictorian. Almost fifty years earlier, this same Father Hesburgh stood shoulder to shoulder and linked hands with the Reverend Dr. Martin Luther King Jr., avatar of the civil rights movement, at a Chicago rally in support of the Civil Rights Act of 1964. That was the same Martin Luther King Jr. who, as a Morehouse undergraduate, had had his vision and voice shaped in part by my great-uncle C. D. Hubert.

In that moment on that brilliant Sunday morning in 2010, two legacies—my family's and Notre Dame's—were symbolically unified. I am forever grateful for the rich heritage that I share with black Notre Dame students and alumni—starting with Frazier Thompson—who have blazed many trails and cleared the path for future generations.

My commencement address was a historic milestone. However, in the years since graduation, many humbling moments remind me that there is more work to be done. The following words, spoken about C. D. Hubert after his passing, inspire continued reflection on the road ahead:

> But like Amos and Micah he brooded and agonized over the wrongs and injustices of society. The injustices in the economic order disturbed him. He could never reconcile himself to war. He brooded over the plight of his people: ignorance, Jim Crowism,

discrimination, segregation, and disfranchisement. Only those of us close to Hubert knew how these sins wore on his heart and mind.

I'm grateful that graduation day was one of many symbols that our world has progressed beyond Jim Crowism and many forms of discrimination. However, disenfranchisement and injustice have taken on new forms in our social, political, and economic systems. I am often reminded of the children—in our country and around the world—who are systematically denied opportunities to learn and prosper. In schools throughout the country, including Notre Dame, many young people still feel unprepared, isolated, and inadequate. As we celebrate all that we have accomplished in the seventy years since Frazier Thompson enrolled at Notre Dame, I am confident that black Notre Dame alumni and students will continue to inspire, to promote change, and to reach back to help others do the same.

CRAIG A. FORD JR.

(Class of 2010)

Craig A. Ford Jr. came to Notre Dame in autumn 2006 from Phoenixville, Pennsylvania. He majored in philosophy and theology and was active in campus ministry and a member of the Glee Club. After graduation, he pursued a master's degree in religion at Yale Divinity School. He currently is pursuing a PhD in theological ethics at Boston College. He lives in Massachusetts.

WHEN I ARRIVED AT NOTRE DAME, I DIDN'T REALLY HAVE A clue about what the words "black, gay, Catholic, and man" meant all next to each other. And had I continued in the Mendoza College of Business after my first year, I probably would not be much closer to giving these words my own meaning. Pursuing a marketing major, even accompanied by a second major in psychology (what better for effecting self-discovery?), left me with a hollow feeling at the conclusion of my second semester.

To the dismay of the prophets of "practicality," I found myself fulfilled in the two majors that generate as many questions about their ability to put food on the table as they do about the nature of truth: theology and philosophy. How I loved what I studied! Declaring the theology-philosophy joint major was like a homecoming for me, an experience that was like only one other that I had had in my life to that point: the decision to become Catholic. I made that decision at the age of eighteen, after having been nourished in the Baptist tradition since childhood.

Day after day in my theology classes I immersed myself in translating complicated concepts with centuries of commentary into the sturdy faith vocabulary given to me as a child. The shouts and praises of my youth turned into theses on Christology and ecclesiology. The most concise, rhythmic presentation of the Gospel that I know—Jesus loves me, this I know, for the Bible tells me so!—became the foundation for statements that prioritize goodness in the articulation of any theological anthropology. And the passionate preaching that first taught me about the grace and love of God became the foundation for my own prioritization of inclusive love in the development of any theology worthy of the name "Christian."

In my philosophy classes I learned that giving answers to some of life's most vexing questions—What does it mean to be human? How do we make the most of life?—is the birthright of every single person, but to study answers to these questions, and even to append to them some of my own, that was a privilege and a joy. As I read more, I discovered more, and, in this process, concepts that were not my own became my own.

Of course, there was a personal dimension to all of this as well. As I was harmonizing and internalizing with my own meaning concepts that belonged to the philosophical and theological "exterior" (words like "ontology" and "epistemology"), so was I also beginning to give meaning to those identities to which I felt drawn, but which still seemed uncomfortably distant. Although I felt attracted to them—black, gay, Catholic, man—they didn't yet, at that point in my sophomore year, fit together in such a way that they radiated from the interior of my being like the simple wholeness of my name "Craig."

I was making progress, though. In the *Scholastic*, for example, I gave an interview on the subject of being both gay and Catholic. Because the magazine had a campus-wide circulation, this had the side-effect of outing me to everyone I knew in South Bend—and many others whom I did not know! So at the very least, I broadcasted to the world that I had made peace with at least two of these identities: gay and Catholic. These words came from me because they were me: I was gay and Catholic; gay and Catholic was I.

"You can't be gay and Catholic," said some of my colleagues in theology. In so doing, they attempted to divide me once again into parts.

"Why not?"

"Because being gay is a lifestyle, a lifestyle fundamentally in opposition to the teaching of the church. It is a lifestyle that embraces and promotes the enacting of homosexual acts. If you're truly Catholic, you're not gay; no, you're a person living with same-sex attraction."

In many ways, the ending of this small dialogue describes the Roman Catholic Church's official position with respect to gay people: homosexuals don't really exist; at bottom there are only healthy heterosexuals and defective heterosexuals, called either to a sex life in marriage or to no sex life at all.

This was a teaching that I wholeheartedly rejected. But what could I do about it? After looking back on my Notre Dame career, I realized that the better question was: What didn't I do about it?

How could someone not notice that I was a gay Catholic rather than some supposedly sexually misguided person living with "same-sex attraction" navigating his way through an oversexualized culture? How could people not notice the gay Catholic who served as Zahm Hall's (absolutely fabulous, I might add) music minister for three years? How could people not notice the gay Catholic who served as a music leader for campus ministry's "Sophomore Road Trip"? How could people not notice the gay Catholic who served as cantor at the noon mass in Malloy Hall, a mass I attended daily? What about the fact that, instead of fleeing as far away from the church as I could, I dedicated my entire senior year to writing a thesis on the subject of including same-sex relationships within the church's theology of marriage?

Are these not precisely the actions of a gay Catholic? For those who had eyes to see, they certainly were. For others . . . well, I just started to ignore them. When orthodoxy degenerates into skepticism about new movements of the Spirit, there is nothing more that can be done. But the Spirit gives life—life to proclaim in a vocabulary that was all my own, from the inside outward, that I was both gay and Catholic.

Yet there was more to be done. During my junior and senior years at Notre Dame, I began to realize that one identity was yet to be integrated into me: my race. Heck, I was at a loss even to know how to effect such an integration. Although I knew that the number of gay Catholics at Notre Dame was large enough to form a small community, not many of them identified as black. People who identified as both black and Catholic were many at Notre Dame, but I didn't feel comfortable enough talking about issues of sexuality with them. And with respect to those who identified as black, Catholic, and gay, I had befriended two of them, only one of whom was a man.

So, not having anyone at Notre Dame whom I could regard as a positive role model of a black, gay, Catholic man—and also having no one in my family of whom I was aware who could fill this role—I didn't feel like I had the resources to confront the issue of integrating my race into my identity. And I didn't. At Notre Dame, I felt as if I had mentally accepted my identity as a gay Catholic who was black—I accepted it from the outside in—but I did not understand my race to be a constitutive part of myself, from the inside out. It would only be during my years *after* Notre Dame, at Yale Divinity School, where my racial identity would become my own.

While at Notre Dame, though, I accepted my racial identity deeply enough to understand that Notre Dame was, and continues to be, the perpetrator of a real injustice. The injustice lies in the wording of Notre Dame's nondiscrimination clause, which protects blacks, among others, from discrimination with respect to "employment, educational programs, admissions policies, scholarship and loan programs, athletics, recreational, and other school-administered programs," but does not guarantee any such protections for people who are not heterosexual.

Reminiscent of my conversation with my theology department colleagues who sought to divide the gay "part" of me from the Catholic "part" of me, this nondiscrimination clause, in refusing to protect sexual orientation along with race, sought to protect the black "part" of me while disregarding the gay "part." But I have no such parts! There is only I, Craig, singular and whole, all of whose identities—black, gay, and Catholic—are equally worthy of dignity, respect, and protection.

As I write this, I stand four years removed from my Notre Dame experience. On one hand, I regard it as a time of tremendous growth: intellectually, spiritually, and socially. Had I not gone to Notre Dame, I would not be where I am today, studying moral theology at Boston College and thinking in and with the Catholic Church that I know and love. Had I not gone to Notre Dame, I would not have met some of my closest friends. Had I not gone to Notre Dame, I would never have discovered the unique form of camaraderie and support that came from being a member of the Notre Dame Glee Club. And, of course—

how could I forget?—had I not gone to Notre Dame, I would never have had the opportunity to be part of the best dorm on the planet: Zahm *House*!

On the other hand, Notre Dame was a place of challenge and disappointment. While I learned to own my identity as a gay Catholic man at Notre Dame, I did this largely on my own, outside the structures both of residential life and campus ministry that were always—because they had to be—ambiguous in their support for my sexual orientation. And with respect to race, I did not feel that Notre Dame helped me understand myself at all.

My situation now is different. Now, when people ask me who I am—and when disclosing my "identities" as a black, gay, Catholic man are relevant—I tell them without any anxiety whatsoever. The anxiety is gone because all of these words no longer come upon me from the outside in. I no longer fear them as intruders seeking to divide me into parts, each with its role to play. Instead they come from the inside out. They come from me, a person affirmed in God's love, for the Bible tells me so.

BRITTANY SUGGS

(Class of 2012)

Brittany Suggs came to Notre Dame in autumn 2008 from Hampton, Virginia. She majored in psychology. After graduation, she enrolled at George Mason University to pursue a master's degree in public health. After earning her master's, she plans to pursue a doctorate in the same field.

THERE I WAS, AT THE BEGINNING OF THE SPRING 2009 SEMESTER, staring academic probation right in the face and asking myself: "How in the world did I get here?" I was striving for academic excellence; I never thought this would happen to me.

Then I questioned: "Was I actually supposed to be at Notre Dame? Was I destined to be a member of the Fighting Irish?"

Truthfully, until the year before, my mind had been fixated on attending Georgetown University for my undergraduate years. I knew essentially nothing about the University of Notre Dame until I had a conversation with my younger brother about *U.S. News & World Report*'s "best colleges" rankings. My brother, an enthusiast of all things pertaining to higher education and college sports (second to his love for Christ), suggested that I should "give Notre Dame a shot and apply."

I was extremely resistant to the idea. A first glance at the website sent my mind whirling into thoughts of, "Goodness! I will be spending my undergraduate years at yet another prep school." Moreover, my first glimpse of the Notre Dame website, outside of the university's strong Catholic presence, found only scant traces of what I envisioned for my undergraduate experience.

Nevertheless, I applied and was pleasantly surprised to find myself quickly growing in love with the thought of becoming a "University of Notre Dame undergraduate student." It took only one visit to the campus during spring visitation weekend and I was hooked. I found such an internal peace while venturing throughout Our Lady's campus that I knew, without hesitation: "I am home. This is the place God has chosen for me."

Somewhere in the midst of my euphoric first semester experiences, I found myself spiraling into a whirlwind of academic challenges as a biology major. I gave it my all: met with professors during office hours; attended tutoring sessions; studied with students who seemed to have a better grasp of the material; attended exam review sessions; and, as a very last resort, signed up for a lesson in study skills. With the support of my parents and my First Year Studies advisor, I switched majors, from biology to psychology, with a minor in Africana studies.

With academic probation still looming, I could only fix my lips to inquire: "Father-God, why in the world was I led here? What purpose is there for me to be at Notre Dame?" If I have learned anything since that moment, it is to be careful of the questions one asks of our Lord. He will certainly deliver on His promises to provide an answer.

On February 20, 2012, I was making my usual rounds between the Student Activities Office and the Office of Multicultural Student Programs and Services (MSPS), keeping tabs on various affairs for the Black Student Association (BSA) and First Class Steppers. Typically, a periodic check of the groups' mailboxes tends to be a pretty mundane task. This time, however, to my shock and surprise, I discovered that a member of the Notre Dame community had placed fried chicken wings and patties in the BSA mailbox. I later learned that this was not the first time this had happened. The same thing had happened nearly a week earlier to the African Student Association (ASA).

Appalled and unsure how to proceed, I immediately sought counsel from staff members in MSPS and the Student Activities Office (SAO), which ushered in strategies that both addressed and prevented future tampering with all organizations' mailboxes. Additional efforts were implemented by the Notre Dame Security Police, who launched an investigation in an attempt to identify the person or persons who did the tampering. Shortly thereafter, a campus-wide email was issued by the Office of Student Affairs and the Office of the Provost, calling the mailbox incidents "two deplorable incidents of racial harassment."

From that moment on, my senior year experience drastically changed. I believe I walked—no, I catapulted—right into the purpose God intended when He led me to Notre Dame. I prayed: "Lord, I wanted to be used by You. I wanted to serve You in a greater way. Yet I would never have guessed You would ask this of me!"

The response He laid on my heart came through a popular reference when questions of *purpose* and *destiny* come into play: "Jonah ran from God . . . Gideon was insecure . . . Martha was a worrier . . . Sara was impatient . . . Moses stuttered . . . Abraham was old . . . I do not call the qualified. I qualify the called."

I still vividly recall the day when I was overwhelmed by calls from the media begging for a story, hearing a mixture of sentiments and complaints from individuals who wished I would have taken a more *radical and defiant* approach, receiving praise and support from those who were thrilled that I took a quieter stance, and being somewhat uplifted by those who were just happy that I took any stance at all.

In the midst of all the voices and opinions around me, I remembered the still Voice placing the following words from Proverbs on my heart: "You make your plans, but I determine your steps." There was something quite freeing in that assurance that I would not have to make all the decisions on my own. I not only rediscovered why exactly God was gracious enough to keep me at Notre Dame, but I also rediscovered that I was merely a vessel for a greater plan He had all along.

The BSA continued working around the clock with SAO, MSPS, Student Affairs, the Offices of the President and the Provost, Campus Ministry, NDSP, Student Government, and student leaders from various organizations on campus to address racial insensitivity, as well as other potential forms of discrimination.

The most notable outcome of their efforts was a first-ever campus-wide town hall meeting to discuss the incidents involving the ASA and the BSA and to gather input regarding a plan of action for handling any future incidents of discrimination on campus. As a result of the town hall meeting, a "Call to Action" committee was formed as a bridge between Notre Dame students, professors, faculty, staff, and administrators to usher in the plan of action.

My experiences at the University of Notre Dame already have had a profound influence on my life, and will continue to do so in the future. Serving as chair of the Black Student Association fueled my passion to lead as Christ exemplified, through service. To that end, I am pursuing a master's degree in global and community health at George Mason University. My desire is to further serve and inspire the collaborative efforts of other health care providers, varying in ethnic and socioeconomic competencies, in promoting the welfare of individuals both nationally and abroad.

Beyond academic and professional development, I believe my experiences at Notre Dame brought me to a deeper level of spiritual realization and growth in my relationship with Christ. Romans 3:23 is a stark reminder that we all fall short sometimes, and we all have "missed the mark" at some point or another in our lives. Therefore, to imagine for even a second that we possess sole autonomy of our destiny or are capable of "true perfection" in life's pursuits is to believe that we are able to save ourselves. Instead, when we make the choice to trust in Christ, we can rest assured that we are made "complete," or "perfected," in Him, and He remains faithful to perfect us in His perfect timing and in accordance to His will. "For He knows the plans He has for us . . . plans to give us hope and a future" (Jeremiah 29:11).

To this day, I still feel so truly blessed to have embraced the campus of the University of Notre Dame. God remained faithful and so gracious to me during my undergraduate years. I could never repay Him in any magnitude for every experience, opportunity for growth, and for every influential friend, peer, professor, faculty mentor, and administrator He placed in my life. With pride and so much love in my heart, I boldly exclaim our motto to all who will listen: "God. Country. Notre Dame."

OLEVIA BOYKIN

(Class of 2014)

Olevia Boykin came to Notre Dame in fall 2010 from Sheboy-gan, Wisconsin. She majored in political science and sociology. She currently is a student at Yale Law School.

IT SEEMED LIKE A SIMPLE AND STRAIGHTFORWARD INTERVIEW. "Do you feel like you have been discriminated against at Notre Dame?" the USA Today reporter asked. "How is the university doing at diversity efforts? What has been your experience being black at Notre Dame?"

I answered honestly: "I don't think I would describe my experience as discriminatory. . . . The university could be doing more to increase diversity and make life easier for its minority students. . . . It's exhausting to be black at Notre Dame."

To this day, I think it would be difficult for many black students to disagree with my statements based on content. It is fairly well established that it is not easy to be black at Notre Dame, regardless of whether you are fully enveloped in the black community, completely separate, or somewhere in between. Further, most of us know two versions of the life of black students at Notre Dame: the version we talk about with nostalgia to prospective students, and the real version, which is much less rosy. Nevertheless, the context of my interview, the fact I spoke the wrong version, got me into trouble.

I've spent my time at Notre Dame in a precarious position. I'm black, but I grew up in a small, basically all-white town in Wisconsin.

Being light-skinned, and with most of my close friends both from home and at Notre Dame being white, I struggled to feel "black enough" at Notre Dame. In fact, I have never felt fully accepted into the black community at the university.

At the same time, I'm clearly not white, nor am I upper middle-class like most of the white students at Notre Dame. I often felt that, in order to be fully accepted into either community, the black or the white, one would basically need to entirely neglect the other. But I didn't want to do that, so I straddled the two as best as I could. While my close friends remained mainly white, I was on the board of the Black Student Association and participated in events and social life accordingly.

When the interview was published in *USA Today* in March 2013, responses among members of the Notre Dame community were polarized. The black alumni association reached out to me to discuss how they could help improve the experience of black students at Notre Dame. I was supposed to recruit some black students to talk with a few alumni at a roundtable. It seemed harmless; in fact, I was excited.

In the end, only one other black student came, and there were six or seven alumni. While it was not their intent, I felt attacked by them, as if I were in a lion's den. The alumni were defensive; my words were used against me; it became a cohort of fairly disconnected alums telling me why I was personally inadequate at handling life at Notre Dame.

Several students and administrators weren't happy either. Many of my fellow BSA board members echoed the alumni's feelings. I was told I needed to do better at handling life here, that it wasn't my place to publicize my personal issues.

At the same time, there were students, professors, and administrators who reached out to me, empathized with me, and stood up for me. In fact, this was the spring semester of 2013, the semester I won the Frazier Thompson scholarship. That helped me feel like I wasn't universally disliked by the larger black community and has significantly eased my financial stress in my final year.

I think most of us learn how and get used to adequately navigating the waters of race at Notre Dame: ignoring ignorant comments, being the only black person in class, being ever-conscious of how we are perceived. But this was the most emotionally straining learning experience for me, as I lost any semblance of cohesion with the black community.

Fortunately, while being black at Notre Dame and its accompanying trials and takeaways have been important, they are not the most salient or defining of my experiences at Notre Dame. I have had the opportunity to get close to professors who challenge me, who have excited in me a passion for academia. I have worked with a professor from the onset of a paper idea through its publication, learning the process of academic inquiry. I got to do archival research at Howard University, teach a financial literacy course, and design a website for another professor. A directed readings course with yet another professor was the most intellectually challenging and informative class of my college career.

Working with these brilliant and passionate professors—who challenge me and care about me; who tell me when I am flat wrong or when I need to do or be better; who will buy me a book I badly need to read, take me out to eat to celebrate or mourn a score on the LSAT, and give me honest advice; who have become some of my closest and most cherished friends—has been the most formative part of my experience at Notre Dame.

Second to my experience with professors in shaping who I am today was studying abroad. I went to Athens, Greece, after previously having never left North America. Besides traveling all around Greece, I went to London, Paris, Istanbul, Madrid, Rome, and Granada. I gained a new perspective on the importance of understanding language and culture as well as paying attention to international news. At the same time, while in a program with seventy-two other students that resembled the diversity of Notre Dame, within a homogeneous country notorious for racism, I felt liberated from my color. All the friends I made, from African immigrants to my Greek barista, showed me how similar all people are, how race, as part of our identity, ought to be trivial. This feeling of liberation made me realize that I had felt burdened at some point.

When I thought back to my time at Notre Dame—"the happiest place in the world," as a best friend would call it—I became disillusioned. I realized how different Notre Dame could be. By "different" I mean easier for black students. Being in Athens showed me that there should not be a line to straddle between racial communities.

Surely, when I came to Notre Dame I did not anticipate any of the experiences I have highlighted here. In fact, thinking back, I had relatively poor reasons for coming to Notre Dame. My boyfriend wanted to stay in the Midwest, a desire that severely limited our options. Notre Dame sounded fun; I was drawn to all the tradition, the people seemed genuinely good at heart, and it felt right in my gut. When I got to campus I spent two years basically floundering. I struggled to feel smart, so I overindulged in clubs. As a club leader, I learned that I love having the agency to help people, to make people feel heard. Since then, I have tutored at the Martin Luther King Jr. Center, interned at the local public defender's office, and started a book club with the girls in detention at the juvenile justice center. Next year, I go to law school.

It's funny how over the long term everything weaves together into some sort of serendipitous narrative, even though day to day it all seems to be in disarray. While I felt like I was foundering in freshman and sophomore years, the seeds were being planted for my last two years. I took classes with great professors; was granted the Doan Scholarship, which opened a network of professors while also relieving financial strain; and participated in community service, which illuminated to me my true values. While going abroad was an opportunity I sought to broaden my horizons, it helped me home in on what was important back in the US. The *USA Today* article and the ensuing fallout, for all the stress and mayhem they caused, taught me how to endure criticism and be assertive. My relationships with professors, which grew gradually out of courses or research apprenticeships, have defined me, made me more intellectually curious, independent, and confident.

And so, here we are. I just graduated, and this fall I go to law school. I would argue my story is not unique, either as a student at Notre Dame or as a black student at Notre Dame. Being black at Notre Dame has not been easy; in fact it has been relatively difficult, but I am better for it. The opportunities that have been extended to me through this university—from grant funding for my senior thesis and research apprenticeships, to developing close relationships with professors, to study abroad—all have had a hand in shaping me into the person I am today. As I move forward, I bring these lessons with me, both the personal and intellectual growth I have experienced and the friends I have made along the way.

Tai-ler "TJ" Jones

(Class of 2014)

TJ Jones came to Notre Dame in the spring semester of 2010 from Roswell, Georgia. He majored in film, television, and theatre and was a key performer on the football team, including the team that played for the 2013 BCS National Championship. He graduated in December 2013.

MY FATHER, ANDRE JONES, WAS A STUDENT-ATHLETE AT NOTRE Dame from 1987 to 1991 and was fortunate enough to play on the 1988 National Championship football team. He met my mother, Michele Jones, at Notre Dame, where she was beginning graduate school after having graduated previously from the University of Minnesota. The fact that both of my parents attended Notre Dame and that my father had made a name for himself on the football field are the reasons why, initially, I did not want to attend Notre Dame.

Growing up I was known solely as "Dre's son TJ," not just "TJ." I decided that when I finally left the house for college, I didn't want to be known solely for who my father was. I wanted the opportunity to make a name for myself, to create my own footprints, not just follow in my father's footsteps.

The desire to branch out and create my own name is why in April of 2008 I committed to play football at Stanford University on a full athletic scholarship. This was only a verbal commitment, meaning I was able to change my mind without any repercussions before the National Signing Day, which is the first Wednesday in February. The following fall, of 2009, I decided to de-commit from Stanford after being told that they do not and never have accepted mid-year enrollees. A few days before my official de-commitment, in November 2009, I took one last visit to Notre Dame. This ended up being the first and last visit I would take before committing to another university.

That wasn't my first visit to the Notre Dame campus, but for some reason there was a significant difference between this time and every other time I had visited. From the game day atmosphere of Notre Dame playing USC to seeing the relationships my father had formed with his former teammates, attending Notre Dame seemed like the only choice for me. It was then that I realized I had a handful of my father's former teammates whom I considered family and who would be there for me for my entire time in college and thereafter.

With Notre Dame being a Catholic institution, I had already assumed what I thought it would be like to be an actual student. I felt I would be forced to follow Catholicism and that people would know as soon as they saw me that I wasn't Catholic. I feared being treated differently or frowned upon because my family wasn't Catholic.

But after my four years of attending Notre Dame, I realize I couldn't have been more off with my assumptions. This campus is one of the most diverse environments I've ever been submerged in, from religion to cultural backgrounds. It's mandatory for student-athletes to live in the dorms for their first three years. At first every athlete is opposed to the idea. But that requirement forces the athlete to interact with the general student population and partake in the activities that they do. It is surprising the number of people you befriend and find similarities with just in your dorm. I realized that there are many people who come from backgrounds similar to mine and who hold themselves to the same moral standards.

The great thing about Notre Dame is that it recruits the same caliber of person in every student it accepts, no matter where they come from. Each student is one of, if not the very best, from his or her high school and strives for greatness in everything they do. They do not discriminate in any manner and are open to forming relationships with everyone. Regardless of where you're from, your individual background helps to form these relationships as opposed to limiting whom you may or may not get along with.

For example, one of my first roommates and now best friends is Nick Fitzpatrick. Nick was just a regular student for a year before walking on to the football team. Since he is from Granger, Indiana, I have spent much time with his family and now consider them my own. Any holiday that I couldn't go home for I spent with Nick's family. And when my father passed, his family was there for me when I returned to school. It's these priceless and lifelong relationships that are formed by chance with people you meet in the dorms and around campus.

Now it is no secret that the black population at Notre Dame is not large, so one would think that the black students and athletes would gel together from the jump, but often that isn't the case. Other students, seeing a black person on campus, will assume the person plays a sport and that's how he or she got accepted into the university. It is because of this assumption by other students that the black non-athletes try to disassociate themselves from the black athletes on campus. They do so in a variety of ways, including wearing shirts that bear the words "Irish Non-Athlete." They find the stereotypical assumption offensive, and this initially builds a wall between the black students and athletes. But eventually that wall is broken down when each finds similarities with the other. It's just unfortunate that it can't be that way from the beginning because of a stereotypical assumption of what it means to be black at Notre Dame.

In the same regard, being a football player at Notre Dame also brings along its own stereotypes when in the classroom. Some professors may love football players, some may dislike them, and some may be indifferent to them. In my personal experience I have dealt with professors who have either loved me or disliked me based on their interactions with football players in the past. The good thing about their not liking you is that you can always change their perception by being polite and hard-working.

One professor I have formed a relationship with is Karen Heisler, who teaches in the film, television, and theatre department. It wasn't until I began to take the courses she taught that I genuinely enjoyed learning in the classroom. From my first class with her to my last, we have had a genuine relationship that goes further than the classroom. She wants nothing more than my well-being in general, not only in the classroom, as do I for her and her family. She sees me as much more than just a football player, while I see her as much more than a professor; she is also a mentor and a caring mother figure. It is the ability to form these kinds of relationships with your professors that makes learning an enjoyable experience at Notre Dame.

I graduated in December 2013 and have already begun to see the strength that the Notre Dame degree holds in all facets of life. The ability to network, not only for business connections but also for cordial relationships, is second to none. That degree and your experience on campus are easy conversation starters that can lead to any sort of blossoming relationship. So I can honestly say that with the friends I've made, my experience in whole, and what is to come in the future, I would choose Notre Dame every time if I could do it all over again. This university not only gave me the opportunity to follow in my father's footsteps, but also to do so while making a name for myself. It wasn't until I enrolled that I understood what it meant to be and how to embrace being a legacy child at Notre Dame. Being able to uphold the legacy my late father began is more than I could hope for. For that I will forever be grateful for the opportunities Notre Dame presented me.

DENISE UMUBYEYI

(Class of 2014)

Denise Umubyeyi came to Notre Dame in autumn 2010 from Glen Ellyn, Illinois. She majored in political science with a minor in international development studies. After graduation, she plans to return to the Chicago area to work for an executive search firm.

PLUNGING FROM THE TOP OF MY CLASS IN LUSAKA, ZAMBIA, to the bottom of my class in Glen Ellyn, Illinois, was a daunting experience. Not only did I have to learn how to write complete sentences, read my first book, and adapt to a whole new education system at the age of thirteen, but I also had to learn how to operate within a new and different environment. However, I was no stranger to new and different.

My story starts in the small city of Gitarama in the small African country of Rwanda. At the time of my birth, my mother and father, who were very successful business partners, imagined a bright future for me, which would have included a series of private schools and an excellent university education somewhere in the US or Europe. Never would they have guessed that their dreams for me and my then-unborn siblings would be diverted by acts of hatred, betrayal, and mass killing that left thousands dead and millions more displaced in the horror that was the Rwandan genocide.

In 1994 my family fled to Tanzania, where we lived for a few years until we were forced to move. Unfriendly relations between the Rwandan and Tanzanian governments made it dangerous for us and other Rwandans to stay in Tanzania. So, in a white pickup truck, with suitcases that had seen better days and the little money my father could stuff in his socks, we moved—making a long drive across borders and cities to Lusaka, the capital of Zambia. There my parents replanted seeds for what they hoped would be a successful future for their children.

My parents, my four younger siblings, and I were each other's companions as we moved from home to home due to fluctuating political and financial circumstances. Eventually, my parents decided to apply for a chance to emigrate to the United States through the United Nations High Commission for Refugees. So after eight peaceful but financially difficult years in Zambia, my family flew to the United States on September 29, 2005, to begin a life that my parents felt was sure to open multiple opportunities for their children.

One thing that remained constant amidst the instability of our circumstances was our continued search for more and better educational opportunities. This value is engrained in my parents, who are aware of the benefits of education, since my father did not even finish the third grade and my mother only finished high school. Both have accomplished much but still say, with a hint of regret, "I could achieve more had I received more educational opportunities."

My parents' hard work and perseverance in the service of finding opportunities for their children has inspired in me an unquenchable thirst for education. I believe, as my father says in his broken English, "Education is opportunity . . . you can do anything you like."

This thirst has driven me from being at the bottom of my class, unable to write a complete sentence, to being in the top 20 percent of my high school's graduating class of over five hundred students, speaking at our senior honors convocation, and attending one of the most prestigious universities in the nation.

I was introduced to the University of Notre Dame through my participation in the QuestBridge Scholar application process. This very competitive program matches bright, low-income students with the nation's best colleges and universities. I knew that I wanted to attend a university that was prestigious, close to home but far enough away for me to be independent, and that fulfilled my mom's wishes for me to attend a Catholic institution.

Against many people's judgment and a teacher who would not let me take a day off school to visit because he thought Notre Dame was unattainable for me, I visited the campus in the fall of my senior year. I was awestruck by the magic that permeated the air around campus. Even as the chilly fall air brushed my cheeks and nipped at my ears, the beauty of the campus, the smiling faces of students, and a growing hunger to one day walk upon this campus was not lost upon me.

I was not accepted as a QuestBridge scholar, but I was made aware of my acceptance to Notre Dame through the regular admissions process during a spring visitation weekend where my life as member of the Fighting Irish family began.

It would be a lie to say that my close to four years at Notre Dame have been a breeze, because they have not. I could recount the number of times I felt inadequate, surrounded by people who I felt would never be able to understand me and I them, the number of times I called home telling my mother it was too hard, the number of times I faced my own identity-crisis nightmares as I tried to fit into different cultures—white, African-American, and just plain American—to all of which I felt I never belonged. The nights I would miss out on social events because I had to work ten to fifteen hours a week, fill out my taxes, and make sure my FAFSA wasn't late. The one time I sincerely feared I would not be able to come back the next semester because my school fees were late.

From these hardships, I learned the best lessons in life: how to be resilient and independent; what true friendship means; how to agree to disagree; what diversity means; and, most importantly, how to let pride go and ask for help when it is needed. As I look forward to graduation, I know I will leave Notre Dame knowing that I made the right decision.

Many would never know that at the center of cornfields and plains for miles is a place where one has the world at their fingertips. At Notre Dame, I have seen more of the world than I ever thought I would. This has been through my classes with renowned US and international scholars, students with diverse experiences and backgrounds, and speakers and guest lecturers from around the world.

With generous funding from Notre Dame, I have had the beautiful opportunity to explore my interests and use the world as my classroom. My participation in seminars in Washington, D.C., and Appalachia in my freshman year exposed me to international development institutions that I aspired to one day work with, and also to the underbelly that is poverty in the US.

I have had the great opportunity to not only study abroad in the United Kingdom and intern for a former minister and current member of Parliament, but also to access parts of Europe I might have lived a lifetime never knowing. At Notre Dame, I have exercised my ability to effect change through my research and work for three years at an after-school program helping low-income minority students from the South Bend community.

One of the most impactful experiences was my trip, during the summer of 2013, to my birthplace of Rwanda, which I left at the young age of two, to conduct research that qualified for my International Development Studies minor capstone.

When I applied to Notre Dame, I concluded my personal statement essay with these words: "I will continue to strive each day to live up to the name Umubyeyi, to honor my parents' sacrifices for me and to become the leader whom they saw in me at birth. I am looking forward to the next level of challenges that college studies will bring and to further developing my education and leadership skills. Along the way, I hope I can inspire other children like me to reach for and achieve their dreams too."

In more ways than I can ever begin to explain, I have fulfilled and exceeded my goals for my time at Notre Dame. I know that my education, exposure to the world, and connections that I have made at Our Lady's university together have prepared me for whatever the world throws at me after graduation.

COREY ROBINSON

(Class of 2017)

Corey Robinson came to Notre Dame in January 2013 from San Antonio, Texas. He majored in the Program of Liberal Studies and was a member of the football team. In his senior year he served as student body president. After graduation he plans to pursue a career as an art dealer in New York City.

I NEVER KNEW ANYTHING ABOUT NOTRE DAME AS A CHILD. I never heard, thought, or talked about it. Never dreamed of studying there, much less playing football there.

It wasn't as if I disliked Notre Dame growing up. My ambivalence simply stemmed from ignorance. During my childhood in Texas, only a handful of schools were mentioned by my family and friends: the University of Texas at Austin, Texas A&M, Texas Tech, and the service academies. The overwhelming majority of my childhood friends went to one of these schools. Almost no one from my high school, San Antonio Christian High School, ever went on to play Division I sports. Never did I imagine that I would leave Texas for college or play collegiate sports. Then, during my junior year, I received a phone call.

It was my dad, David Robinson. He was wondering if I wanted to go with him to see his alma mater, the Naval Academy, play Notre Dame at Notre Dame Stadium. It had been a childhood ambition of mine to attend the Naval Academy, so I eagerly agreed. Notre Dame wasn't the attraction for me; it was simply a vehicle for me to watch my favorite university.

And then I got to the campus. The sharp October air filled my lungs. Massive trees adorned with multihued leaves signaling the changing seasons towered over me. An unmistakable electricity permeated the campus—football was in the air.

Navy got crushed that day. While sitting in Notre Dame Stadium wearing my Navy gear, I felt something I had never experienced before: a mystical merging of past tradition, present ambition, and future glory in a stadium that had previously meant nothing to me. As we went home, I uttered to my father in fascination, "I want to be a student here." He understood. Honestly, I think he had the same feeling.

I had just finished my junior football season when my coach heard about the Army All-American Combine, a national collegiate football scouting event. He encouraged me to sign up for the weekend and test my mettle against the top players in the country. Why not? So I registered for the combine, got my cleats, and ran some routes. Three days later, Notre Dame offered me a full scholarship to play football.

I couldn't believe it! Since I knew nothing about the history of Notre Dame, I did the logical next thing: I watched the movie *Rudy*. One hour and fifty-four minutes later, I was hooked. I had to see this magical place again—this fantastic vision of a great American university. I took a visit in the spring and ran into one of my future teammates. After practice ended, Malik Zaire and I were following the players off the field.

"Wouldn't it be great if we both came here?" Malik said. "I can hear it now, Zaire to Robinson! And the crowd goes wild!"

"Yeah, Malik," I replied. "Wouldn't that be something."

After I and my new teammate and roommate Steve Elmer arrived on campus as freshmen in spring of 2013, things became more difficult. Football was extremely demanding—physically, mentally, and emotionally. Academics challenged me more than I ever could have imagined. Between early-morning practices, five classes, mandatory study hall, homework, film sessions, and treatment, Steve and I barely had time for sleep and friends. I struggled that year with finding a good balance of commitments, responsibilities, and free time. It was truly a trial by fire, but gradually I learned how to manage my time. Football and academics were going pretty well. Both Steve and I were playing as true freshmen and made the Dean's List our first year.

Despite my initial success, however, something still felt incomplete. One morning I woke up and it hit me: I had been in college for one year and I had done nothing on campus except catch footballs and take tests. I felt ostracized from the community I had seen on that mid-October Navy gameday a couple of years earlier. A whole year of community service, clubs, and dorm events had passed me by.

It was at that moment that I made a critical decision: I would not let another year of college go by without taking advantage of the incredible resources a university has to offer.

Mike Harrity, the senior associate athletics director for student-athlete services, encouraged me to apply for a position on the Student Athlete Advisory Committee (SAAC) as a team representative of football. SAAC provided me the outlet for community engagement and service that I desperately needed. Finally I was surrounded by brilliant and passionate students who wanted to use their influence to make a mark on campus. Getting to know the other athletes, hearing their training regimens and perspectives on NCAA policies, and watching them excel on game days are by far some of my fondest memories of college. SAAC allowed me to feel like a contributing member of the Notre Dame community. Without SAAC I would have missed out on the full Notre Dame experience. For that, I am eternally grateful to Mike and his staff at Student Welfare and Development.

After a couple of years in SAAC, I felt like something else was missing. I knew the student-athlete world pretty well, but there are so many facets to university life other than athletics. Mike encouraged me to ask Alex Coccia, the student body president in 2014–2015, how he managed to juggle collegiate fencing and campus involvement. I did, and from that conversation on, Alex became a fixture and mentor in my life. He inspired me to apply for athletics representative in student government to get a taste of the diverse facets of student life at Notre Dame. I spent the next year basking in the brilliance and passion of young student leaders resolved to better their community. It amazed me to see my peers developing gender policy, organizing vigils and prayer services for victims of sexual violence, and implementing programs to promote the safety of students on campus. My time in student government proved to me that students can make a difference on campus if they are well organized, passionate, and persistent.

During my sophomore year, Joe Schmidt and Cam McDaniel, two of my good friends and teammates, introduced me to a former student-athlete who worked at the Notre Dame Investment Office. Rick Buhrman opened up a cornucopia of inter-disciplinary learning, widening my perspective to the nth degree. His natural curiosity, patience, and genuine love for learning is second to none. Rick's unique manner of applying general principles of physics and biology to investing fascinated me. Through our friendship, I learned to approach complicated issues through an interdisciplinary lens and, most importantly, to strive to be a life-long learner.

Thanks to mentors such as Mike, Alex, and Rick, I discovered new communities that broadened my horizons and fostered my personal development. Looking back, I can't imagine four years here without my friends from football, SAAC, or student government. Each community taught me invaluable lessons, informed my worldview, and inspired me to better serve my community.

After the Fiesta Bowl against Ohio State on New Year's Day 2015, I had to make a decision. I could either graduate in May and get a job, or come back to school for my final year of eligibility. I remember sitting on a beach in Los Angeles thinking through my options, and the biblical book of Jonah came to mind. Like Jonah, I needed to make the difficult decision and embrace my role as a servant leader. Although it would have been easier to graduate with my degree from a Top 20 university, get a job, and move on, something wasn't right. My work at Notre Dame wasn't finished just yet. So I decided to come back and find the best avenue for me to serve the student body.

Earlier that academic year, I had met a remarkable student in Becca Blais. She was a young student leader who asked me if I would be interested in running for student body president with her as my vice president. Initially I said no. But in January I gave her a call saying I had changed my mind. We immediately got on Skype and spent the next six days before school writing our platform and organizing our team. One exhausting month of campaigning later, we emerged victorious. We made history: I was the first football player elected student body president and the second African-American student body president in the history of Notre Dame.

This year our administration has two central goals: to serve the student body to the best of our ability and to better the student experience. Our platform focuses on five primary issues: sexual assault prevention; sustainability; diversity and inclusion; community engagement; and health and wellness. This October we are organizing the first Race Relations Week in Notre Dame's 175-year history. Injustice, violence, hatred, prejudice, and fear have plagued the past eight months. Our Race Relations Week will address racial injustice through the lens of psychology, politics, opportunity, and sexual assault. It is extremely important that we, as student leaders at the premier Catholic school in the world, take the time to deeply discuss the problems plaguing our nation, stand in solidarity with our brothers and sisters who are suffering injustices each passing day, and seek solutions.

One of the more underreported concerns of students at Notre Dame is the lack of an entrepreneurial culture. We have brilliant students who are passionate about positively impacting communities across the nation and globe. But we currently don't encourage or support their entrepreneurial pursuits. Who knows what could happen if we provided funding, mentorship, work space, and publicity to our student entrepreneurs? If we fostered a culture of innovation on campus where people come from all over the world to celebrate ingenuity and creativity? If we found ways to get students involved with start-ups on campus? Might Notre Dame be responsible for the next Bill Gates, Ruth Porat, Steve Jobs, or Rosie Rios?

Notre Dame has allowed me, a black minority and student-athlete, to find a home in South Bend. It wasn't easy, but through my experience on campus I can honestly say I will never be the same. My football team, SAAC, and student government experiences have taught me how to lead, follow others, create social change, and make a difference in my community. And as long as God continues to move me to serve, I will answer.

INDEX